The School Improvement
Planning Handbook

Praise for *The School Improvement Planning Handbook*

"Despite calls for school improvement coming from nearly all directions, school leaders often struggle to find practical guidance for facilitating the process. Duke, Carr, and Sterrett have helped fill that important gap with this important, hands-on approach. Leaders truly committed to authentic, meaningful and sustainable school improvement will benefit from this practical and accessible book."—**Nicholas J. Pace**, EdD, author of *The Principal's Hot Seat: Observing Real-World Dilemmas*

"Attaining genuine and meaningful school improvement is an exceedingly difficult process, and not for the faint of heart. Dan Duke, Marsha Carr, and Bill Sterrett have provided an instrument that all school leaders can relate to and appreciate. The thought provoking case-studies are immensely valuable and 'spot on' in terms of applying multiple data sources and a process orientation, to the heavy work associated with school improvement. *The School Improvement Planning Handbook* is a breath of fresh air within a misguided environment that seeks quick fixes and easy solutions to very difficult problems."—**David C. Jeck**, superintendent, Greene County Public Schools, Stanardsville, Virginia

"The school improvement process is an annual necessity for schools, yet it often remains a difficult process for school leaders and staff. This book will help you get beyond the lengthy discussions about school problems, and enable teams to focus on actions that will lead to tangible improvements for students. This is a book that will help plans become meaningful actions."—**Curt Rees**, elementary school principal in Wisconsin

"If developing a plan to school improvement has distressed your organization in the past, this book has the roadmap to success, guiding the pathway to raising student achievement. I am recommending this book to every colleague who genuinely is in search of the cause of low performing schools in their communities."—**Kevin J. Baker**, Title I program coordinator

"With authentic scenarios, intentional step-by-step guides, and high-quality planning tools, this handbook serves as a powerful reference for change agents looking to root their school improvement plan in a balanced system of instruction, assessment and accountability."—**Nader Imad Twal**, Milken National Educator, California 2003; Linked Learning project director, Long Beach Unified School District

"School turnaround is the most difficult and complex task for school leaders. Having a guide like *The School Improvement Planning Handbook* to provide concrete solutions for implementing change has already benefited my practice as a school leader. The tactics in this book create artifacts that truly measure improvements to student achievement and school climate."—**Thomas W. Taylor**, principal of Charlottesville High School, Charlottesville, Virginia, adjunct professor of educational leadership at the University of Virginia

"This step-by-step guide for principals and their school leaderships teams is chock full of specific strategies for developing a meaningful school improvement plan that can truly be a guiding document for the school. A distinguishing feature of this book is the acknowledgment of the importance of differentiated school improvement planning aligned to the need for school turnaround, school transformation or continuous improvement. Specific and authentic examples of real school scenarios and strategies are shared to address reading, math, English language learned, students with special needs and student indicators of success such as student attendance and school culture."—**Ann Blakeney Clark**, deputy superintendent, Charlotte-Mecklenburg Schools

"Education, like anything else, requires effective leadership to be successful. Schools need the high performance only planning can provide. This book uses effective leadership to guide schools in planning for success."—**Martin Cain**, retired professor of financial management

The School Improvement Planning Handbook

Getting Focused for Turnaround and Transition

Daniel L. Duke, Marsha Carr, and William Sterrett

Rowman & Littlefield Education

A division of
ROWMAN & LITTLEFIELD PUBLISHERS, INC.
Lanham • New York • Toronto • Plymouth, UK

Published by Rowman & Littlefield Education
A division of Rowman & Littlefield Publishers, Inc.
A wholly owned subsidiary of The Rowman & Littlefield Publishing Group, Inc.
4501 Forbes Boulevard, Suite 200, Lanham, Maryland 20706
www.rowman.com

10 Thornbury Road, Plymouth PL6 7PP, United Kingdom

British Library Cataloguing in Publication Information Available

Library of Congress Cataloging-in-Publication Data
Duke, Daniel Linden
 The school improvement planning handbook : getting focused for turnaround
and transition / Daniel L. Duke, Marsha Carr, and William Sterrett.
 p. cm.
 Includes bibliographical references and index.
 ISBN 978-1-61048-631-6 (cloth : alk. paper)—ISBN 978-1-61048-632-3
(pbk. : alk. paper)—ISBN 978-1-61048-633-0 (electronic) 1. School
improvement programs. I. Carr, Marsha, 1957– II. Sterrett, William. III. Title.
 LB2822.8.D85 2013
 371.2'07—dc23   2012041354

Printed in the United States of America

Contents

Acknowledgments

The authors would like to extend gratitude and acknowledgments to the following for their insights and contributions to this work: Corrie Kelly, Kristen Williams, David Bittner, Pete Fiddner, Chandra Lynn Roughton, Eric Sheninger, Salena Rabidoux, Thomas Taylor, N. Eleni Pappamihiel, Janna Siegel Robertson, Martin Wasserberg, Bethany Meighen, and The Center for Mental Health in Schools at UCLA.

Introduction

If you are a school principal or a veteran teacher, the odds are that you have participated in the process of planning for school improvement. Do you have strong feelings about school improvement planning? Many educators do. Some look at the process as a colossal waste of time. Others acknowledge that planning has the potential to improve teaching and learning, but their experiences with the process have been largely unproductive. Still others consider planning to be an important and essential professional responsibility that leads to demonstrable gains in student achievement. We believe that significant and sustained school improvement is impossible without careful and continuous planning.

We also believe that planning, in and of itself, is no guarantee of success. As with anything else educators undertake, planning can be done poorly or planning can be done well. This *School Improvement Planning Handbook* is designed for principals and teachers who are committed to high-quality planning and who are motivated to get better at the planning process.

The subtitle of our book—"Getting Focused for Turnaround and Transition"—provides some important clues about its contents. "Getting focused" refers to what is arguably the primary reason for planning. Few educators leave school at the end of the day without feeling that more could have been done to help students. The peculiar curse of education is that there is always more to do than time available to do it. Without "focus," there is no way to ensure that the most important things get done. Planning provides the opportunity to determine what are the most important things and to develop the means for ensuring that they get done.

"Turnaround" and "transition" refer to a pair of challenges facing contemporary educators that absolutely require "getting focused." "Turnaround" is a reference to the quest for "quick and dramatic" improvements in the lowest-performing schools. Without such improvements, the futures of hundreds of thousands of young people are in serious jeopardy.

The need for planning, of course, does not cease once a school has turned around. "Transition" refers to the challenge of sustaining improved performance. Many turnaround schools soon slip back into old patterns of low performance, underscoring the fact that they have failed to effect a transition to continuous improvement—the desired state for all schools.

Throughout this book we employ the term School Improvement Plan to describe the product of the planning process. We realize that this terminology may not be used in some locations. Related terms of which we are aware include Campus Improvement Plan, School Strategic Plan, School Turnaround Plan, and Strategic and Continuous School Improvement and Achievement Plan. Regardless of the wording, all of these terms are concerned with providing educators with a focused set of goals and objectives and a plan for achieving them.

TO PLAN OR NOT TO PLAN? THAT IS NOT THE QUESTION!

School improvement planning in most school systems is not an option. States and school districts typically require all schools to develop and submit for review an annual School Improvement Plan. Regulations often govern the kinds of goals and objectives that must be included and the format to be used in presenting the plan. Additional planning may be mandated for chronically low-performing schools. The annual evaluation of principals and, increasingly, teachers is tied to the achievement of School Improvement Plan goals and objectives.

The No Child Left Behind Act of 2001 provided an important impetus for school improvement planning. Concerned that far too many low-performing schools continue to languish, the drafters of the bill established a prescription to be followed by all Title I schools that fail to meet adequate yearly progress benchmarks for two or more years. These schools are said to be in "school improvement" status and are required to develop a School Improvement Plan. Every plan has to address ten specific components.

Ten Requirements of a School Improvement Plan under the No Child Left Behind Act

A School Improvement Plan must:

1. Incorporate strategies based on scientifically based research;
2. Adopt policies and practices that ensure all student subgroups meet the state's proficiency level of achievement;
3. Allocate funds for the high-quality professional development of teachers and principals;
4. Specify how federal funds will be used to remove the school from school improvement status;
5. Establish specific and measurable annual objectives;
6. Describe how the school will provide written notice about its status to parents;
7. Specify the school improvement responsibilities of the school, the district, and the state education agency;
8. Include strategies to promote effective parent involvement in the school;
9. Incorporate provisions for before school, after school, extended school year, and summer activities; and
10. Incorporate a teacher mentoring program.

Provisions such as those specified in the No Child Left Behind Act reveal the lengths to which policymakers are prepared to go in order to hold educators accountable for improving the lowest performing schools. Even though in 2012 the Obama administration granted waivers for various sections of No Child Left Behind, the focus on school improvement for troubled schools has persisted. But, what about schools that are not in serious academic difficulty? Education officials and legislators in many states have taken the position that *all* schools can benefit from a continuing engagement in school improvement. The state of Washington, for example, clearly states the expectation for continuous improvement for all schools in *School Improvement*

Planning: Process Guide (2005), issued by the state superintendent for public instruction:

> School improvement is a continuous process schools use to ensure that all students are achieving at high levels. All schools, in collaboration with families, students, and communities, can create better environments so that all students are successful. Continuous improvement of public schools is essential to providing increased student performance and quality results. (p. i)

Like most of its sister states, Texas expects all schools (campuses) to engage in improvement planning. Section 11.253 of the Texas Education Code mandates that every year principals must develop, with the assistance of a campus school improvement committee, a plan "for the purpose of improving student performance for all student populations." The regulations go on to outline the elements of a plan, including performance objectives, objectives for special needs populations, the means by which objectives will be achieved, the personnel and resources needed to achieve objectives, and time lines for the achievement of objectives.

The basic elements of school improvement plans do not vary a great deal from state to state. Common features include goals and objectives, strategies for achieving the goals and objectives, and time lines. Depending on the state, plans also may be required to include goals and objectives addressing specific subjects, provisions for monitoring progress, individuals responsible for particular objectives, and professional development activities. For the sake of clarity, key terms in the planning process are defined below.

GOAL: A comprehensive and relatively long-range outcome requiring the achievement of multiple objectives.

OBJECTIVE: An intermediate and measurable outcome, the accomplishment of which contributes to the achievement of a goal.

STRATEGIES: The means by which an objective is achieved.

TIME LINE: A schedule for tracking the implementation of strategies and progress toward the achievement of objectives and goals.

Imagine that a high school faculty is concerned about the high number of students who drop out of school. The principal and School Improvement Planning Committee decide to focus on the *goal* of increasing the number of entering ninth graders who receive a diploma in four years by 25 percent. After a careful analysis of student performance data over the preceding five years, committee members conclude that three powerful predictors of failure to graduate are 1) a failing grade in Algebra 1, 2) a failing grade in English 9, and 3) a high rate of absenteeism in ninth grade. The School Improvement Planning Committee chooses to focus on three objectives for the coming year:

1. Reduce the failure rate in Algebra 1 by 10 percent for the coming school year.
2. Reduce the failure rate in ninth grade English by 15 percent for the coming school year.
3. Increase average daily attendance for ninth graders by 8 percent for the coming school year.

In order to accomplish these objectives, a variety of research-based strategies are identified. To increase students' chances of passing Algebra 1 and English 9, for example, the courses will be double-blocked for struggling students, thereby providing them with twice the instructional time. Algebra and English teachers will receive focused professional development on how to use additional instructional time to greatest advantage. Teachers also will be trained in classroom assessment methods so they can monitor student progress and target assistance in a timely manner. Students who, despite these efforts, fail either or both courses will be required to attend summer school in order to earn a passing grade.

To improve attendance, the School Improvement Planning Committee chooses two proven strategies. First, parents will be notified immediately when their child is not in school. Parents of chronically absent students also will be informed that the school system is prepared to refer them to the court system if absenteeism persists. Second, students who miss school for non-approved reasons will be required to make up missed time by attending Saturday school.

The School Improvement Planning Committee draws up a detailed time line to guide the implementation of all the strategies. The time line indicates when teacher training will take place and the points during the year when the progress of each strategy will be checked. The committee members are prepared to make adjustments in the School Improvement Plan if certain strategies do not appear to be working.

GOOD PLANNING BEGINS WITH SOUND THINKING

Planning often is regarded as a set of skills. Educators who engage in planning school improvement should be adept at diagnosing problematic conditions, analyzing student achievement data, and evaluating program effectiveness, among other skills. But good planning depends on more than skills. How people *think* about planning and their ability to make sound judgments also are critically important.

Let's face it—some people dislike planning. They may resent the time it takes away from performing duties they regard as more impactful. Or they may find planning pointless because they believe plans rarely lead to constructive action. Then there are individuals who seem to have an attachment to spontaneity. They think that planning deprives them of opportunities to seize the moment and act creatively.

It is true that spontaneity has its benefits. Getting together with friends on the spur of the moment, for example, can be a great pleasure. But should schools be run in such an ad hoc manner? When the lives of young people depend on how well educators do their jobs, we believe that planning is not only important, it is essential.

There are many reasons why schools are unlikely to improve spontaneously. Resources typically are limited when it comes to schooling. Careful planning can ensure that available resources are directed to priority concerns, not to random requests and "squeaky wheels." Another reason why spontaneity is ill-suited to the work of educators involves the sheer complexity of the problems educators confront. Addressing reading deficits for a group of children, for example, requires forethought and careful consideration of instructional interventions. Adopting the first supplementary reading program that a vendor happens to recommend is probably unwise. Students are not guinea pigs for whom spontaneous experimentation is acceptable.

The quality of thinking that goes into planning for school improvement is often manifested in *judgment calls.* A judgment call is a "tough choice." Perhaps the difficulty concerns the lack of unambiguous information about a particular course of action. Or maybe the choice is hard because it involves competing objectives or opposing values. Consider the judgment calls listed below. Each question represents a decision that a principal ultimately may need to make as part of school improvement planning.

Judgment Calls

Is low student achievement in mathematics due to an unsuitable mathematics program, inadequate instruction, or a combination of the two?

Should a teacher experiencing difficulty at one grade level be assigned to another grade level, or is the teacher unlikely to be effective at any grade level?

Is targeted professional development likely to help a teacher improve, or is it simply going to delay replacing the teacher?

Is it better to increase instructional time for a subject with which students are struggling or focus on making better use of existing instructional time?

Will better classroom management result in fewer instructional problems, or will better instruction result in fewer classroom management problems?

Is a new program failing because it was poorly designed or because it was not implemented properly?

There are no easy answers to questions such as these. Still, they may have to be answered in order to develop a School Improvement Plan. Arriving at sound judgments regarding such questions often requires school leaders to take into account what is legal, what is feasible, what is ethical, and what has been shown to work. When these considerations are aligned, a judgment call may not be especially difficult. But when they conflict, educators can lose a lot of sleep deciding what to do. Consider, for instance, a planning decision where the choice that is legally defensible is unlikely to be effective or where the choice that is most likely to work is not feasible given existing resources. We cannot tell readers what judgment calls to make, but we can and will identify the kinds of issues with which educators frequently grapple as they engage in school improvement.

THE NECESSITY OF EFFECTIVE PLANNING

The need for effective school improvement planning has never been greater. The economic downturn that began with the mortgage and banking crisis of 2008 has deprived school systems of resources desperately needed to meet the challenges of an increasingly diverse population and a highly competitive global economy. Though funding for education is shrinking in many localities, expectations for schools have never been greater. Educators now are expected to ensure that substantial percentages of students achieve proficiency in the Common Core Standards. Schools are supposed to provide opportunities for students to develop advanced skills of inquiry and innovation that will enable the United States to compete with rapidly developing nations.

Another obstacle concerns the achievement gap between white and Asian American students, on the one hand, and African American and Hispanic American students, on the other. It is not uncommon for double-digit differences to characterize the test performance of these groups. These differences in test success are also reflected in differences in dropout rates. The percentage of students who complete high school and earn a diploma in the United States has hovered around 75 percent for years, and in many urban areas the figure is closer to 50 percent. A disproportionately high number of those who do not graduate are African American and Hispanic American students.

School improvement planners need not search for long to identify overarching goals for their plans. Three goals are of surpassing importance for America's future: 1) raising the overall level of student achievement, 2) reducing and eventually eliminating achievement gaps, and 3) increasing high school completion rates.

When educators zero in on the reasons why many schools are struggling to achieve these goals, they identify a variety of concerns: Student deficits in reading, writing, and mathematics. Instructional practices that do not reflect what is known about effective learning. Programs that do not adequately address the needs of English language learners. Interventions that fail to provide timely and targeted assistance. Outdated and underused technologies. Chronic absenteeism. Disorderly and unsafe schools and classrooms. School cultures characterized by low expectations and demoralization. Lack of parent and community involvement. Low rates of high school completion, especially in urban areas.

Deciding which of these problems are *causes* of low performance and which are *symptoms* can make the planning process particularly challenging. Are disorderly classrooms preventing students from becoming proficient readers, or is the fact that students struggle with reading, leading them to act out and disrupt class? Planners who focus on symptoms rather than root causes frequently discover that problems persist, despite their well-intentioned efforts.

Although School Improvement Plans invariably are associated with efforts to overcome persistent problems, educators should be aware that planning is also important for sustaining success. There are many high-achieving schools in the United States. To maintain and extend their accomplishments, these schools also need to engage in continuous planning. Even the most successful schools are subject to slippage if past accomplishments are taken for granted and groundwork is not laid for future improvements.

ORGANIZATION OF *THE SCHOOL IMPROVEMENT PLANNING HANDBOOK*

The term "handbook" appears in the title of this volume because we intend it to be a ready reference—a resource that can be kept close "at hand"—for principals and teachers engaged in school improvement planning. This is a practical book for practitioners, not an academic work. We purposely avoid highly technical language and lengthy citations from studies. We focus instead on actual examples of successful planning and research-based best practices.

The book opens with a section devoted to the planning of school improvement planning. Yes, even planning, to be effective, can benefit from planning. The first chapter provides an overview of the essential steps involved in developing a School Improvement Plan. Plans are no better than the data on which they are based; so chapter 2 examines various types of data that can be used to diagnose school conditions that may need to be addressed in a School Improvement Plan. Section I concludes with a chapter devoted to troubleshooting the planning process and pinpointing its potential pitfalls.

The second section constitutes a unique feature of this book. Many books offer educators an overview of the planning process, but few of these resources go further to examine in detail the actual goals, objectives, and strategies that educators are most likely to focus on when they develop a School Improvement Plan. This book provides such an examination.

Section II opens with perhaps the most ubiquitous focus of school improvement planning—the improvement of reading. Subsequent chapters address such foci as raising mathematics achievement, improving school culture, raising the quality of instruction, assisting English language learners, developing effective instructional interventions for struggling students, and reducing absenteeism. It is very likely that any educator who has been involved in school improvement planning has worked on one or more of these concerns.

The final section of *The School Improvement Planning Handbook* takes a more comprehensive look at school improvement. Just as there are significant differences in the challenges facing different schools, so too there are differences in approaches to planning. The importance of differentiated planning, however, has received relatively little attention in the planning literature. Chapter 11 investigates the planning issues facing educators charged with turning around chronically low-performing schools. Typically "quick and dramatic" improvements are expected in these schools, expectations that place considerable pressure on planners. Once schools are able to reverse a prolonged period of decline, a new challenge arises. How can early gains be sustained over time? The planning needed to maintain momentum is the focus of chapter 12. Given the high hopes Americans have for their schools, becoming a "good" school may not be good enough. Moving schools toward excellence is the last challenge addressed in section III. What do planners need to do to provide young people with a truly exceptional education?

The School Improvement Planning Handbook is best regarded as a set of road maps rather than a collection of recipes. Recipes constitute relatively rigid sets of instructions that discourage deviations. Such approaches to planning can run into problems, however, because every school enjoys a distinct history, culture, and context. We prefer the analogy of a road map to capture our intentions in this book. Road maps present the territory to be covered and alternative routes to a variety of destinations in that territory. There are many possible routes to school improvement. No book can replace the judgment of educators when it comes to determining the most appropriate route.

REFERENCES

McNeil, M. May 11, 2011. Rising proportion of schools falls short on AYP, study says. *Education Week*, 22.

School Improvement Planning: Process Guide. 2005. Olympia, WA: Office of Superintendent of Public Instruction.

PAVING THE WAY TO BETTER SCHOOL IMPROVEMENT PLANS

Successful School Improvement Plans are not merely the private products of savvy principals. They are the result of a number of carefully executed steps, a good deal of teamwork, and lots of open and honest reflection. Section I begins with an overview of seven essential elements of the planning process. Chapter 2 follows with an in-depth investigation of the foundation upon which all successful plans are built—data gathering and diagnosis. The last chapter in this section investigates some of the impediments that may be encountered along the road to planning school improvement.

CHAPTER 1

Seven Steps to Good Planning

PREVIEW

The opening chapter examines seven important dimensions of the school improvement planning process. Readers are introduced to data gathering; diagnosing; assessing context, constraints, and capacity; focusing; determining strategies; developing the plan; and managing and monitoring the plan.

A NEW PRINCIPAL: A NEW PLAN

Mac Thompson[1] is the newly appointed principal of Marshall Middle School in an economically struggling Rust Belt city. It is early July. Thompson's supervisor has told him that student achievement must improve significantly in the coming year or Marshall is likely to be closed. Parents and other community members, many of whom attended Marshall in its "glory days," want the school to stay open. Thompson has looked at student performance on state standardized tests and knows that the percentage of students achieving proficiency in language arts and mathematics has been declining for five years. He is uncertain, however, about the reasons for the decline.

Thompson understands that the school system requires him to develop a School Improvement Plan to guide the faculty over the coming school year. Marshall is not the first low-performing school he has taken through the improvement process. The plan must address several broad goals but be focused enough to provide teachers with an unambiguous course of action leading to improved student achievement. The district-designed template for School Improvement Plans calls for each goal to consist of several measurable objectives. Each objective, in turn, must list the strategies and actions that will enable the objective to be achieved. A time line and list of staff members responsible for each objective also must be included.

At first Thompson thinks he has a clear idea about what to focus on and include in Marshall's School Improvement Plan, but his conversations with several faculty members and parents uncover a variety of explanations for the school's decline. Several blame lack of adequate resources. Others cite lack of leadership. Parents question the competence of some teachers. Teachers, on the other hand, note the lack of parental involvement. Thompson decides it would be a mistake to draft a plan too hastily. More preparation must be undertaken before he will feel comfortable developing and disseminating Marshall's School Improvement Plan. Too much is at stake to rush the planning process or jump to premature conclusions about the causes of school decline.

———

Mac Thompson realizes that drafting a School Improvement Plan is not the first step to school improvement. Even though his previous experience in low-performing schools has led him to favor certain objectives and strategies, he understands that Marshall has its own history and set of circumstances. Thompson also knows that school improvement planning is best regarded as a series of steps, some of which must be taken *before* a plan can be developed. Nor is the completion of a School Improvement Plan the end of the process. Plans must be implemented. Successful implementation depends on managing and monitoring the plan. This chapter provides an overview of seven important steps in the development and implementation of School Improvement Plans.

SEVEN STEPS TO GOOD PLANNING

1. Data gathering
2. Diagnosing
3. Assessing context, constraints, and capacity

4. Focusing
5. Determining strategies
6. Developing the plan
7. Managing and monitoring the plan

DATA GATHERING

Most people would be concerned if they went to a physician because they were suffering and the physician made no effort to collect data on their symptoms and health in general. An accurate diagnosis depends on the availability of a range of data. The wider the range of data, the more possibilities that can be considered and either ruled out or confirmed.

Like physicians, educators today are expected to make data-driven decisions. So, when is a decision not data-driven? Decisions that are based on vague feelings, intuition, or deeply held values are not data-driven. Other decisions may be based on data, but the data is outdated or circumstantial. Not all data is of equal quality. Educators must understand the difference between high-quality data and questionable data. Chapter 2 explores various sources of high-quality data for educators in greater depth.

Deciding what data to gather depends, to some extent, on the conditions that are judged to merit consideration of changes. Among the possible conditions are the following:

* Reasonable progress toward achieving current goals is not being made.
* One stakeholder group or more is dissatisfied.
* The benefits of schooling are not being shared by all student subgroups.
* Educational practices and programs are not in compliance with laws and regulations.
* Certain policies and/or practices are suspected to be harmful to certain groups of students.
* Conditions external to school have changed sufficiently to warrant adjustments.
* New research and/or technology offer alternatives to current practice.

When educators think about gathering data for school improvement, they often have in mind data that relates to deficits and discrepancies. Too many students are being retained at grade level. Too few students are graduating. Desired goals are not being achieved. To be sure, these are conditions that need to be examined. But schools that routinely promote and graduate their students on time and achieve their goals can also benefit from gathering data. Educators in these schools can always gain from examining promising new practices and collecting benchmarking data from higher-performing schools.

The terms "mission" and "vision" are useful in thinking about different approaches to data gathering. Mission refers to what a school is expected and committed to do. Vision, on the other hand, concerns what a school aspires to become. A chronically low-performing school may aspire to become one of the best schools in the state, but first it must accomplish its mission. Determining what is required to accomplish its mission therefore must be the first focus of data gathering. When the mission is clearly being accomplished, attention can turn to matters of vision.

Regardless of the focus of data gathering, planning always benefits from longitudinal data. Without longitudinal data, it is impossible to determine whether the most recent data represents a trend. Negative trends suggest that persistent and pernicious forces may be at work. Such forces can range from personnel and program shortcomings to misallocated resources. Until these forces are understood, lasting improvements are unlikely.

Another key to data gathering involves tapping multiple sources of data. Without data from multiple sources, it is difficult to confirm or disconfirm data-based impressions. Imagine that a student is failing his courses in high school. Without collecting data on how the student functions outside of school, an observer might conclude that the student has a profound learning disability. That judgment would need to be modified, however, if it were discovered that the student has an after-school job in which he uses complicated technology very effectively.

Collecting data from different stakeholders is also important because people have different perspectives on what goes on in school. A principal may observe a teacher three or four times a year. Students in the teacher's classes observe her every day. The teacher's directions may seem perfectly clear to the principal, first because he is an educated adult; and, second, because the teacher has carefully prepared the lessons that are being observed. The students may have a different perspective, however. They realize that most of the time the teacher's directions are vague and confusing. Only by tapping different stakeholders is it possible to identify discrepant perceptions and the potential problems they represent.

Perceptual data is of great value in the planning process, but so too is descriptive data. Descriptive data is relatively free of impressions and possible bias. Daniel Patrick Moynihan is credited with telling a highly opinionated adversary that he had a right to his own opinions but not to his own facts. The number of minutes that a teacher devotes to conducting a pretest review is a *fact*. Whether or not those minutes are used productively is an *opinion*. Descriptive data is helpful in creating a context in which to judge opinions and perceptions.

Some Keys to Data Gathering

- Understand the conditions that justify thinking about improvement.
- Recognize the difference between mission-oriented data gathering and vision-oriented data gathering.
- When possible, collect longitudinal data.
- Gather data from multiple sources.
- Balance perceptual data with descriptive data.

DIAGNOSING

Data collected is not data analyzed. Educators committed to school improvement can compile a wide range of high-quality data, but if a poor job is done analyzing the data, an accurate diagnosis of the problems that must be addressed in order to achieve school improvement is unlikely.

One reason why diagnosing can be daunting is the confusion that often arises between causes, symptoms, and consequences. Consider ineffective instruction, a ubiquitous problem in chronically low-performing schools. An initial diagnosis of teacher observation data suggests that ineffective instruction is the cause of low student achievement. Additional scrutiny of available data, however, reveals that ineffective instruction actually is a consequence of overcrowded classrooms and lack of appropriate instructional materials.

Sometimes distinguishing between symptoms and root causes is difficult. When students act out in class, is their behavior a symptom of ineffective instruction or a cause of ineffective instruction? It may be impossible to determine an answer with absolute certainty, but analyzing student behavior data across various classes and teachers can provide important clues as to the relationship between student behavior and instructional effectiveness.

The primary purpose of diagnosing is the identification of the root causes of school performance. But, which aspect of performance? It is essential that educators engaged in data analysis be clear about what they want to diagnose. Is the focus on understanding why the entire school is doing poorly or just one student subgroup? Does school improvement depend on explaining a long, slow period of decline in student achievement or a drastic drop from one year to the next? Why are some intervention programs at the school working while others are not? Although many diagnostic efforts zero in on problems such as these, it also can be worthwhile to account for dramatic improvements in school performance.

Arriving at diagnoses of school-based problems and progress involves a variety of analytical approaches. The previous example concerned comparisons across classes and teachers. Comparative analysis allows educators to determine if problems are limited to particular teachers and groups of students or they are school-wide. Problems that are school-wide pose special challenges that often require the analysis of data over time, or what is referred to as trend analysis. By determining when a problem began to emerge, it may be possible to identify changes in policy, practice, and/or personnel that could have triggered the problem.

Much of the data analysis that attends school improvement efforts involves quantitative data—scores on standardized tests, retention and graduation rates, attendance figures, and the like. Qualitative data can also offer valuable insights into the causes of school problems. One approach to analyzing qualitative data is content analysis. Content analysis may focus on the curriculum topics that receive the most and the least attention from teachers or the kinds of questions that teachers tend to ask. A special form of content analysis is called null analysis. As the name suggests, null analysis involves determining what is *not* covered during instruction. The fact that teachers fail to address non-Western cultures, for example, may be of great importance when it comes to explaining why some students are uninterested in social studies.

Educators recently have become interested in identifying leading indicators of student success and failure. A leading indicator is data that predicts subsequent outcomes. Leading indicators are often detected as a result of analyzing performance data of a cohort of students over time and diagnosing the causes of any discovered achievement gaps and learning deficits. The earlier in a student's school experience the indicator can be identified, the greater the potential for effective intervention. Predictors of student graduation from high school, for example, have been found to include student behavior, attendance, and grades in elementary school. Students who receive many referrals to the office, miss school frequently, and fail key subjects such as reading and mathematics in the early grades have been shown to be likely candidates for dropping out of high school.

The diagnosing phase of school improvement planning enables educators to pinpoint probable causes of performance-related problems. Once such causes have been identified, educators must judge which causes they are and are not able to affect. Poverty contributes to low student achievement, for example, but educators cannot do much to eliminate poverty. Educators are in a better position, however, to increase instructional time and improve assistance for struggling students should these factors be diagnosed as contributors to low achievement.

Some Keys to Diagnosing

- Agree on what aspects of school performance need to be diagnosed.
- Recognize the possibility that apparent "causes" actually may be "symptoms" or "consequences."

• Draw on different analytical approaches, including comparative analysis, trend analysis, and content analysis.

ASSESSING CONTEXT, CONSTRAINTS, AND CAPACITY

The third step in school improvement planning involves assessing the variety of factors that can affect educators' efforts to address the causes of performance problems. These factors may derive from a school's local context, various constraints to which the school is subject, and gaps in the school's capacity to support school improvement. Ignoring these factors can lead to resistance to school improvement and the ultimate failure of School Improvement Plans.

Context. All schools exist within a local or community context, and this context is characterized by multiple dimensions. One dimension is *historical.* A community's history reveals the origins of expectations for local schools and insights into relations between parents and educators. In communities where school integration has been vigorously resisted by whites, for instance, relations between African American parents and school leaders may be characterized by lingering distrust. Educators in these communities are ill-advised to ignore such feelings as they contemplate school improvement.

Closely tied to a community's historical context is its *cultural* context. Local culture embodies the beliefs, values, and assumptions that shape how people think and act. In some affluent communities where parents are highly educated and where residents pay high property taxes, it is assumed that the schools will prepare students to attend the most highly competitive colleges. By contrast, in many poor and rural communities, graduation from high school is regarded as a more likely outcome.

Cultural values help to shape the *economic* and *political* contexts of schools. A school district's budget, for instance, can be regarded as a manifestation of local values. Whereas one community takes an active interest in supporting the arts in its schools, another community prefers to focus available resources on athletic programs. The condition of the local economy obviously must be factored in to any school improvement effort as well. Improving schools requires resources. Where resources are limited because of high local unemployment, educators may need to reduce the scale of improvement plans or seek assistance from outside the community.

Much of local political activity involves determining how resources will be allocated. Special-interest groups lobby for particular initiatives or press to eliminate school programs they believe are unnecessary or harmful to students. Taxpayer groups urge schools to use resources more efficiently. Political parties seek to influence who is chosen for local school boards, and school board members, in turn, may take an active interest in shaping school improvement efforts.

It is tempting to regard these aspects of a school's local context as checks on educators' freedom to develop responsive School Improvement Plans or even as causes of school-based problems. Principals and teachers need to recognize, however, that the community also can be a significant source of support and assistance. The more educators understand about a community's historical, cultural, economic, and political contexts, the more likely they are to craft School Improvement Plans that receive such support and assistance. Principals should make certain that an assessment of local context is part of the planning process.

Constraints. Constraints represent the laws, regulations, policies, and court decisions that affect how educators plan. Some of these constraints, of course, derive from the community context, but others are associated with state and federal laws and regulations and court decisions. One reason that school districts and, in some cases, state education agencies routinely review School Improvement Plans is to make certain that plans are in compliance with the law. School funding often depends on such compliance.

State education agencies establish guidelines covering such matters as school staffing, school calendars, graduation requirements, and standardized testing. In recent years, states have focused considerable attention on what content must be taught in schools. Concern over disparities in curriculum standards across states led the National Governors Association and the Council of Chief State School Officers to promulgate the Common Core State Standards in 2010. These standards define the knowledge and skills students require in order to succeed in college and workforce training programs. Forty-five states have adopted the Common Core Standards.

Many states have also established relatively specific regulations regarding the content and format of School Improvement Plans as well as the process by which plans are to be developed. Texas, for example, requires that every plan include goals for violence prevention and the encouragement of parental involvement. Most states insist that student achievement goals be included in every School Improvement Plan. The required templates for plans typically encompass broad goals, specific objectives, strategies for achieving objectives, and time lines. In some cases, plans must also indicate who is responsible for each objective and the resources needed to achieve objectives.

Regulations pertaining to school improvement planning in low-performing schools can be even more restrictive, in part because these schools often receive supplementary funding. A certain percentage of these additional funds, for instance, may have to be spent on tutoring for students or professional development for teachers. Virginia and Indiana mandate that low-performing schools develop three-year School Improvement Plans. They also allow schools to petition for waivers of certain rules and regulations. Presumably such an option is meant to encourage innovative approaches to school improvement.

The principal of one low-performing Virginia alternative middle school, for example, petitioned and was granted a waiver that allowed teachers to teach social studies and science in the context of language arts and mathematics rather than as separate subjects. The principal reasoned that little progress in the first two subjects could be made until student achievement in language arts and mathematics was raised. Receiving the waiver allowed her to double instructional time in these two subjects.

Some states go beyond the content and format of plans to direct schools on *how* plans must be developed. One type of regulation requires that schools have a School Improvement Committee to assist principals in developing and monitoring plans. Teacher and parent membership may be mandated for these committees.

In addition to state rules and regulations, school districts often place additional constraints on school improvement planning. A school board, for example, may require every School Improvement Plan to address district goals and priorities. It goes without saying that principals should be familiar with state and district rules and regulations for school improvement planning *before* drafting a plan.

Capacity. The extent to which a school is prepared to implement a School Improvement Plan depends on its *capacity* for change. Research (Duke 2004) suggests that a school's capacity for change is a function of three factors:

1. A facilitative organizational structure.
2. An organizational culture that supports change.
3. Adequate resources to initiate and nurture change.

Educators frequently treat the bureaucratic structure of schools and school districts as an impediment to change. Structure is seen to be the source of red tape, rules, and resistance. There is no denying that the formal structure of a school and especially a school district can make change challenging. Approvals have to be obtained. Plans must be in concert with district mission and goals. Standard operating procedures need to be followed.

The solution, however, is not to abandon structure. Instead, educators must identify the elements of structure that are necessary to support and sustain improvement efforts. Are provisions in place, for example, so that teachers can collaborate within and across grade levels? Does a credible and transparent process exist for developing a School Improvement Plan? Is a process in place for reviewing progress on the plan?

The assessment of structure extends beyond the school to encompass the structure of school district operations. School improvement is contingent on district-level support, so school-based planners need to determine 1) the extent to which units in the central office are prepared to offer assistance and 2) the process by which such assistance is to be secured.

It is easier to assess whether structures are supportive than whether a supportive organizational culture exists. People can claim they support school improvement, but claims are no guarantee that people actually will embrace the need for improvement and the means by which improvement is to be achieved. Some faculties have witnessed so many improvement initiatives come and go that they have grown cynical and resistant to planning.

Planners who set out to assess the extent to which their school culture supports change must find ways of determining what stakeholders do and do not value. People's beliefs about education and school improvement also need to be studied. Do veteran teachers, for instance, embrace the belief that instruction can always be improved? Or do they feel they have mastered what they need to know to be effective instructors? Is a high value placed on never giving up on struggling students? Does the school culture support teacher collaboration and experimentation?

If planners discover that the school culture places a higher value on maintaining the status quo than on school improvement, or if their investigation reveals resistance to professional development and teacher collaboration, they need to rethink the approach to be taken with school improvement. A focus on challenging prevailing beliefs and values may have to precede work on raising student achievement.

The third dimension of a school's capacity for change involves resources. School improvement typically entails various "costs"— time, materials, training, additional personnel, and so on. Before a School Improvement Plan can be completed, planners need to assess the availability of funds to support their efforts. Funds usually must be secured from the school district, but in some cases they also may be derived from competitive grants, community donors, and foundations.

Checking with district officials about the availability of funds for school improvement should indicate the extent to which the central office can be counted on for support. Central office reluctance to fund a summer planning retreat for a School Improvement Team, for instance, should be a "red flag" for planners. If there are no additional funds to support planning school improvement, then securing funds to implement the actual School Improvement Plan is likely to be problematic.

Assessing context, constraints, and capacity is a time-consuming process. Educators may be tempted to skip these steps and get on with developing their School Improvement Plan. Doing so, however, can be a major mistake. This assessment process provides critical information that enables planners to develop a plan that is not only responsive to school needs, but one that stands a realistic chance of succeeding.

Some Keys to Preplanning Assessment

- Study local history, culture, politics, and the economy to understand the context in which planning will take place.
- Identify policy-based and legal constraints on school improvement.
- Clarify state and district requirements for the content and format of School Improvement Plans and the process for developing them.
- Assess school and district capacity to support school improvement efforts.

FOCUSING

Up to this point the steps in the planning process have been all about getting ready to develop a School Improvement Plan. Focusing is the initial step in creating the actual plan that will guide school improvement efforts. Of all the steps in the planning process, focusing is also the one most closely associated with leadership. Leadership is supposed to provide direction, and direction requires a clear sense of priorities.

There is a tendency for planning groups to overidentify targets for improvement. Perhaps this tendency is the result of concern over relegating some areas of the school program to "second-class" status. By setting improvement targets for every content area and aspect of school operations, no one's feelings get hurt. Or perhaps an abundance of improvement goals are identified because planners cannot agree on which goals to focus on. Whatever the reason for overidentification, leadership is needed to remind planners that nothing is a priority when everything is a priority. There is never enough time, energy, and resources for a faculty to focus on improving all aspects of the school program simultaneously. When planners fail to agree on a limited set of targets, principals must be prepared to do three things:

1. Decide which goals to focus on.
2. Ensure that goals are stated clearly and correctly.
3. Provide a rationale for each goal.

Deciding on a limited set of school improvement goals requires a number of considerations. That is why time is devoted to preliminary activities such as data gathering; diagnosing; and assessing context, constraints, and capacity. These activities provide critical information to help in the determination of goals.

It is unlikely that a school can address effectively more than three or four goals during the course of a year. Remember that a goal is "a comprehensive and relatively long-range outcome requiring the achievement of multiple objectives." Some goals are so ambitious they must be carried over from one year to the next. Such a goal might be "to reduce the number of high school dropouts by 50 percent." Obviously this goal requires the achievement of various objectives dealing with such matters as credit tracking, guidance counseling, academic assistance for struggling students, curriculum offerings, extended learning time, and credit recovery.

Deciding on a limited set of broad school improvement goals also means deciding what *not* to focus on. Many of the goals that fail to receive priority status may still be worthy goals. To assure advocates for these goals that they will not be forgotten, principals are advised to develop a multiyear plan in which non-priority goals eventually will be addressed. As priority goals are achieved and retired, non-priority goals can be added to the School Improvement Plan.

Care must be taken that the goals upon which plans are based are stated clearly and correctly. This means that there should be no confusion about the focus of the goal and the basis for determining its accomplishment. Consider the example below:

GOAL: Improve high school attendance

This goal statement is lacking in several respects. First, "attendance" is too vague. Does it refer only to school attendance, or is class attendance also included? It is not unusual, after all, for some high school students to arrive at school but fail to attend certain classes. Second, no target for improvement is indicated. Does a particular level of average daily attendance need to be achieved in order to reach the goal? Or is the real goal to reduce the number of students who miss more than a certain percentage of school days?

The third responsibility associated with goal development involves justifying each chosen goal. Veterans of school improvement planning understand that plans must be "sold" to stakeholders. Individuals typically have "pet" concerns. When they see no goal covering these concerns, they want to know why.

When Matt Landahl, principal of Greer Elementary School, chose to focus reading improvement efforts on fourth and fifth graders, primary grade teachers and parents of primary grade students wondered why (Duke and Landahl 2011). Logic seemed to dictate that improvements would begin with the early grades. Landahl explained that he did not want to send older students to middle school with serious reading deficits. These students' needs were more immediate. Once reading instruction was addressed for the intermediate grades, the focus at Greer then could shift to the primary grades.

Much of the advice pertaining to goal setting applies to the drafting of objectives for each goal as well. Objectives should also be clear and measurable. Since objectives involve the implementation of various strategies, they will be discussed in the next section.

Some Keys to Focusing

- Resist the temptation to elevate all potential goals to priority status.
- Ensure that goals are measurable and unambiguous.
- Be prepared to justify the choice of priority goals.

DETERMINING STRATEGIES

Once goals for a School Improvement Plan have been chosen, planners need to concentrate on each goal, deciding on a series of specific objectives the accomplishment of which will lead to goal achievement. Depending on the complexity of the goal and the duration of the plan, one goal may require many objectives. In their efforts to develop objectives, planners should take into account several considerations.

First, attention must be given to the *difficulty* of achieving particular objectives. Choosing to start with an especially challenging objective increases the likelihood that problems will be encountered and that momentum will be lost. Early setbacks, particularly in chronically low-performing schools, can be devastating. They confirm in the minds of stakeholders that little can be done to turn around the school. Demoralization and loss of hope can result. By carefully choosing initial objectives, ones that are likely to produce some "quick wins," planners pave the way to progress. A quick win might entail adjusting the school schedule so teachers can plan during the school day, replacing outdated technology, or finding local donors willing to support a professional development workshop.

Another consideration involves the *sequencing* of objectives. Certain objectives constitute prerequisites for other objectives. If implementing a supplementary reading program for struggling readers is an objective, it probably should be preceded by extensive professional development. Assuming that teachers will develop facility with the program on their own may be unrealistic.

When planners draft a set of objectives, they also need to consider each objective's *measurability*. If there is no way to determine that an objective has been accomplished, it is less likely to be monitored effectively. With a complex objective, it is better to divide it into several more straightforward objectives so that progress can be tracked more easily. Examples of well-stated objectives include the following:

The percentage of students completing Algebra 1 with a grade of "C" or better by the end of ninth grade will increase by 15 percent.

The number of high school students enrolling in Advanced Placement courses will increase by one hundred.

At least half of this group will earn a 3 or higher on the Advanced Placement test.

These sample objectives could be part of a plan to achieve the overarching goal of increasing the high school graduation rate. In order to accomplish these objectives, planners must identify various strategies to include in the School Improvement Plan. Possible strategies might include double-blocking Algebra 1, creating a Plato Lab where students can get online assistance with algebra, increasing the number of freshmen and sophomores taking honors courses, and creating after-school review sessions two weeks before Advanced Placement tests are given.

Strategies come in various forms and represent the means by which objectives are achieved. To facilitate thinking about the range of possible strategies, the following set of terms is offered as a planning aid:

POLICIES: School-based rules, regulations, and guidelines. Examples: grading policies, homework policies, discipline policies.

PERSONNEL: Staffing arrangements, including individual assignments, job descriptions, team arrangements, and specialists.

PROGRAMS: Formal, school-based offerings intended to address academic and nonacademic needs. Examples: ninth grade academy, supplementary math program, extended day program.

PROCESSES: Organizational mechanisms that support the core functions of teaching and learning. Examples: curriculum alignment, personnel evaluation, classroom observations, school improvement planning.

PRACTICES: Activities related directly to instruction and assessment. Examples: inquiry-based teaching, use of math manipulatives, short-cycle testing.

PROFESSIONAL DEVELOPMENT: School-sponsored training tied to the accomplishment of goals and objectives.

PARENT INVOLVEMENT: Activities related to engaging parents in supporting the school and their children's efforts to succeed academically.

PARTNERSHIPS: Initiatives designed to engage local agencies, businesses, and other organizations in supporting school improvement.

Planners need to consider several factors when choosing strategies for a School Improvement Plan. First of all, is there evidence that the strategy works? Young people are not guinea pigs on whom can be tried any strategy purported to be promising. What is the evidence of effectiveness? Has evidence been gathered through systematic and preferably controlled inquiry? Was evidence collected in schools comparable to the target school? Is the only available evidence based on vendor-sponsored evaluations? Such questions should be answered before determining what strategies to include in the plan.

Examples of evidence-based classroom practices that have proven effective in turning around low-performing schools include the following:

- Reteaching content based on posttest results.
- Differentiating instruction based on prior student performance.
- Ensuring that all students are asked challenging questions.
- Developing, implementing, and reinforcing rules that promote an orderly learning environment.
- Expressing high expectations for all students.

Another consideration for planners concerns whether to adopt, adapt, or create strategies. Although some strategies can be imported and implemented without making any modifications, other strategies need to be adjusted to fit the particular circumstances of a school. On occasion, these circumstances may be so unusual that planners are unable to identify an existing strategy that fits. Local innovation by educators has produced an array of novel strategies that have succeeded in addressing school improvement objectives. Assigning an ex-coach to be a full-time "dropout prevention" monitor, for example, may not have worked in some high schools, but it was the perfect strategy for Fort Worth's South Hills High School. The ex-coach's unique attributes and personal rapport with struggling students enabled him to keep tabs on students at risk of not graduating and make certain they were completing assignments and passing classes.

A third consideration relates to the *compatibility* of strategies. The strategies chosen to achieve a particular objective ideally will reinforce each other. Strategies selected without care, however, actually can have the opposite effect. Pairing student-teacher advisories with a strict set of new school rules, for example, might seem to support a new school safety initiative, but the trust needed for advisories to work is undermined because teachers also are expected to enforce the new rules.

No matter which strategies are chosen for a School Improvement Plan, planners should be prepared to evaluate the effectiveness of the strategies on an ongoing basis. If evidence that a strategy is not working surfaces, steps must be taken to understand why and to adjust or replace the strategy.

Some Keys to Determining Strategies

- Choose some objectives that can be accomplished quickly in order to build confidence and momentum.
- Develop objectives that are measurable.
- When possible, select strategies with a proven record of success.
- Choose strategies that reinforce each other.

DEVELOPING THE PLAN

After deciding on a manageable set of goals to focus on, identifying the objectives that need to be achieved in order to make progress toward each goal, and specifying the strategies that will enable each objective to be accomplished, planners are ready to put the finishing touches on the School Improvement Plan. States and school districts often provide guidelines for drafting plans. Virginia, for example, requires that the following nine topics be covered in three-year plans for schools that are "accredited with warning":

1. A description of how the school will meet accreditation requirements;
2. Specific measures for achieving and documenting student academic achievement;
3. The amount of time in the school day devoted to instruction in the core academic areas;
4. Instructional practices designed to remediate students who have not been successful on state standardized tests;
5. Intervention strategies designed to prevent further declines in student performance;
6. Staff development needed;

7. Strategies to involve and assist parents in raising their child's academic performance;
8. The need for flexibility or waivers to state or local regulations to meet the objectives of the plan; and
9. A description of the manner in which local, state, and federal funds are used to support the implementation of the components of the plan.

Guidelines may also govern the formatting of School Improvement Plans. Connecticut recommends that the improvement goal and related objectives be recorded at the top of the page of the plan. Below the goal and objectives are five columns, each with a different heading:

Column 1:   Identified needs (based on student test results).
Column 2:   Adult actions that will impact student achievement.
Column 3:   School strategies.
Column 4:   How will we monitor and provide evidence of implementation and effectiveness?
Column 5:   Professional development.

The format for School Improvement Plans in the Fairfax County Public Schools (Virginia) calls for an objective located above five columns as well, but these columns are headed as follows:

Column 1:   Strategies.
Column 2:   Person(s) responsible.
Column 3:   Materials needed and costs.
Column 4:   Time line (divided into quarters).
Column 5:   In-process measures.

Although guidelines and formats vary, it is reasonable to expect all School Improvement Plans to include:

• Broad goals (typically requiring a multiyear effort).
• Measurable objectives for each goal (typically achievable in one school year or less).
• Strategies, activities, and/or tasks associated with each objective.

- Resources required to implement each strategy.
- Person(s) responsible for managing efforts associated with each objective and/or strategy.
- Time lines and/or benchmarks for tracking progress on each objective and/or strategy.

Goals, objectives, and strategies have already been discussed. The resources required to implement each strategy range from materials and aligned assessments to additional personnel. The professional development needed to support various initiatives represents both a strategy and a resource. Most resources ultimately involve the allocation of funds, either because people's time is involved or materials come at a cost. It is important for planners to make a careful estimate of the money needed to implement a School Improvement Plan so that the necessary funds can be set aside in advance.

The designation of individuals who are responsible for managing efforts associated with each objective is another critical component of School Improvement Plans. Without designated "project managers," accountability is unlikely. More will be said about this aspect of planning in the next section.

The final element of a plan is the time line for accomplishing each objective and implementing each strategy. Time lines should be accompanied by interim benchmarks or targets to aim for. Examples of possible targets include the percentage of teachers to receive training by a certain date and the percentage of students to pass a particular benchmark test. Time lines and targets increase the likelihood that school personnel will stay "on track" and maintain momentum.

Some Keys to Developing Plans

- Be certain that plans conform to state and district guidelines and formats.
- Identify the human and other resources needed to implement the plan.
- Designate individuals to be responsible for managing each objective.
- Develop time lines and interim targets for objectives and strategies.

MANAGING AND MONITORING THE PLAN

The most carefully developed School Improvement Plan is of little value if stakeholders do not take it seriously or if it is poorly implemented. That is why the seventh phase of the planning process is so important. A School Improvement Plan constitutes a commitment to a school's students and patrons—a contract against complacency. Just as a contract must be managed and monitored to ensure that its provisions are being observed, so it is with School Improvement Plans.

School Improvement Plans are often managed and monitored by the school principal. In the case of chronically low-performing schools, district and state officials may also participate in this process. Although principals are accountable for everything that goes on in their schools, holding them solely responsible for managing and monitoring School Improvement Plans is not necessarily the only, or the best, option.

An effective alternative is the project management approach. A project manager other than the principal is designated for each objective in the School Improvement Plan. Project managers can be assistant principals, counselors, specialists, and teachers. Project management constitutes a means for distributing leadership, cultivating collective accountability, and broadening involvement in the school improvement process.

Each project manager is charged with the responsibility of forming a project management team, typically consisting of three to six individuals. Teams should be comprised of people with expertise related to the target objective. Team members need not be limited to school staff, but can include parents, community members, and higher education faculty. It is each team's initial task to work out a day-to-day plan for tackling its objective.

Monitoring the progress of project teams becomes the responsibility of the Project Management Coordinating Committee (PMCC). The PMCC can be chaired by the principal or another member of the school staff. Sometimes the PMCC's members are also the individuals who drafted the School Improvement Plan. The PMCC meets on a regular basis—every two to four weeks—to hear updates from each project manager. When work on particular objectives (projects) is slowed by unexpected impediments and other problems, the PMCC is supposed to offer guidance and support.

School Improvement Plans often are developed to cover a year or more. Planners sometimes wait until the end of a school year to assess how well the plan is working. This approach means that students will not benefit from any adjustments or modifications in the plan until the following year. By that time some students may have "fallen through the cracks."

To prevent the school improvement process from bogging down or proceeding in an unproductive direction, provisions are needed for midcourse corrections. Scheduling a review of progress at the end of the fall semester creates an expectation that the School Improvement Plan may require changes based on what happened between September and December. A review may lead to abandoning or replacing certain strategies, revising particular objectives, and adjusting time lines. Some schools have even substituted ninety-day plans for yearlong plans in order to encourage staff members to revisit objectives and strategies on a regular basis.

Managing and monitoring the School Improvement Plan is the seventh phase of the planning process, but it should not be regarded as the last phase. Instead, the planning process should be considered to be continuous. Managing and monitoring lead to more data gathering, which then occasions diagnosing, and so forth. The ultimate goal is to create a culture of continuous improvement, one in which educators are committed to seeking new and better ways to promote learning.

Some Keys to Monitoring and Managing Plans

- Involve others besides the principal in managing and monitoring plans.
- Consider project management as a way to distribute responsibilities for School Improvement Plan objectives.
- Schedule periodic reviews of progress and be prepared to make midcourse corrections when plans are not working.

CHAPTER REVIEW

The purpose of this chapter has been to present a seven-stage model of the school improvement planning process and to identify key elements of each stage. The stages include data gathering; diagnosing; assessing context, constraints, and capacity; focusing; determining strategies; developing the plan; and managing and monitoring the plan. The stages form a continuing cycle of activities. Managing and monitoring lead back to data gathering and a repetition of the stages of planning.

To summarize the key elements of each stage and provide readers with a convenient way to reflect on school improvement in their own school, the following School Improvement Checklist is provided.

SCHOOL IMPROVEMENT CHECKLIST

Data Gathering

1. Do planners understand the conditions that justify thinking about improvement?
2. Do planners recognize the difference between mission-oriented and vision-oriented data gathering?
3. Has longitudinal data on student achievement been collected?
4. Has data been gathered from multiple sources?
5. Does data include both descriptive and perceptual data?

Diagnosing

6. Do planners agree on which aspects of school performance need to be diagnosed?
7. Do planners recognize the difference between causes, symptoms, and consequences of problems?
8. Have planners used different analytical approaches?

Assessing Context, Constraints, and Capacity

9. Have planners examined local history, culture, politics, and economics?
10. Have planners identified policy-based and legal constraints on school improvement?
11. Are planners aware of state and district requirements for School Improvement Plan content and format and for the process of developing a School Improvement Plan?

12. Have planners assessed school and district capacity to support school improvement?

Focusing

13. Have planners limited goals to a small number of high-priority goals?
14. Are all goals measurable and unambiguous?
15. Are planners able to justify their choice selection of priority goals?

Determining Strategies

16. Have planners chosen some objectives that can be achieved quickly in order to boost confidence and build momentum?
17. Are all objectives measurable?
18. Have strategies with a proven record of success been selected?
19. Have strategies that reinforce each other been selected?

Developing the Plan

20. Does the School Improvement Plan conform to state and district requirements?
21. Have the human and other resources needed to implement the School Improvement Plan been identified?
22. Have individuals been designated to manage each objective in the School Improvement Plan?
23. Have timelines and interim targets been identified for all objectives and strategies?

Managing and Monitoring the Plan

24. Are individuals besides the principal involved in managing and monitoring the plan?
25. Have planners considered using the project management approach?
26. Have planners scheduled periodic reviews of progress?

SCHOOL IMPROVEMENT PLAN OBJECTIVE: Increase student achievement in reading through professional collaboration and community involvement. Ninety percent of students will either (1) meet end-of-year benchmark accountability standards or (2) make approximately one year's growth in reading achievement.

Improvement Strategies	Person(s) Responsible	Materials Needed and Costs	Time Line				In-Process Measures
			Check the projected quarter for implementing the strategy this school year.				
What we will do to achieve the objective	Person(s) who will monitor the strategy	What materials will be used to implement the strategy? What are the costs?	1st Qtr.	2nd Qtr.	3rd Qtr.	4th Qtr.	How we will monitor progress
K–6: Within Collaborative Learning Teams, identify area(s) of focus and achieve a SMART goal based on June and September data. Identify, share, and implement strategies to accomplish the goal.							
Kindergarten Increase student proficiency in sound recognition, resulting in at least 90 percent of kindergartners meeting or exceeding the kindergarten benchmark.	K teachers and related specialists	Basal text and supporting materials	✓	✓	✓	✓	Daily oral language informal observation

Small-group guided reading anecdotal notes

Biweekly classroom assessments |

• The School Improvement Plan format is based on the plan elements developed by Fairfax County (Virginia) Public Schools (http://www.fcps.edu). This format incorporates most of the elements found in School Improvement Plans across the United States.

NOTE

1. Names—including characters, schools, and/or locations—in the case studies in this book are fictitious and intended to illustrate relevant issues facing schools today. Cases are not intended in any way to depict actual people, places, or events.

REFERENCES

Duke, D. L. 2004. *The Challenges of Educational Change.* Boston: Pearson.

Duke, D. L., and Landahl, M. 2011. Raising test scores was the easy part: A case study of the third year of school turnaround. *International Studies in Educational Administration*, 39(3), 91–114.

Finding a Focus for School Improvement

PREVIEW

As data gathering goes, so goes diagnosing; and without accurate diagnoses of school problems, school improvement efforts are unlikely to succeed. So crucial are data gathering and diagnosing to the improvement process that chapter 2 is devoted to these two planning essentials. Readers will discover a variety of data sources and how to tap them in order to identify the root causes of school performance problems.

"THESE KIDS SHOULD BE DOING MUCH BETTER"

All heads nodded in agreement when Shelley Saunders pointed to the PowerPoint slide with the latest state test results and sighed, "These kids should be doing much better." Seated around the conference table in Saunders's office were the teacher leaders at Riedlinger High School. They had been invited by Saunders, principal of Riedlinger for the past three years, in order to generate possible explanations for the substandard passing rates on end-of-course tests in a variety of subjects, including algebra, American history, chemistry, and government.

Sophia Sanchez complained that the state had changed some of the content for the American history test. Saunders agreed, but noted that Riedlinger's history teachers had known about the changes for more than a year. Besides, she pointed out, student scores had dropped in a variety of subjects besides American history.

Several teachers noted the increasing percentage of Riedlinger students from families qualifying for free or reduced-price meals. Saunders acknowledged that the banking crisis and the downturn in the local economy had hit Riedlinger hard. "Is your judgment that our performance on the state tests is the result of the economic situation?" she asked. Erin Greene pointed to the PowerPoint slide and observed that the pass rates in English had not dropped. "I don't see why changing economic circumstances would affect performance in some subjects but not others," she said. Callie Jones, chair of the English department, chimed in at this point, "Please don't think I'm bragging, but we initiated a new review process this year. Two weeks before the end-of-course tests in English 9 and 11, every English teacher organized systematic reviews of key content for students with a cumulative grade of C or lower."

Shelley Saunders turned to teachers from the history, mathematics, and science departments and asked if they had organized similar review sessions. Milton Adams, a veteran algebra teacher, responded that he had undertaken such a review, but he was not sure his colleagues had done so. Without even pulling up Adams's score reports, Saunders knew—as did everyone at the table—that Adams's students, on average, outperformed other sections of similarly grouped students who had other teachers.

Bill Rodriguez, a respected science teacher and member of the governing board for the local teachers union, spoke up at this point. "I'm opposed to comparing teachers when it comes to student performance on state tests." Saunders asked him to state the reason for his objection. "Because," Rodriquez replied, "we don't randomly assign students to teachers. In fact, some of our best teachers are assigned the toughest students, students who are years behind their peers. How can we compare a teacher with lots of highly motivated students and a teacher with a bunch of struggling students?"

Meetings like the one at Riedlinger High School occur on a regular basis in schools across the United States. Teachers and administrators review data and seek understandings of why some students are doing better than other students and why their school's trend line on tests is going down or up. Experienced educators do not always agree, of course, on the reasons for student achievement trends. It is useful, up to a point, to get all the possible explanations out on the table, and that was exactly what Shelley Saunders tried to do. Once everyone had a chance to express his opinion, however, Saunders needed to direct the group on what data to gather in order to be able to rule out certain explanations and support others. The purpose of this chapter is to identify various data sources that groups such as the one at Riedlinger High School can tap in their quest to pinpoint the likely causes of lower-than-expected student achievement.

ACCURATE DIAGNOSING DEMANDS DILIGENCE

Most experienced educators have their pet notions about why students do poorly or well in school. These notions, if allowed to go unchallenged, can lead to a "rush to judgment" by school improvement planners. Schools, after all, do not have full-time planners. Members of School Improvement Committees typically have demanding jobs as teachers and administrators. No one wants to put in a lot of extra time arriving at the possible causes of school problems. Most educators are characterized by a bias for action. Knowing that time is precious, they want to move quickly from diagnosing to implementing improvement plans.

What these educators may fail to realize, however, is that a lot of valuable time can be wasted if they misdiagnose the reasons behind particular problems. It is interesting to note that a study comparing the problem-solving approaches of "expert" and "nonexpert" principals found an important difference between the two groups (Leithwood and Stager 1989). When they encountered highly complex problems, expert principals devoted much more time to diagnosing and defining the problems than the nonexpert principals. The latter group arrived at a diagnosis relatively quickly, then, took more time to identify possible solutions. Because the expert principals took more time to understand the causes of problems up front, they spent relatively little time zeroing in on solutions.

One reason why accurate diagnosing can be so time consuming concerns the importance of tapping multiple sources of data whenever possible. Veteran educators appreciate how much trouble can result when they jump to conclusions after hearing only one side of the "story." There are almost always competing versions of every story. Prudence and fairness dictate that all sides should be heard *before* a causal judgment is made.

Let us consider the range of possible data sources that school improvement planners should think about tapping.

Data sources can be divided into two categories—descriptive data and impressionistic data. Descriptive data is relatively objective and factual. Quantitative data such as enrollment figures, time spent on various subjects, and test scores belong to this category, but so do observational accounts that are free of judgment and speculation.

Impressionistic data, on the other hand, is subjective in nature. People's opinions about other people and events are an example of qualitative data that is impressionistic, but quantitative data also fits into this category when individuals are asked to give a numerical rating to something, such as teaching performance or school climate. Impressionistic data frequently is gathered through interviews, focus groups, surveys, and questionnaires.

Data collected by questioning people in person, through the use of surveys and questionnaires, or by phone or e-mail can be supplemented by observational data, collected by watching a live "performance" or a videotaped version of a live performance.

Observational data can be recorded in a variety of ways, some more subjective than others. Imagine that a teacher is to be observed conducting a 45-minute lesson. One option is to take extensive *descriptive* notes, focusing on such "objective" matters as the content of instruction, instructional activities, the length of time spent on different activities, and student responses to teacher questions. A second option involves recording *impressions* of the lesson, including judgments about student interest and engagement, teacher effectiveness, and the appropriateness of lesson content.

Besides recording notes, either descriptive or impressionistic, observers may decide to provide a more focused representation of the lesson by counting, checking, coding, rating, or mapping observational data.

COUNTING: The observer decides on certain actions or behaviors to focus on and then counts the number of times they occur during the lesson. Example: The teacher asked students fourteen times not to interrupt during the lesson.

CHECKING: The observer develops or uses a ready-made checklist and records checks when items on the checklist are observed. Example: A check is made because the teacher began the lesson by stating the lesson's objective.

CODING: The observer uses a coding system to identify and classify certain phenomena during the lesson. Example: Every time the teacher asks a question, the question is coded as either "divergent" or "convergent."

RATING: The observer gives a numerical rating to what is observed, using some type of scale. Example: A five-point scale ranging from "never" to "always" is used to rate the extent to which the teacher provides positive reinforcement after students answer questions correctly.

MAPPING: The observer creates a floor plan for the instructional space and then uses one or more of the techniques listed above to record information on the floor plan. Example: A map with all students' desks is drawn and a check is written in the box representing a student's desk each time the student is asked a question by the teacher.

Each of these five ways of collecting observational data is characterized by strengths and weaknesses. Checking, for example, is simple to do, but it is poorly suited to data that is not dichotomous. Coding offers the potential for greater detail, but observers need to be trained in how to apply the codes accurately.

The great benefit of observational data is that it is collected at the time action is occurring. This strength also constitutes a limitation, however. An observer cannot observe what has already happened (unless videotape is available) or what is yet to happen. Collecting data on past actions usually involves asking individuals to respond to questions or statements that require them to remember. To guard against the possibility that an individual may have forgotten important information, it is best to collect data on past events from a number of individuals.

The availability of video recording devices can greatly enhance the task of collecting certain kinds of data. Multiple observers, for instance, can watch the same video footage and share their impressions. Video also enables the technique of stimulated recall to be used. Imagine that a teacher's lesson has been video recorded. Soon after the lesson, the teacher is asked to review the video with an observer. The observer stops the video at certain points and asks the teacher what he was thinking at that moment or why he chose to act in a particular way. Stimulated recall also can be used with students to better understand what they were thinking during a lesson.

Debriefing students after they have completed a lesson, unit, or even an entire course offers another way to obtain valuable data. Asking students what they learned, for example, provides an opportunity to ascertain what content "stuck" and how students reconstruct past learning. Do students, for instance, use a framework or "scaffold" to assist in recalling content? Students' responses to post-lesson debriefing can provide valuable information on how the lesson was taught. Planners should not overlook the contributions that students can make to the school improvement process.

Because students are in classes on a more regular basis than observers, they are able to address issues of instructional continuity and coherence. Student judgments about such matters as the clarity of lesson objectives and teacher directions and the availability of assistance can be extremely important when planners focus on instructional improvement goals.

Another approach to gathering data about students involves the use of "focal students" (Boudett and Steele 2007). Planners choose a sample of students in order to track their progress in a particular subject or across various subjects. Perhaps there is concern that students "in the middle" are not receiving as much attention and assistance as high-achieving and low-achieving students. Selecting several "average" students on whom to collect data may provide insights into their classroom experiences that lead to school improvement initiatives.

At times planners may want to look ahead and learn about students' perceptions of the future. Interviews, surveys, and questionnaires can be used to gain insight into student aspirations, hopes, concerns, and fears. Similar data also can be collected from other stakeholders, including parents and teachers.

Another source of data involves artifacts. Most of the artifacts that planners are likely to inspect are written documents, but in some cases they also may be objects, such as student projects. Documents range from official reports to course syllabi to student work samples. Planners can get a good idea of the issues that their predecessors considered to be important by reviewing previous School Improvement Plans. Other useful official documents include accreditation reports, evaluations of school programs, and school budgets.

To gain insight into what teachers are doing and have done, planners can request course syllabi, lesson plans, and teacher-made tests. Such material provides one basis for determining the extent to which teachers cover required content and align content within and across grade levels. Copies of student assignments provide further information about instructional practice. Teachers of the same subject, for example, can be asked to provide samples of student work that they regard as exemplary, typical, and below average. By comparing these samples, planners can judge the extent to which teachers share common expectations for students.

Given the vast range of potential sources of data, planners can easily find themselves overwhelmed with information. To avoid information inundation, planners should conduct a preliminary assessment of probable concerns in order to be able to focus data collection efforts. It is better to collect a lot of data about the most pressing concerns than a little data about dozens of relatively low-level concerns.

ASKING THE RIGHT QUESTIONS IS CRUCIAL

One of the most valuable tools in a planner's tool kit is a good question. Sometimes a good question represents the unexpected. At other times a good question can be surprisingly simple and straightforward. This section presents a variety of questions that planners may find useful as they go about the task of gathering data. The initial set of questions pertains to student achievement. Subsequent questions address the range of school-based efforts to support student achievement.

How are students doing? Student achievement can be investigated in a variety of ways—by subject, teacher, grade level, cohort, student subgroup, and program. A sample of possible questions to guide inquiry into student achievement is offered below.

QUESTION: Is student achievement greater in some subjects than in others?

Planners need to know whether the level of student achievement is comparable across the curriculum. Comparability can be based on standardized test scores, analyses of work samples, teacher grades, and systematic observations. A school where many students are struggling with mathematics but not with other subjects may need to approach planning quite differently from a school where students have difficulty in a variety of content areas.

QUESTION: Is student achievement greater in some teachers' classes than in other teachers' classes?

Although some teachers resent comparisons across teachers, such comparisons can reveal problems with instruction, efforts to help struggling students, and even the way students are assigned to teachers. Teachers may do all right covering content for most students, but they may not provide effective assistance for a small number of students who have difficulty with the content. In some schools, certain teachers may be assigned larger numbers of struggling students than other teachers, thereby presenting them with greater challenges than other teachers. Pinpointing large variations in student achievement across teachers, especially teachers of the same grade level and subject, can lead to a variety of follow-up questions aimed at determining the reasons why.

QUESTION: Does student achievement vary across an individual teacher's classes?

Although variations in student achievement across teachers are important to identify, planners should not overlook variations across an individual teacher's classes. Such variations may result from scheduling issues, intentional assignment variations, the timing of each class, differential expectations, and other factors. School improvement efforts need to include a close look at the daily schedule, how students are assigned to classes, and how teachers approach each of their classes.

So far the questions have focused on variations in student achievement during a particular school year. Other questions entail examining student achievement over a number of years. Analyzing longitudinal achievement data provides important clues to a school's performance history.

QUESTION: Has student achievement been improving or declining over the past five years?

Finding trends in student achievement over time is a critical element in the diagnostic process. Sustained improvement or decline can be the result of systemic factors such as a leader-directed focus on a particular subject or high teacher turnover in an academic department. Student achievement typically does not vary a great deal from one year to the next, so when planners look at data over time and find a dramatic increase or decrease in achievement, a closer investigation is warranted. Did a precipitous drop in student achievement coincide, for example, with the redrawing of school boundaries or an influx of new students? Did an unexpected achievement gain in a particular subject occur after the adoption of a new textbook series or a supplementary curriculum?

QUESTION: What does student achievement look like when students who are recent transfers from another school and students who have been absent more than twenty days are removed?

Although every school is responsible for educating all of its students, the truest test of a particular school's instructional effectiveness involves an examination of the achievement of students who have attended the school for at least a year and who have not accumulated large numbers of absences. Planners should make every effort to disaggregate data in order to determine the performance of students who have been exposed to a school's instruction on a consistent basis over time.

QUESTION: What is the pattern of achievement for a particular cohort of students over a five-year period?

Many teachers believe that every cohort of students has its distinctive "personality." Sometimes a cohort possesses an abundance of school-spirited students who work hard and take their classes seriously. At other times, a cohort lacks positive student leadership. Tracking a cohort of students over a long period of time provides an alternative to cross-sectional analyses in which the achievement of students in different grade levels is examined for the same year. Cohort analyses over time offer clues regarding the performance of the same group of students as they progress from one grade to another.

QUESTION: What is the track record of students who are retained at grade level for one or more years?

Compelling evidence shows that students who are retained at grade level are much more likely to drop out of school. Given such a dire possibility, it is important for planners to track the impact of retention on students. If the data indicate that retention is associated with failure to graduate, planners should consider alternatives to retention.

QUESTION: Are some student subgroups achieving at significantly higher levels than other student subgroups?

With the advent of the No Child Left Behind Act and various state accountability systems, educators are expected to examine the performance of student subgroups on state standardized tests. When achievement gaps are found between subgroups, efforts must be made to 1) understand why the gaps exist and 2) close the gaps. Among the subgroups for which gaps are of greatest concern are African American, Hispanic, English language learner, low socioeconomic status, and special education students.

QUESTION: In what subjects and grade levels is the greatest progress being made in closing achievement gaps?

Planners should not focus exclusively on negative data. By examining achievement gaps by subject matter area and grade level, planners may discover particular subjects and grade levels where gaps are narrowing. When such encouraging findings are revealed, an effort should be made to determine what teachers are doing to raise the achievement of under-performing subgroups. This information can be of great value in developing strategies for School Improvement Plan objectives.

QUESTION: Do student grades reflect their performance on state standardized tests?

If teachers are grading students appropriately, grades should be reasonably accurate predictors of student performance on state standardized tests. When teacher grades and scores on standardized tests are not highly correlated, planners need to determine why.

QUESTION: Has the number of students identified for special education services been increasing over the past five years?

An upward trend in the number of students identified for special education can be a cause for concern. Some educators see special education as a way around the contemporary focus on test performance. Special education students, depending on the state, may qualify for special testing provisions and modified diplomas. Planners should investigate the possibility that students are being overidentified for special education services.

The preceding questions illustrate a variety of student achievement topics that can be investigated by planners interested in creating successful School Improvement Plans. Once planners identify any issues regarding student achievement, they need to focus on school-based factors that help to explain these issues. It is to these school-based factors that we now turn.

What is the school doing to support learning? In order to promote learning, schools are expected to employ qualified professionals and establish effective programs, processes, and practices. In this section we present a sampling of questions that planners can use to guide their inquiry.

QUESTION: Are there indications that some teachers have not been properly assigned?

The No Child Left Behind Act called for schools to be staffed by highly qualified teachers. Although important, this provision does not ensure that highly qualified teachers necessarily are assigned in ways that maximize their impact on student learning. Planners, of course, should determine whether teachers are teaching subjects for which they are qualified, but in addition they need to look at student achievement on a teacher-by-teacher basis. Do struggling students have access to the most-skilled teachers? Are some teachers' students better prepared to move to the next grade or course than other teachers' students? School improvement, after all, depends on the capabilities and commitments of teachers.

QUESTION: What is the evidence that specialists are contributing to student achievement?

Contemporary schools, especially chronically low-performing schools, frequently employ various specialists, including Title I teachers, reading and mathematics specialists, and instructional coaches. Planners should gather data on how these individuals spend their time and to what effect. Is there data to indicate that students who receive assistance from specialists are benefiting? Do teachers feel that specialists are contributing in meaningful ways to school effectiveness?

QUESTION: Are teachers using proven instructional practices?

Most research on effective schools points to sound instruction based on proven practices as a key to success. Little else matters if teachers fail to 1) organize instruction in ways that promote efficient learning, 2) engage students in meaningful activities, and 3) employ sound classroom assessment practices on a regular basis. The challenge for planners is to gather accurate data on how teachers are teaching. School administrators can share their overall impressions of instructional practices based on periodic classroom observations, but planners also may want to collect student perceptions of teaching, review videotapes of instruction, and conduct their own observations that target particular practices. It goes without saying that instructional practices are suspect in chronically low-performing schools, but planners also must not assume that instruction is necessarily effective in high-performing schools. Good teaching involves so many variables and complexities that ways always can be found to improve instructional practice.

QUESTION: Do teachers differentiate instruction in order to address the needs of various students?

One aspect of instructional practice that is receiving considerable attention is differentiated instruction. Given the range of student ability and prior knowledge in most classrooms, teachers need to be able to make adjustments in instruction for individual students based on their success (or lack of success). Adjustments may involve various grouping formats, the use of peer and adult tutors, alterations in the pacing of instruction, access to special software programs, customized assignments, and texts geared to different reading levels.

QUESTION: What programs and interventions are available for struggling students and how effective are they?

It is not unusual for schools to provide a variety of programs and interventions to help students address learning issues and other problems. What is less typical is to find schools that can produce a comprehensive list of these programs and interventions. Rarest of all are schools that regularly evaluate the effectiveness of their programs and interventions. Planners should make a point of compiling an inventory of programs and interventions and all available data on their effectiveness. An important focus for school improvement might well be the modification or replacement of ineffective programs and interventions for struggling students.

QUESTION: Do struggling students receive timely and targeted assistance based on regular assessments of their progress?

Waiting until end-of-year and end-of-course testing to determine that certain students need help is inexcusable. Planners need to focus on the frequency with which teachers track student progress and the immediacy of their efforts to provide help. When students are assessed on an ongoing basis and given immediate assistance to address problems, they are much less likely to fall behind their peers and eventually give up. Contemporary efforts to implement Response to Intervention (RtI) represent recognition by educators of the benefits of timely and targeted assistance.

QUESTION: Do teachers meet on a regular basis by grade level and subject matter area to analyze student performance, identify struggling students, and coordinate intervention efforts?

Schools that successfully address the needs of struggling students often have established regular occasions when teachers meet to review how students are doing. These meetings can be organized along various lines—teacher teams, academic departments, all teachers from a particular grade level, cross-grade teams, and teams of specialists. Planners first need to find out which groups of teachers meet, how often they meet, and for what purposes they meet. Beyond these basic questions, however, are questions regarding how the meetings are conducted and their actual impact. Just because teachers meet to track student progress is no guarantee that the meetings are productive. Observations of these meetings can provide planners with important data on their effectiveness.

QUESTION: Does an analysis of disciplinary referrals reveal any trends as to when and where problems occur?

Many schools require disciplinary referral forms to be filled out when students are sent to the office for misconduct. These referrals offer planners valuable information regarding when and where behavior problems take place. Problems, for example, may tend to arise at certain points during the school day, on certain days of the week or certain times of the year, in particular locations within or outside the school, and in the classes of particular teachers. Because misconduct interferes with teaching and learning, identifying patterns and trends in disciplinary data can provide a springboard for targeted intervention.

QUESTION: What professional development have teachers been provided over the past three years, and how is the focus of this in-service work related to areas of concern at the school?

Professional development is frequently an important component of School Improvement Plans. Planners should inquire about recent professional development initiatives and their relationship (or lack of relationship) to the most pressing concerns at the school. How teachers feel about the value of professional development initiatives should be determined before launching any new efforts. Planners also need to search for evidence that previous professional development has made a positive impact on teaching and learning.

QUESTION: What effort is the school making to involve parents in supporting teaching and learning, and how successful has it been?

Highly effective schools usually find a variety of ways to inform and involve parents. From student progress reports and school newsletters to active parent-teacher organizations and regularly scheduled conferences for concerned parents, these schools reach out to parents and find ways to enlist the support of even the busiest parents. School Improvement Plans frequently contain at least one goal or objective related to parent involvement; so the more data planners can collect on the current level of parent involvement, the better they can pinpoint areas of need.

QUESTION: When parents contact the school, what questions do they tend to ask?

When parents are thinking about sending their children to a particular school or when they are worried about how their children are doing at school, they are likely to contact the school and ask a variety of questions. The questions they ask of principals, guidance counselors, secretaries, and teachers represent a valuable source of information regarding parental interests and concerns. By reviewing the most frequently asked questions, planners can increase their understanding of what parents think about when deciding where to send their children to school and whether to withdraw their children from a particular school.

The questions in this section are only a brief sampling of the possible queries that planners can ask in order to gather data regarding the extent and effectiveness of school-based efforts to support teaching and learning. Additional questions, of course, can focus on factors beyond the control of the school, such as conditions at home and in the community. Although the data gathered from such questions may help to explain why some students are not experiencing success, planners are advised to concentrate their efforts on the concerns they are most likely to reduce or resolve.

School-to-school comparisons. There is one additional source of data that can provide planners with insights regarding how to focus their improvement efforts. In every state a variety of schools are similar in grade configuration, size, and student composition. By identifying a sample of these schools, planners can obtain data for comparative purposes. It is important for planners to know how their school measures up to similar schools. Are students at similar schools performing at higher levels in certain subjects? Are fewer students suspended at these schools? Is the graduation rate higher?

Locating similar schools with better track records is an effective antidote to making excuses. Investigating what these schools are doing to achieve better results can lead planners to focus on implementing comparable measures in order to improve outcomes. While school-to-school comparisons are especially important for chronically low-performing schools, they also are useful for boosting achievement and motivating staff at relatively high-performing schools.

CONVERTING DATA INTO DIAGNOSES

Contemporary planners often find themselves awash in data. The data is of little value, however, if it cannot be used to arrive at accurate diagnoses of the root causes of concerns. But the diagnostic process can be daunting. The point has been made already—distinguishing between causes and symptoms is challenging. It is tempting, for example, for planners to agree on "causes" that they already know how to address, even if these are not the real sources of problems.

Consider an example. Planners decided that a cause of low graduation rates at a high school was student unwillingness to attend "help" sessions after school. The planners failed, however, to continue asking "Why?" Why didn't students attend "help" sessions? If they had probed deeper, they would have discovered that many students had after-school commitments and other students simply were tired of school at the end of a long day. Why didn't school staff explore alternative ways to deliver assistance, for instance a "zero" period tutorial at the beginning of the school day or a required "help" session during students' free periods?

Asking "Why?" is the most critical part of diagnosing. Why is teacher turnover so high? Why aren't teachers using proven instructional practices? Why don't all teachers address reading comprehension problems? Why is so much instructional time lost to classroom disruptions?

One technique for generating "why" questions involves activity tracking. Imagine listing all significant changes at a school during the past three to five years. A time line is created and on it are noted the points at which major changes in personnel, programs, policies, practices, and processes took place. Also noted are school-wide professional development activities and any newly created partnerships with community organizations. A separate line on the time line is created for each of these changes, and the duration of the change is recorded. A supplementary reading program was tried for two years. A math coach was assigned to the school for nine months. Workshops on classroom management were offered for all teachers during July of the third year.

Once all changes have been tracked on the time line, planners then record student achievement on state tests over the same three-to-five-year period. If interim test data is available for periods leading up to state testing, that data also can be recorded. Planners then take note of any changes in the slope of the lines representing student achievement in various content areas. Do these changes in achievement correspond to any changes in personnel, programs, policies, and so on? If so, inferences can be made regarding possible causes for changes in achievement. Did language arts scores drop following the loss of three veteran English teachers? Did math scores rise after a math coach was hired to work with the mathematics department? Was there no change in test scores or disciplinary referrals following school-wide classroom management training?

Having asked a variety of "why" questions based on a preliminary analysis of the data, planners eventually must make some judgments about the probable causes of concerns that will be addressed in their School Improvement Plan. As the examples below suggest, these judgments can be difficult. Planners may lack some information that could be useful in arriving at a judgment regarding the true causes. Still, at some point a determination or "best guess" must be made and used as the basis for developing goals and objectives, and selecting strategies for the School Improvement Plan. If problems persist despite these efforts, planners may need to go back to the drawing board and consider additional or alternative causes.

JUDGMENT: Is low student achievement more a function of inadequate time for instruction or inadequate use of existing instructional time?

If what students are expected to learn has increased dramatically without a corresponding increase in time for learning, declining achievement might be time-related. First, however, planners must rule out another possibility—that teachers have not made appropriate adjustments in their use of the available time for instruction. Diagnostic judgments invariably entail eliminating some possible causes. To determine whether instructional time is being used efficiently and effectively, planners may need to rely on classroom observation data and the assessments of trained observers.

JUDGMENT: If a program is not accomplishing what it is supposed to accomplish, is it because the program is not well designed to address student needs, the program has been poorly implemented, or other reasons?

Because significant school resources go into running a variety of programs, it is important for planners to identify programs that are producing disappointing results. The next step is to determine the likely reason or reasons why. If a program is poorly designed to address the needs of a school's target population, it probably should be replaced. If the program is not succeeding because it has been implemented incorrectly, another judgment must be considered:

JUDGMENT: If a program has been implemented poorly, is it because of teacher resistance, inadequate resources, lack of teacher training, or other reasons?

Just because a program is not living up to its potential is no reason necessarily to scrap it. If the program is likely to succeed with the proper training, more resources, or a different group of teachers, planners should consider objectives and strategies that address these issues. In some instances, a new program just needs more time to take hold. Although isolating probable causes for program implementation problems is rarely easy, planners should not back away from making the effort.

Arriving at judgments does not cease when planners have isolated the probable causes of problems. Additional judgments must be made regarding which improvement strategies to try. Section II of this book addresses a variety of strategic judgments associated with specific areas of school performance. One judgment, however, applies to all improvement efforts:

JUDGMENT: Which leadership style is best suited to the improvement challenges that face the school?

Making a judgment regarding the best leadership style for the circumstances can be tricky, especially when the individual making the judgment is the principal. Different circumstances, though, call for different approaches to leading. Sometimes a principal needs to become highly directive, giving staff explicit assignments and holding them to strict time lines. In other cases a more collaborative approach is warranted with various staff members assuming leadership roles. Before putting the finishing touches on a School Improvement Plan, planners are advised to spend time considering the leadership style best suited to implementing the plan.

CHAPTER REVIEW

School Improvement Plans that actually lead to improved student achievement derive from accurate diagnoses of the causes of achievement problems. Accurate diagnoses, in turn, depend on 1) the collection of high-quality data regarding student achievement and school-based efforts to promote and support it and 2) careful analyses of this data. Such analyses focus on continually asking "Why?" and on recognizing the difference between symptoms and causes.

A variety of sources of data are described in this chapter. They include student test results and other data concerning student achievement; observational data collected in classrooms; data collected from stakeholders using interviews, focus groups, surveys, and questionnaires; and artifactual data. Examples are offered of the kinds of questions that planners can ask in order to focus data collection on key areas of school performance and operations.

Arriving at data-based diagnoses of school problems requires sound reasoning and good judgment. Several tough "judgment calls" are examined in order to illustrate the challenges planners face when they try to identify the root causes of problems. When these causes are beyond educators' control, planners may have to concentrate instead on addressing symptoms that educators are able to impact.

REFERENCES

Boudett, K. P., and Steele, J. L. 2007. *Data Wise in Action.* Cambridge, MA: Harvard Education Press.

Leithwood, K., and Stager, M. 1989. Expertise in principals' problem solving. *Educational Administration Quarterly*, 25(2), 126–161.

CHAPTER 3

Planning and Implementation Problems

PREVIEW

"Forewarned is forearmed" is good advice for school improvement planners. There are plenty of impediments along the road to better schools. This chapter reviews a variety of problems that can derail school improvement planning and the process of implementing plans. By anticipating the possibility of these problems, planners can reduce the likelihood of frustration and failure.

"WHAT WENT WRONG?"

As he sat alone in his office on the last day of school before the summer break, Jeff Jones kept repeating the same question to himself. "What went wrong? I thought we had a great School Improvement Plan. What went wrong?"

One thing was clear. Palomar Elementary School had failed to hit its School Improvement Plan targets in both reading and mathematics. The goals of reducing disciplinary referrals and absenteeism were missed as well, though not by much. Jones was disappointed with the lukewarm response to the goal of establishing a professional learning community at Palomar. Teachers also had balked at embracing full inclusion for Palomar's special education students, another School Improvement Plan goal.

Jones asked Jasmine Reed, his instructional coach, to step into his office. Together they tried to recall where their plans might have gone awry. Reed wondered if teachers had needed more professional development before implementing the new reading series that had been adopted. Jones admitted he had not been impressed with the publisher-sponsored workshop that had been provided for teachers the previous August.

"What about the PLC initiative?" Jones asked. "Remember when we added it as a goal? We thought it would be a great foundation for improving reading and math." Reed agreed, noting that the focus on collaborative analysis of student data should have led to a team approach to delivering assistance to struggling students.

"And what about inclusion?" Jones added. "I thought that we made it crystal clear to the staff. Palomar needed to raise the achievement of its special needs students if it was to meet state benchmarks."

"You did make it clear," Reed replied, "but I think some teachers are fundamentally opposed to the idea of inclusion." The two administrators discussed how they could address resistance and whether there were viable alternatives. Reed suggested they explore the possibility of implementing Response to Intervention in the fall. Jones responded that he was reluctant to try anything new until they understood why they had failed to achieve their goals for the current School Improvement Plan.

Jones and Reed sat in silence for several minutes. "Do you think we tried to do too much?" Jones asked. "Or did we try to do the wrong things?" Reed responded.

◆

When school improvement efforts produce disappointing results, it may be impossible to determine precisely why, but reflecting on the possible reasons is still worthwhile. Jeff Jones and Jasmine Reed raised two possibilities at the end of the vignette. They probably did attempt too many ambitious goals for one school year. Perhaps Palomar would have experienced more positive results if they had chosen a few less ambitious goals, ones they would have been certain to accomplish. That way, the staff could have celebrated their accomplishments and used the momentum to tackle more challenging goals. School leaders, however, are always under pressure to address a wide variety of concerns.

Many of the problems that undermine the success of School Improvement Plans arise during planning when decisions must be made about what to focus on and what not to focus on and what improvement strategies to try. Additional problems can occur when plans are put into action. We refer to these as implementation problems. This chapter takes a look at some common planning and implementation problems that planners would do well to anticipate.

PLANNING PROBLEMS

In chapter 1 we presented a seven-stage model of the planning process. Six of the stages take place prior to implementing the School Improvement Plan, and problems can arise at each of these stages. Problems that arise early in the planning process and go undetected or are not addressed effectively can compound over time, reducing the likelihood of School Improvement Plan success.

Problems with data gathering. Educators are busy people, and planning is not their primary purpose. The temptation therefore may be great to take shortcuts when collecting the data upon which School Improvement Plans are to be based. We strongly urge planners to think twice before doing so. A School Improvement Plan will be no better than the data used to identify areas in need of improvement.

Focusing too much on collecting one type of data represents one potential problem. Perhaps the focus is on standardized test data and not a balance of test data and other indicators of student performance. Or the focus is on data from one year instead of data from several years. Some planners may be tempted to rely exclusively on opinions instead of balancing this data with more objective observational data. In any case, planners should always strive to collect multiple types of data.

A second problem concerns overreliance on data from one source. Sometimes, for instance, a School Improvement Plan is based almost exclusively on the perceptions of the principal and members of the school leadership team. It is important for planners to gather data from enough stakeholder groups to enable them to determine the extent to which groups agree on important issues. Excluding teacher, student, or parent views can lead to plans that miss critical concerns.

Although planners should pursue an inclusive policy when tapping data sources, they also need to know which questions to address to which groups. Asking certain stakeholders questions they are not in a position to answer contributes nothing to the planning process. It makes little sense, for example, to ask students technical questions about the accuracy of the taught curriculum. On the other hand, students who have completed a curriculum unit may be able to offer important insights regarding how well content was organized and covered.

Knowing the right questions to ask is especially important when planners conduct needs assessments. People frequently confuse needs and desires. Helping respondents to understand the difference can improve the quality of needs assessment data. People also may not always be aware of what they need. If teachers, for example, have never heard of new software for students who struggle with Algebra 1, they cannot indicate that they need to learn how to use it. To maximize the usefulness of needs assessments, therefore, planners should increase stakeholder awareness of possible needs and available options for addressing them *before* conducting a needs assessment.

Another data-gathering problem concerns focusing too much on data from one point in time. There are various reasons why such data can be misleading. Perhaps key personnel had just been replaced or the school community recently had faced a crisis. Regardless of the reason, data representing an extended time period is preferable to data from one point in time. Such data enables planners to spot long-term trends and pinpoint the circumstances surrounding the onset of problems.

Collecting too much data is another problem that planners should guard against. There is no benefit to being inundated by an abundance of data. Most schools have a limited capacity for processing and analyzing data. To conserve resources and avoid overwhelming people, planners should consider a two-phased data collection process. Phase 1 involves a relatively quick overview of existing data, including student achievement data and other "school report card" information. Using this data to identify several prominent areas of concern enables planners to move to Phase 2, where they can undertake a very focused effort to collect additional data related specifically to targeted areas of concern.

Data-gathering Problems

- Collecting too much of one type of data.
- Overrelying on one source of data.
- Asking questions that respondents are in no position to answer.
- Focusing on data from one point in time.
- Collecting too much data.

Problems with diagnosing. Good data does not automatically lead to good diagnoses. Mention already has been made of the possibility that planners will treat symptoms of school problems as causes. Although addressing symptoms can produce some short-term improvements, long-term gains depend on getting at root causes.

One reason why planners confuse symptoms with causes is that they stop asking "Why?" too soon. Imagine that planners are trying to diagnose the causes of a drop in the number of fourth graders passing the state reading test. When a fourth grade teacher is asked "Why?," she responds that too much instructional time was lost because of classroom management problems. When asked why so much time was lost, the teacher identifies a group of five boys who were regularly inattentive and disruptive during the previous school year. One more round of asking "Why?" reveals that the boys, all struggling readers, had been together since kindergarten. It is likely, therefore, that the five boys developed patterns of dysfunctional behavior that only could be broken by placing them in different classes.

Another reason for inaccurate diagnoses involves the assumption that a correlation constitutes a cause. Just because two phenomena enjoy a statistical relationship does not prove that they are causally linked. Class size, for example, may be correlated with student achievement, but this does not necessarily mean that the number of students in a class determines student achievement. How teachers respond to class size is more likely to be the determining factor.

While on the subject of statistics, it is important to recognize how "data averaging" can mislead planners. Averages can conceal as much as they reveal, especially when the performance of various individuals is being averaged. Consider the case of a teacher pilot testing a new science curriculum. When student test scores are examined at the end of a year of the new curriculum, the average test score is little changed from the preceding year (when the old curriculum was in place). Automatically concluding that the two science curriculums were comparable would be a mistake, however. When the scores of each student are investigated, planners discover that most students who were exposed to the old curriculum had scores clustered around the mean. As for the new curriculum, roughly half of the students posted very high scores, while the other half posted very low scores. The averages may have been comparable, but the actual impact of the two curriculums on individual students was quite different.

Given the complexities of the education process, it is unlikely that any significant school problem is the result of a single cause. Planners, therefore, should resist the temptation to oversimplify their diagnoses. Take the example of a drop in student achievement in Algebra 1. When each student with a poor score on the end-of-course test is put under the microscope, a variety of likely causes emerge. Some students did not take advantage of pretest review sessions. A subset of these students also had a large number of absences during the second semester. Another group of students had a substitute teacher for three weeks in February. Before choosing strategies to improve performance in Algebra 1, planners must determine which causes to focus on.

Sometimes oversimplification of causes is the result of generalizing too much. In other cases, planners pin their hopes on a particular cause of a problem because that is the cause they are best prepared to address. A principal, for example, may decide that students who are struggling in mathematics need a double dose of math instruction. If the problem has more to do with inadequate instruction than exposure to math content, then doubling the time can only compound the problem. The principal may have reasoned, however, that it is easier to double-block math classes than improve the quality of math instruction or hire more skilled math teachers.

The diagnostic process can also be undermined by denial. In certain instances planners may purposely overlook certain causes in order to protect special interests. Politics often gets a bad name because politicians are perceived to spend too much time trying to pin the blame for problems on their opponents. Planning also can have a similar "political" dimension. No one likes to be blamed for contributing to a problem. Some teachers, for example, may try to shift the focus for low student achievement from instructional problems to lack of parental support and inadequate resources. In order for school improvement planning to be regarded as a credible process, planners must make every effort to avoid explanations that cater to special interests.

Problems with Diagnosing

- Confusing symptoms with causes.
- Neglecting to keep asking "Why?".
- Assuming that a correlation constitutes a cause.
- Relying exclusively on data averaging.
- Oversimplifying the identification of causes.
- Overcommitting to a particular cause.
- Ignoring particular causes in order to protect individuals or groups.

Assessing context, constraints, and capacity. The most serious mistake that planners can make with regard to this third phase of the school improvement process is to skip it. Chronicles of failed improvement initiatives frequently reveal that planners simply assumed stakeholders would be supportive. The rule of thumb for school improvement planning, as with most things, should be "never assume."

Educators involved in trying to improve chronically low-performing schools, for example, are often willing to implement untested reforms on the grounds that "things can't get any worse." Unfortunately, things can always get worse, at least for certain individuals. Planners must never lose sight of the fact that, no matter how bad the situation, some individuals are likely to benefit from the status quo. In every struggling school, there are teachers who are doing a solid job of teaching and students who are succeeding. These individuals may not welcome reforms. Nor may teachers who, despite not being especially effective, have grown comfortable with their circumstances and complacent.

Planners make a mistake when they do not expect some level of resistance to school improvement efforts. The focus of the third phase of the school improvement process is to determine possible sources of resistance. This means looking at the past as well as the present. What has been the local response to previous school improvement efforts?

Which individuals and groups have challenged these efforts and what were their reasons?

School culture constitutes another potential impediment to improvement efforts. Culture, by nature, is an inertial force, resistant to change. Made up of traditions, norms, and beliefs, the culture of a school may stand between planners and successful improvement efforts. When planners fail to understand school culture, they place their improvement efforts at risk. A good first step in assessing school culture is to determine which aspects of the school have remained unchanged over the years. These aspects typically represent what members of the school community have come to take for granted. Changing these aspects is likely to be the greatest challenge for any school improvement initiative.

Identifying important elements of a school's culture is not necessarily a simple, straightforward process. This is especially true for planners who have been associated with the school for a long period of time. Because culture represents what people take for granted, veterans of a school staff may not even recognize key elements of their school's culture. The best insights into school culture actually may be gleaned from individuals who are new to the school or even outsiders. Planners therefore should not rely solely on input from longtime staff members in order to learn about school culture.

Another aspect of the third phase of school improvement planning involves determining the capacity of the school district to support school improvement. Here, again, planners can run into problems. One major problem concerns overestimating the district's capacity for support. Before getting too far into the planning process, planners should schedule time with central office personnel in order to determine what resources they are willing to commit to school-based improvement. If assurances of sustained support cannot be obtained, planners need to moderate their improvement plans or seek support from other sources.

Problems with Assessing Conditions

- Assuming that all stakeholders will embrace improvement efforts.
- Failing to understand school culture.
- Overestimating the capacity of the school district to support improvement efforts.

Focusing. It is likely that data gathering and diagnosing will reveal a variety of concerns that need to be addressed in a School Improvement Plan. This does not mean that planners should try to tackle every concern, at least not in the same plan. A common mistake, however, is for planners to include a long list of goals in order to avoid accusations that they neglected some concerns. Although such action is understandable, it can be self-defeating. Creating a School Improvement Plan that overwhelms school personnel serves no one's interests.

Focusing on a manageable number of goals—typically three to five goals—may be a key to the success of a School Improvement Plan, but it alone does not ensure success. Planners can decide to focus on the wrong goals. Deciding to address problems over which school personnel exercise little or no control, for example, leads only to frustration. Poverty clearly creates challenges for schools, but schools typically are not in a position to reduce poverty or its impact on the lives of students when they are not in school.

Planners can also undermine School Improvement Plans by choosing to focus on long-term goals instead of short-range and intermediate goals. The best School Improvement Plans specify goals that can be achieved in a year or two, thereby generating feelings of accomplishment and building momentum to tackle additional, more challenging goals. Trying to undertake long-term goals in an annual School Improvement Plan serves only to increase the likelihood of failure and frustration with the improvement process.

Another common mistake during the focusing phase of school improvement involves setting goals that are difficult to measure. Planners find it hard to determine if progress is being made when goals are stated in vague or highly generalized terms. The inability to determine progress, in turn, can lead to the abandonment of goals and a sense of futility for school personnel.

Goals for which no sense of urgency can be generated also pose a problem for planners. One reason for the third phase of the planning process— the phase involving the assessment of context, constraints, and capacity—is to determine whether local conditions are likely to support efforts to improve a particular aspect of schooling. When it seems unlikely that school personnel will rally behind a particular improvement goal, then building support to tackle that goal becomes the first order of business.

One other problem during the focusing stage should be mentioned. Because principals' evaluations are often tied to the success of school improvement efforts, some school leaders attempt to "game the system." They opt to focus on modest goals or goals that already have been accomplished in order to ensure a positive evaluation. Such action obviously does little or nothing to produce genuine school improvement.

Problems with Focusing

- Focusing on too many problems at one time.
- Focusing on problems over which school personnel have little or no control.
- Focusing on long-term goals instead of short-term or intermediate goals.
- Setting goals whose progress cannot be measured.
- Setting goals for which no sense of urgency is felt.

Determining strategies. Once planners decide on the concerns that should be addressed in the School Improvement Plan, they turn to the selection of strategies that are likely to improve conditions. Here, too, care must be exercised.

One problem that can arise during this phase is expecting one strategy to address all facets of a complex problem. Take the problem of a high dropout rate. Students drop out of school for a variety of reasons, ranging from credit deficiencies and struggles with particular subjects to feelings of alienation and isolation. One strategy, such as a summer credit recovery program, may assist certain students in remaining in school but fail to meet the needs of other potential dropouts. Planners should target a specific group of potential dropouts or, if they want to cover all possible causes of dropping out, identify a variety of strategies.

Planners also must be careful not to identify too many strategies for a particular goal or objective. Every strategy must be managed and monitored. Choosing a large number of strategies can overtax school personnel and reduce the likelihood that any single strategy will be implemented successfully.

Many strategies, especially those associated with special instructional materials and methods, require considerable training. Planners make a mistake when they underestimate the professional development required to implement a strategy. The history of educational reform is littered with examples of sound strategies that failed to make a difference because teachers were not given sufficient time and training to master the reforms.

Strategies come in various forms, ranging from comprehensive programs that include curriculum materials and instructional guidelines to policies aimed at a very specific issue such as absenteeism. Planners frequently learn about strategies by talking with colleagues in other schools and school systems and by attending professional conferences. In other cases, vendors contact schools to promote their products. Time pressure can lead planners to select strategies without checking to see how well the strategy has worked in other settings. Such hasty action is very risky. The negative consequences of choosing the wrong strategy are great and include wasted time, energy, and resources. In some cases, students actually can be harmed by the selection of an inappropriate or untested strategy. No strategy should be chosen without consulting others who have used it and investigating any independent evaluations of the strategy.

When choosing strategies that have been developed in other settings and strategies that are marketed by commercial firms, planners need to determine if the strategies have to be adapted to local circumstances. Every school is characterized by certain features that are unique. The size, student makeup, curriculum, level of teacher expertise, past history and experience with school improvement, and community expectations of a school are all variables that can impact the implementation of a strategy. Considering these variables *before* choosing a strategy can reduce the likelihood of a mismatch.

In some cases, no amount of adaptation is likely to improve the prospects of success for a strategy. The fact is that the strategy is ill-suited to the school improvement goal. Still, planners sometimes select such strategies. Why they do so may have to do with how the strategy is marketed or the desire of planners to implement something new and exciting. How often have principals returned from conferences with an innovative strategy that they cannot wait to try? Enthusiasm for a particular strategy always should be tempered by a careful examination of the problems it is supposed to address and the likelihood that it will make a difference.

Problems with Determining Strategies

- Expecting one strategy to address all facets of a complex problem.
- Identifying too many strategies for one goal or objective.
- Underestimating the training needed to implement a strategy.
- Failing to check on the track record of a strategy.
- Failing to adapt a strategy to local circumstances.
- Choosing a strategy that is ill-suited to a goal or objective.

Developing the plan. School Improvement Plans are developed in various ways. Sometimes an effort is made to involve the entire staff of a school. At other times, a specially designated School Improvement Team is charged with the responsibility. In some cases, principals tackle the task by themselves.

The success of a School Improvement Plan depends, to a great extent, on whether the school staff and members of the school community feel a high degree of ownership in the plan. Although it is not always efficient to engage all these individuals in the actual drafting of the plan, opportunities for widespread input from stakeholders should be provided. Those responsible for drafting the plan should be open about the reasons why they chose certain goals and objectives and rejected others.

Problems can arise as a result of how various details in School Improvement Plans are handled. A common mistake, for example, concerns the creation of unrealistic time lines. Plans must be implemented by individuals who typically have full-time jobs teaching students and supporting learning. Working on a School Improvement Plan constitutes an additional responsibility. Planners need to be sensitive to the workload of staff members assigned to particular goals and objectives. Whenever possible, releasing these individuals from some of their duties is advisable.

Principals as well as staff members can become overloaded as a result of duties associated with school improvement. Some principals, in order to maintain control over school improvement or to avoid over-extending staff, assume responsibility for every School Improvement Plan goal and objective. Such action is ill-advised for various reasons, including the potential negative impact on principals' other responsibilities and the missed opportunity to cultivate a culture of collaboration around school improvement.

In order to avoid overloading individuals with school improvement responsibilities, principals sometimes assign particular goals and objectives to a group of staff members. This strategy, while seemingly logical and well intentioned, can backfire. When more than one person is responsible for supervising work on a school improvement goal or objective, confusion can arise. According to the project management approach advocated in this handbook, one individual should be designated as the "manager" for every objective in the School Improvement Plan. Each manager, in turn, creates his own project team to help work on the objective, but only the manager is ultimately responsible for providing direction, maintaining momentum, and reporting back to the principal on progress.

One other detail needs to be addressed. The success of a School Improvement Plan generally is contingent on the acquisition and allocation of resources. Sometimes the resources are materials and equipment. In other cases resources represent personnel or funds for training. Regardless of the type of resources required, planners need to avoid underestimating what resources will be necessary to support school improvement efforts. Having progress stalled because of failure to anticipate resource needs can undermine morale and derail efforts to address important concerns.

Problems with Developing Plans

- Failing to get input from all stakeholder groups.
- Creating unrealistic time lines.
- Overloading individuals with too many responsibilities related to the plan.
- Assigning more than one manager for each objective.
- Underestimating the resources needed to accomplish each objective.

IMPLEMENTATION PROBLEMS

Each of the planning stage problems discussed in the preceding section can undermine the successful implementation of a School Improvement Plan. Even when planners are careful to avoid these problems, however, the possibility exists for other problems to arise once work begins on implementing the School Improvement Plan. And addressing these implementation problems effectively is not the end of the story. The successful implementation of a School Improvement Plan is no guarantee that improvements will be sustained. The potential for slippage and backsliding requires that school leaders remain ever vigilant.

The importance of managing and monitoring School Improvement Plans was stressed in chapter 1. When principals and project managers become distracted and turn their attention away from managing and monitoring plans, the likelihood of implementation problems increases. Just knowing that key personnel are regularly checking on the progress being made on School Improvement Plan goals and objectives is enough to keep many staff members focused and motivated.

Over-managing and over-monitoring the implementation of School Improvement Plans, of course, can also be a problem. Staff members must be accorded a degree of trust and discretion in order to enact strategies. The key is to establish a process whereby implementers report on their progress and receive periodic constructive feedback on their efforts. When progress is stalled, assistance should be readily available.

A variety of problems can impede the progress of implementation efforts. Attempting to implement all strategies in a plan simultaneously, for example, can overtax resources and the capacity of leaders to provide constructive feedback. When certain strategies are especially complicated, pilot testing them before requiring full implementation may be advisable. Such a preliminary step provides an opportunity to identify impediments and iron out any kinks.

Another problem concerns the premature cessation of professional development training. Implementing various strategies associated with school improvement, especially when new curriculums and instructional methods are involved, requires more than a summer workshop or two. Planners make a mistake when they expect training to end when new strategies are launched. Training that continues throughout the year is the best insurance against improper implementation and eventual abandonment of improvement strategies.

Sometimes when new strategies challenge teachers' cherished beliefs and familiar practices, professional development needs to provide opportunities to "unlearn" (Sarason 1982). It is naive, in other words, to expect teachers who have spent years developing particular practices and beliefs to set them aside immediately when asked to change. Planners should provide, as part of the training associated with implementing a School Improvement Plan, occasions when teachers identify their beliefs and practices and discuss why they may not be well suited to their current assignments. When planners fail to make such provisions, teachers frequently revert to their familiar practices and beliefs as soon as the new strategies encounter difficulties.

There is no reason, of course, to expect newly implemented strategies to work perfectly at first. All School Improvement Plans entail some "growing pains" as staff members learn new methods and programs. In certain cases, however, these "growing pains" are the result of poorly designed strategies and inappropriate goals and objectives. When school leaders determine that elements of the School Improvement Plan are unlikely to produce desired improvements, it is essential that they make midcourse corrections. Waiting until the end of the school year to adjust elements of the plan can waste precious resources as well as jeopardize the educational experiences of students.

Sometimes midcourse corrections involve relatively minor changes such as adjusting the timetable for implementing strategies or modifying the pacing guide to be used with a new curriculum. In other cases, however, corrections may call for replacing a new program that proved to be a poor match for student needs or abandoning an intervention that failed to help students raise their achievement.

Even with midcourse corrections and awareness of the kinds of problems that can arise during the implementation of School Improvement Plans, planners sometimes are powerless to prevent some backsliding. Researchers have dubbed this process "the implementation dip" and warned school personnel not to be surprised if it occurs. The reasons for slippage are not clearly understood, but some observers have attributed it to "reform fatigue." Implementing a School Improvement Plan invariably entails more training, more meetings, and more effort in general. People get tired, especially when they fail to see sizable gains in student achievement. Other observers believe that the implementation dip may result from teachers exhausting their reservoir of skills and knowledge regarding the challenges they face. Without additional skills and knowledge, improvement efforts are likely to plateau or even diminish.

Although it may be impossible to avoid some backsliding, the impact of such a reversal of progress can be mitigated by raising awareness that it can occur and by encouraging stakeholders to take a long-range view of school improvement. Such a view requires individuals to see a School Improvement Plan for a given school year as one step among many. The greatest hope for sustained improvement resides in a school community's commitment to continuous improvement.

Implementation Problems

- Neglecting to manage and monitor school improvement efforts.
- Overmanaging and over-monitoring.
- Implementing too many strategies at the same time.
- Ending professional development training too soon.
- Failing to make midcourse corrections when improvement plans are not working.
- Losing momentum when desired outcomes are not achieved.

CHAPTER REVIEW

Problems can arise during any stage of the school improvement process. Problems that occur during planning and go uncorrected are likely to undermine efforts to implement School Improvement Plans. Various examples of planning problems were reviewed in the chapter. They ranged from failing to collect enough data on school concerns to confusing symptoms and causes of problems. Other issues included failing to understand school culture, electing to focus on too many problems, and underestimating the training required to undertake improvement strategies.

The ultimate success of School Improvement Plans also depends on how well the plans are implemented. Among the problems that can derail improvement efforts during implementation are under- and over-managing the process, trying to implement too many strategies simultaneously, and failing to make adjustments when particular strategies are not producing desired results.

REFERENCE

Sarason, S. B. 1982. *The Culture of the School and the Problem of Change.* 2nd ed. Boston: Allyn and Bacon.

SCHOOL IMPROVEMENT SCENARIOS
Key Concerns for Planners

Contemporary school improvement efforts can focus on a broad range of concerns, including raising student achievement in reading and mathematics, improving school culture and instruction, providing targeted assistance to English language learners and other at-risk students, and reducing absenteeism. The chapters in section II offer overviews of each of these concerns, summaries of current research, and promising strategies for planners to consider as they go about the work of improving their schools.

Each chapter concludes with a sample School Improvement Plan, including goals, objectives, and strategies.

CHAPTER 4

Reading Improvement
Raising Reading Achievement at Lincoln Elementary School

PREVIEW

The opening case illustrates a school facing challenges in reading achievement. An overview of what experts say about the five main areas of reading is presented, followed by ten strategies for improving reading achievement. Sample reading improvement objectives are provided that illustrate School Improvement Plan work at the elementary, middle, and high school levels. Additional resources for schools to consider when addressing reading improvement are also provided.

Principal Jackson Roberts double-clicked the attachment and shifted his weight in his office chair nervously. This file was not a letter from an upset parent, nor was it bad budget news. It was 6:15 in the morning, and he had hurried to school, anxious to receive this e-mail. School had ended just one week ago, and the "ghost town" feeling of the empty, silent building was soothing relief to the exhausted man who had just finished his first year as principal.

Thirty-one years old and energetic, Roberts had replaced a well-loved principal who had served fifteen years at the school before retiring. Ann Lincoln had served in the school district for an astounding fifty years. She passed away the week after her retirement reception at seventy-three years of age. The governor of the state gave an impassioned speech at her funeral, and letters from former students and staff poured in. Three days after Roberts signed on to take the helm, the school was renamed after his predecessor.

In the midst of this emotional transition time, Roberts wisely followed the advice from his dissertation adviser not to make immediate momentous changes, but instead to focus on building relationships with the school community, assessing the school's current state, and achieving "quick wins" to make the school an effective and efficient operation.

During his first year, Roberts encountered some challenges. Lincoln had gone from being, as the school nurse confided to him, a "country club" to being "a barbell school" where "there's a lot of students at both ends [of the socioeconomic spectrum] and not much in the middle." The numbers bore this out. Due largely to recent redistricting as well as quickly shifting population dynamics in the largely working-class school community, Lincoln was now a Title I school with a "majority minority" population.

In terms of academic achievement, Roberts realized, as he took the "pulse" of student achievement by walk-through observations, reviewing assessment data, and listening to team discussions, that the school did not have a clear focus. And due to rising accountability benchmarks, his school had only narrowly made progress targets the previous year. Students in all subgroups had to achieve a 75 percent pass rate in the 2010–2011 year, but in Roberts's first year (2011–2012) the state had raised the benchmark to 85 percent in keeping with rising proficiency targets. Thus, not only was Roberts filling the principal chair of a larger-than-life icon, he was also grappling with a school that had changing demographics and lacked a clear plan for addressing the needs of newcomers.

Roberts's first year was occupied with building trust, firming up a workable schedule, redefining team professional learning community (PLC) expectations, and relying on formative data to give him a reading on student progress. What his review of data revealed worried him. In reading, students were not comprehending grade-level text, and fluency rates were lower than expected.

Table 4.1. Student Ethnicity by Percentage

	2009–2010	2010–2011	2011–2012
African American	19	27	34
Caucasian	67	52	39
Hispanic	7	13	17
Other	7	8	10

When Roberts shared the data with the PLC teams, veteran teachers shrugged it off. One team leader said, "Dr. Roberts, we're in the trenches with this data at the middle of every year. And every June, our students pull it off and we'll be just fine." He had enlisted the help of division coordinators and coaches, but teachers were "wary of outsiders." In faculty meetings, Roberts spoke of increased proficiency benchmarks and current trends that he noticed in the student data, striving tirelessly to generate a meaningful dialogue, but he usually received glazed-over expressions and, at best, polite agreement.

Roberts stared at the e-mail. As the "urgent" attachment from the division testing coordinator opened, Roberts sighed. It was just as he had feared—no, it was worse. His school had not only missed proficiency targets in reading, but it had missed targets in multiple subgroups. In some grade levels, students were not even close to benchmarks. Roberts detected a glaring achievement gap between white students and other subgroups.

As a school, the overall pass rate for students came in around 80 percent, which, in past years, was deemed acceptable, if not "good," and no cause for further consideration. This year, Roberts and his school would have a large "failing school" indicator stamped on the Lincoln Elementary report card. As Roberts reflected in the quiet office, he smiled. He recalled a politician saying, "Never let a crisis go to waste" and thought to himself, "Perhaps we had to fail in order to be able to succeed." In the days, weeks, months, and semesters ahead, Roberts knew there would be serious reflection and work to be done in order to move the school forward.

Table 4.2. End-of-Year Reading Exam Pass Rates by Grade Level and Ethnicity

	Student Pass Rate by Cohort (%)*
Third Grade—All Students	76
Third Grade—Non-Caucasian	58
Third Grade—Caucasian	89
Fourth Grade—All Students	80
Fourth Grade—Non-Caucasian	61
Fourth Grade—Caucasian	94
Fifth Grade—All Students	83
Fifth Grade—Non-Caucasian	68
Fifth Grade—Caucasian	95

*85 percent needed to make proficiency targets

As Roberts "unpacked" the data, his previous concerns were confirmed. In terms of comprehension and reading fluency, students were struggling across the board. In fact, many students who had passed the state reading tests only did so narrowly. Students clearly did not understand what they were reading. Roberts resisted the urge to quote team leaders who had promised "that every year we pull it off in June" when the test results came in. He would need their help, along with many others, in the days ahead.

KEY ISSUES: IDENTIFYING SCHOOL IMPROVEMENT PLANNING GOALS AND OBJECTIVES FOR INCREASING READING ACHIEVEMENT

Principal Roberts assembled his School Improvement Planning team in the weeks following "the data dump" in order to proactively frame an overarching goal and specific objective to address student reading achievement. This two-day mid-June workshop included key team leaders (each grade level was represented), specialists, a parent representative, and a district liaison. Roberts delicately noted there would be "more of a presence from the division and the state" now that the school had been labeled, and this news seemed to generate a sense of genuine urgency as the team worked through the data.

Roberts carefully organized the workshop (see table 4.3) to ensure as much buy-in and shared leadership as possible and to incorporate the seven steps to good planning. He had an idea of what needed to happen, but he wanted to ensure that there was a true sense of ownership and purpose in this work. He also knew that others had "been there, done that," so he created an advisory "reflective panel" comprised of a subject matter expert (a university professor who had considerable consulting experience with schools in similar positions), a principal and teacher who had similarly navigated through this work in a neighboring school with similar demographics, and a parent with experience on a school improvement planning team.

As the workshop came to an end, Principal Roberts knew that significant work lay ahead in the months to follow. This work would require thoughtful reflection and support in order to sustain meaningful

Table 4.3. School Improvement Plan Summer Workshop at Lincoln Elementary

School Improvement Workshop Agenda
June 20–21, Lincoln Elementary Media Center

Day One	Agenda Item	Day Two	Agenda Item
8–9 a.m.	Welcome, introduction, overview of School Improvement Planning work, setting norms for work	8–9 a.m.	Reflection on work, establishing goals, purpose of the day (to clarify a goal and establish measurable outcomes)
9–10	**Step 1: Data Gathering**—Unpacking the data by grade level, strand, class section. Consider lack of reasonable progress being made and look closely at subgroups.	9–10	**Step 3: Assessing Context, Constraints, and Capacity**—What is our current context in regards to school culture? What state and district requirements exist regarding this SIP work? What is in place for the district to support the school's plan?
10–11	General reflections within breakout groups	10–11	**Step 4: Focusing**—Begin discussion on what goals to focus on.
11–12	Lunch/break	11–12	Lunch/break
12–1 p.m.	Shared reflections and thoughts	12–1 p.m.	**Step 4: Focusing (cont.)**—Are our goals clearly stated? Does rationale exist for each goal?
1–2	Reflective Panel (professor, local principal and teacher, parent) discuss/share "what other schools have done to respond to this challenge."	1–2	Reconvene Reflective Panel to reflect on goals, offer advice and insights on our work so far. What strategies address the goals?
2–3	**Step 2: Diagnosing**—What aspects of reading need to be diagnosed? Considering different analytical approaches.	2–3	**Step 5: Determining Strategies**—What must be considered regarding the "Eight Planning P's?"—Policies, Personnel, Programs, Processes, Practices, Professional Development, Parent Involvement, and Partnerships?
3 p.m.	Adjourn until tomorrow (Day 2).	3 p.m.	First Five Steps completed. The principal will outline **Step 6 (Development of Plan)** and present to School Improvement Planning team prior to school year. **Step 7 (Managing and Monitoring the Plan)** will begin during pre-week in extensive work with staff and communication with school community members.

change. Fortunately, others had successfully navigated these waters before him.

WHAT EXPERTS SAY ABOUT READING ACHIEVEMENT

Sir William Curtis was born in 1752 and was the son of a sea biscuit manufacturer who stamped an oft-repeated phrase into the history books when he gave a speech at a board of education meeting and emphasized the "three R's of readin', 'ritin', and 'rithmetic" (Ramsgate 2011). Since Curtis's time, much focus has been on the importance of teaching reading. Reading instruction has been heavily scrutinized, debated, and legislated.

The Common Core State Standards (CCSS) include "anchor standards" for reading, writing, speaking, listening, and language that are designed to help students in the following capacities:

- Independence in comprehending, evaluating, and becoming self-directed learners;
- A better understanding of content knowledge;
- Being able to address varying demands of audience, task, purpose, and discipline;
- Being able to comprehend and critique;
- Being able to cite evidence;
- Using technology and digital media;
- Understanding other perspectives and cultures (National Governors Association Center for Best Practices 2010, p. 7).

The Standards are organized into three main sections as follows: K–5 language arts, 6–12 language arts, and 6–12 content areas (social studies, science, and technical education). Information about these standards can be found on the Core Standards website (www.corestandards.org). The reading standards foundational skills section includes, for grades K–5, competence areas such as print concepts, phonological awareness, phonics and word recognition, and fluency (National Governors Association Center for Best Practices 2010, pp. 15–16).

Some districts, such as the West Haven School District in Connecticut, have compiled their Language Arts Common Core-aligned units on the Web (http://www.whschools.org/page.cfm?p=5892), complete with "unwrapped" concepts, skills, and Bloom's levels outlined in chart form. As described in the later strategies section, CCSS implementation requires careful planning and professional development.

The National Institute for Literacy, citing findings from the National Reading Panel (NRP), released a guide for educators titled *Put Reading First: The Research Building Blocks for Teaching Children to Read* (Armbruster, Lehr, and Osborn 2001). The guide focused on the following five key areas of reading instruction: phonemic awareness, phonics, fluency, vocabulary, and text comprehension. Experts generally agree that learning to read requires development of these five areas.

Fluency

Reading fluency "is most often defined as the ability to read text quickly, accurately, and with appropriate expression" (Meisinger et al. 2010, 1). Fluency is of utmost importance when considering learning to read. Rasinksi, Homan, and Biggs (2009) note that difficulties in reading fluency can contribute to general reading problems. The authors note that fluency in any activity—including sports and performance arts—requires repetitive training drills and much practice.

Rigorous "direct instruction" can benefit the young or struggling reader. As readers advance in their learning, greater independence in reading is then established. Fluency can be taught in preschool with repeated practice with objects such as shapes (reading them from "left to right" as one would in reading text) to gain proficiency in accomplishing a task.

Grabe (2010) notes "reading fluency has been associated with reading comprehension in a wide range of research studies over the past 20 years" (p. 72). Fluency, Grabe contends, depends on skills such as "rapid word recognition, rapid reading rate, extensive 'exposure to print' (large reading amounts), accuracy in comprehension, and incremental learning" (p. 72). He observes that these skills require developing automaticity, recognizing vocabulary, and extended periods of implicit learning.

Many reading skills—such as "automatic word recognition, a large recognition vocabulary, skilled grammatical processing, and the formation of basic meaning propositions units for reading comprehension—only emerge as an outcome of *implicit* learning" (p. 73, emphasis added), which comes from meaningful time spent in reading text.

Phonemic Awareness

Phonemic awareness (PA) is defined as "the ability to notice, think about, and work with the individual sounds in spoken words" (Armbruster, Lehr, and Osborn 2001, p. 2). Students must be familiar with speech sounds (known as phonemes) and recognize that the "smallest parts of sound in a spoken word make a difference in the word's meaning" (p. 2). PA can be seen by breaking a word into segments. Breaking the word *ball* into three separate parts "/b/, /a/, /ll/" or recognizing that the beginning sound in "bat" is "/b/" and the ending sound is "/t/" require a student to have phonemic awareness.

Phonemic awareness is not the same as phonics. The authors of the *Put Reading First* report distinguish the two components as follows:

> Phonemic awareness is the understanding that the sounds of *spoken* language work together to make words. Phonics is the understanding that there is a predictable relationship between phonemes and graphemes, the letters that represent those sounds in *written* language. If children are to benefit from phonics instruction, they need phonemic awareness. (Armbruster, Lehr, and Osborn 2001, p. 3)

Therefore, phonemic awareness, like fluency, can be considered an essential, foundational component that must be emphasized in teaching reading. Kamil (2005) notes that PA is a reliable predictor of reading ability, but that "the most important point here is that while every student needs to be phonemically aware, only a relatively small number of students need PA instruction. The students who need PA instruction tend to be those who are labeled 'at-risk'" (p. 5). Here, PA is best offered in small groups for small amounts of time. In fact, Kamil notes, "something on the order of a maximum of 20–25 hours of instruction seems to be the optimal point for benefits from PA instruction. However, this seems to be most effective for students in kindergarten and first grade" (p. 6).

Phonics

Phonics takes phonemic awareness in another direction—a written one—as students link the sounds such as "/b/, /a/, /ll" into the written word *ball*. Students must gain an "understanding that there are systematic and predictable relationships between written letters and spoken sounds" (Armbruster, Lehr, and Osborn 2001, p. 12). They can benefit from a systematic, explicit approach that is grounded on "the direct teaching of a set of letter-sound relationships in a clearly defined sequence" (p. 13).

Phonics instruction is most beneficial when taught early, thus primary teachers are in a unique position to help students make great gains in this regard. Kamil (2005) adds that "phonics instruction is an important part of early reading instruction that research shows is effective for a wide range of students. It seems to be less effective for older students and for students who already have some degree of reading skill" (p. 7).

Vocabulary

The National Reading Panel defines vocabulary as "the words we must know to communicate effectively" (Armbruster, Lehr, and Osborn 2001, p. 34) and identifies four components of vocabulary as follows:

1. Listening vocabulary—the words we need to know to understand what we hear,
2. Speaking vocabulary—the words we use when we speak,
3. Reading vocabulary—the words we need to know to understand what we read, and
4. Writing vocabulary—the words we use in writing (p. 34).

Students must be actively engaged in learning vocabulary in order to grasp the varied, nuanced meanings of words. Strategies such as meaningful repetition, combining modes, and reading aloud in a dialogic style can effectively help students learn (Jalongo and Sobolak 2011). Vocabulary is also important for comprehension, fluency, and overall reading achievement (Bromley 2007). Researchers point out that whereas most vocabulary is learned indirectly (such as from hearing a parent in conversation), some vocabulary must be taught directly. Here, direct instruction is again relevant in the following two ways:

1. Providing students with specific word instruction; and
2. Teaching students word-learning strategies (p. 36).

Kamil (2005) adds to this, saying that "direct instruction of vocabulary is effective in improving both vocabulary and comprehension. The implication is that *both* direct, explicit instruction *and* learning from context are important. A further implication is that explicit instruction *may* be useful in closing the gap between the students with the highest levels of vocabulary knowledge and those with the lowest" (p. 9).

Comprehension

The NRP states "comprehension is the reason for reading. If readers can read the words but do not understand what they are reading, they are not really reading" (Armbruster, Lehr, and Osborn 2001, p. 48). Key findings from research indicate that comprehension strategies allow students to become conscious, deliberate, and active readers who can master their own reading comprehension. NRP outlines six strategies that have strong scientific bases for improving text comprehension. These include monitoring comprehension, using graphic and semantic organizers, answering questions, generating questions, recognizing story structure, and summarizing text (Armbruster, Lehr, and Osborn 2001, pp. 49–53).

TEN STRATEGIES FOR IMPROVING READING

Much ground has been covered when it comes to reading achievement. We noted five agreed-upon areas of reading instruction (fluency, phonemic awareness, phonics instruction, vocabulary, and comprehension). However, strategies must extend beyond these five facets that are often, but not entirely, addressed by choosing a reading program. This section includes the following ten strategies for improving reading:

1. Choosing a New Reading Program
2. Using an Intervention Program
3. Adjusting Time Spent in Reading
4. Developing Flexible Reading Groups
5. Implementing RtI with Reading Focus
6. Increasing Student Engagement
7. Ensuring Parent Buy-in and Help
8. Reading across the Curriculum
9. Using Technology to Improve Reading
10. Emphasizing Writing Instruction

Strategy One: Choosing a New Reading Program

In 1983, researcher Jeanne Chall noted that most elementary schools use basal reading series, which include textbooks with reading selections and workbooks for students and a teacher's manual or guide, as "the major vehicle" (p. 105) for teaching reading. This remains true in current times (Ediger 2010).

The positive aspects of basals are that teachers have access to a consistent, planned approach developed by experts and often accompanied by support structures based on collaboration and professional development (Wiggins 1994). The negative aspects are that the basals do not always meet the needs of individual learners, specifically when there are great discrepancies within a class (Chall 1983; Ediger 2010). Teachers may also become too dependent on basals and not infuse their teaching with other effective strategies (Kelly, personal communication 2011).

In the states where the Common Core Standards have been adopted, any reading program should be carefully scrutinized to ensure alignment. Kendall (2011) suggests that educators complete a "crosswalk" to compare state standards that are in place with the Common Core Standards to ensure alignment. Kendall (2011) notes that "schools can't expect to adopt the Common Core in a day" and that using transition documents can allow for a deeper understanding for planning instruction (p. 43). Grade-level and department teams must carefully analyze how the standards align with instruction. Planning questions that focus on transition and turnaround could include four that Kendall (2011) offers:

1. How is this content that I am teaching today, in this lesson, addressed differently in the Common Core?
2. Would this lesson plan or activity work for the Common Core content? If not, can it be revised? If so, is the lesson or activity demanding enough?
3. Do I need to rethink how I go about teaching this content?
4. Does the change in content present a new area for professional growth? (pp. 48–49).

Because many schools rely on basals as a foundation, they are worth considering in light of the five main areas of reading. They should also be considered in terms of alignment with the K–5 language standards found in the Common Core (National Governors Association Center for Best Practices 2010). When considering adopting a new reading program, the following fundamental considerations should be reviewed:

- Cost—What funds are available? Are supplemental resources (consumable workbooks, teacher extension books, technology supplements) affordable?
- Training—What professional development will be necessary for teachers to be equipped to use this program for students?
- Addressing the Reading Components—Does this particular program address the needs that were identified in the planning process? If applicable, is this program aligned with the Common Core State Standards? Are intervention components included that may target specific needs that have been identified?
- Similar School Comparison—Knowing how similar schools have fared is worth noting when considering programs. What does the experience of others reveal regarding a particular program at a school with similar characteristics?

Reading programs can provide a foundation of consistency and common goals for teachers, but they should not be seen as a one-size-fits-all solution. Planners should consider a variety of options including technology-based, targeted programs and differentiated approaches to reading instruction.

Strategy Two: Using an Intervention Program

Students who are reading below grade level often require a special intervention to improve their achievement levels. Many schools offer intervention programs in which students either miss a portion of reading instruction (usually independent work time) or nonreading instruction to work alone or in small groups with trained staff, but there are also strategies in which a teacher can intervene in class.

Using guided notes and "pre-teaching" (providing an introduction to new concepts and vocabulary words) can serve to engage the struggling reader. Going over pronunciation, acquainting students with the text, and using question/answer dialogue in advance can boost confidence and allow students to benefit from whole-class instruction.

Out-of-class intervention programs, such as *Reading Mastery* at the elementary level, and *READ 180* at the secondary level, often include short lessons that are centered around a topic in a subject such as social studies, art, or science. Professional development is of utmost importance when adopting such intervention programs (Slavin et al. 2008). At the primary level, intervention groups should be kept small (generally no more than six students), and the intervention sessions should last from twenty to thirty minutes.

When considering the use of interventions, the role of a reading specialist should be considered. Not all schools have reading specialists due to funding or organizational priorities, but schools that have a professional who is certified as a reading specialist can bolster instruction and student success. Rather than simply assigning the lowest-achieving students to the reading specialist, the master schedule should accommodate times for the specialist to "push in" to the regular classroom and provide targeted instruction in one or more of the five key areas.

This arrangement provides for a collaborative framework for reading specialists and classroom teachers to share strategies and dialogue regarding instruction and student learning. Reading specialists also should attend and participate in grade-level meetings in which student learning is discussed. These meetings should examine the effectiveness of interventions and targeted support as well as the format of instructional delivery to ensure student learning is maximized.

Planners should take into account how interventions are aligned with student needs, the instructional format of programs (Do they require the expertise of a teacher or specialist or could a paraprofessional or volunteer handle them?), the availability of instructional technology, and embedded assessment (Kelly 2011). In addition, teachers should continually seek ways to incorporate interventions into their instruction to maximize benefits of instruction.

Strategy Three: Adjusting Time Spent in Reading

Researchers generally agree that a minimum of ninety minutes is needed for language arts instruction at the elementary level (Allington 2001). When allowing for writing instruction along with various transitions, the total amount of time may be closer to two hours. Of course, how teachers structure the time spent in reading (and writing) is of utmost importance.

Principals should make certain that the ninety minutes is uninterrupted (by bells, announcements, etc.). Allowing for two hours of language arts leaves approximately four hours for other instruction in a six-hour instructional day. Having an Extended Learning Time (ELT) block built into the schedule can provide time for focused reteaching, pre-teaching, and conferencing with students who need assistance.

Federal mandates require states to provide out-of-school-time (OST) in order to assist low-achieving and at-risk students in reading (Lauer et al. 2004). Although it is ideal to have knowledgeable, highly qualified staff in place to support learning, the reality is that volunteers, teachers-in-training, and assistants must often be used to provide after-school instruction.

In their book *Book Buddies: Guidelines for Volunteer Tutors of Emergent and Early Readers*, the authors note "quality instruction can be delivered by community volunteers if they are properly supported" (Johnston, Ivernizzi, and Juel 1998, p. 6). The authors contend that effective after-school tutoring involves children learning in meaningful contexts, receiving differentiated instruction tailored to their needs, being taught in conjunction with writing and spelling, and being immersed in a social context in which they learn through interacting with each other.

The onus is on the principal to ensure that these components are in place. Principals should not assume that optimal learning is occurring simply because an extra hour or two have been added to the instructional day. Professional development for tutors is needed to promote consistency. A coordinator (other than the principal) should serve as a "point person" to assist in providing plans, materials, and oversight of the other necessary details in order to make the most of extended learning and out-of-school-time programs:

1. Linking Attendance to Achievement—More time on task will result in higher student performance. Token-based rewards and game-like cooperative activities are examples.
2. Ensuring Staff Quality—The tutors, whether they are volunteers or paid staff, must possess an understanding of the reading process and how to teach beginning readers along with the belief that all students can learn.
3. Program Duration—The data indicate that OST strategies have significantly positive effects when implemented for at least 45 hours but less than 210 hours.
4. Preventing Loss and Sustaining Gains—OST can be effective during the summer months in terms of preventing the "summer slide," but only with consistent attendance (Lauer et al. 2004).

Instructional time is a valuable resource that must be continually examined to ensure that students are receiving maximum support. By creatively considering in-school options, such as extended learning time and a protected schedule, as well as OST, principals and teachers can work together to ensure that reading instruction is a priority and that time is well spent to bolster student learning.

Strategy Four: Developing Flexible Reading Groups

It is vitally important that educators recognize that their classes are comprised of learners with varied abilities and interests (Tomlinson and McTighe 2006; Wiggins 1994). Grouping students is important, but when grouping is based solely on ability, it can negatively impact learning, especially if there is little consideration given to students' prior knowledge and readiness levels (Castle, Deniz, and Tortora 2005; Tieso 2003; Flood and Lapp 1992).

A large group instruction/small group follow-up approach can enhance learning when initial reading instruction (introduction of the lesson and components) is taught to the whole class and then reinforced as the teacher meets with small ability-based groups (to review, identify learning targets, and enrich based on the needs of the individual learners) (Wiggins 1994).

There are various bases for grouping learners (e.g., skill level, age, interests, and diversity), different formats for groups (small vs. large, teacher-led, student-led), and different materials for groups (e.g., same material for all groups, different levels of material with similar theme, or different topics) (Flood and Lapp 1992). These varied approaches should be considered in light of the specific needs of a class or cohort.

Strategy Five: Implementing RtI with Reading Focus

Congress reauthorized the Individuals with Disabilities Education Act (IDEA) in 2004 and included Response to Intervention (RtI) as a *general* education instructional process that involves multiple tiers of instruction and intervention (Cole and McCann 2009). The model includes universal screening and ongoing formative assessment. Allington (2011) notes that the model has a "dual focus" that allows intensive expert reading instruction support for students who are struggling and identifies students who have difficulties even after receiving the extra support.

This begs the question, *How can teachers be equipped to teach reading to students effectively and understand how to respond when students are not learning?* For this question to be answered, a fundamental understanding of teaching reading and a model for reaching students who are not successful are imperative. The staff must be clear on the model and the process that is in place in their school. RtI should not be seen as "the solution" that will "fix" students, but instead as a process to align resources within the school to enable greater learning.

The Institute of Educational Sciences (IES) identified interventions that are considered effective. The IES report provided a list of recommendations for the early identification of reading problems:

• Screen all students for potential reading problems at the beginning of the year and again in the middle of the year. Regularly monitor the progress of students who are at the elevated risk for developing reading disabilities.
• Provide differentiated reading instruction for all students based on assessments of students' current reading levels (Tier 1).
• Provide intensive, systematic instruction on up to three foundational reading skills in small groups to students who score below the benchmark score on universal screening. Typically, these groups meet between three and five times a week for twenty to forty minutes a time (Tier 2).
• Monitor the progress of Tier 2 students at least once a month. Use this data to determine whether students still require intervention. For those students still making insufficient progress, school-wide teams should design a Tier 3 intervention plan.
• Provide intensive instruction on a daily basis that promotes the development of the various components of reading proficiency to students who show minimal progress after reasonable time in Tier 2 small group instruction; this intensive approach is considered Tier 3 (Gersten et al. 2008, pp. 9–10).

When considering implementing RtI as part of a School Improvement Plan, the availability of support must be assessed. RtI should be seen as a means to an end, not simply an end in and of itself. Instituting universal screening to better understand where all students are in terms of reading achievement allows educators to understand and address student needs (Buffum, Matto, and Weber 2010). Recent books (Fisher and Frey 2010; Searle 2010) offer resources for the school leader interested in implementing RtI as a way to boost student achievement in reading.

Strategy Six: Increasing Student Engagement

If students are struggling with some aspect of reading, they are unlikely to enjoy reading. An important strategy, therefore, involves building student interest in reading. Engaged students are more likely to devote the time and attention necessary to address their reading problems.

One reliable method for increasing student interest in reading is to provide reading materials that address topics about which students express interest. Another technique is to have students watch a film in a foreign language with English subtitles. Stopping the film periodically and asking students what is going on is a good way to assess their comprehension. A third option involves encouraging parents to read with their children at home. Teachers can also promote student interest in reading by providing access to computer games that involve written instructions and commentary.

Planners who choose to focus on increasing student engagement in reading need to include provisions for identifying subjects about which students want to learn more and acquire appropriate materials. Consideration should be given to promoting high-interest activities that require students to read and write. Such activities might include publishing a class newspaper, operating a weekly videotaped news program, and collecting biographies of relatives and fellow students.

Strategy Seven: Ensuring Parent Buy-in and Help

Parent involvement can serve as an effective support for bolstering student success. Schools that find ways to engage parents regularly often find that students become more interested in learning. The federal government offers a useful guide titled *Family Involvement in Children's Education: Successful Local Approaches*. The book provides suggestions and tips for educators looking to engage parents and families in their children's learning.

Regardless of which program is developed and implemented, it is imperative that the program inspires, excites, and motivates not only parents but also the staff to participate. Often this kind of positive energy is the very mechanism that promotes a healthy school environment and nurtures participation from the community at large. Involving local businesses that are willing to provide coupons or gift cards as incentives for students (and parents) who are meeting goals related to a new literacy program, for example, can build interest in and support for the initiative.

Strategy Eight: Reading across the Curriculum

Teaching language arts cannot be relegated only to reading teachers. Researchers advocate at least ninety minutes of reading instruction per day in an elementary school, but exposure should involve instruction in other subjects such as science, math, music, and social studies (Manning 1999). Sanacore and Palumbo (2010) note that this approach broadens the student's knowledge base, and they offer the following suggestions for all content teachers:

- Provide time for actual reading,
- Help students to experience different types of text,
- Extend students' in-school reading to at-home reading,
- Engage students in drama-based activities, and
- Build and activate students' vocabulary.

A science teacher, for example, might provide a periodical (e.g., *National Geographic* or *Time*) that is relevant to a specific topic students are learning about. By focusing on specific vocabulary in the article, students can become engaged in the subject matter.

Department heads and administrators should consider how to align resources in order to provide a variety of materials for students to use in the classroom setting. Each subject and grade level will have a unique focus. A CCSS content reading standard for focusing on "key ideas and details" serves as an example. In grades 9–10 a student in science is expected to "follow precisely a multistep procedure when carrying out experiments . . . attending to special cases or exceptions defined in the text" (National Governors Association Center for Best Practices 2010, p. 62), whereas in history/social studies, the student would "analyze in detail a series of events described in a text (and) determine whether earlier events caused later ones or simply preceded them" (p. 61). Team planning will enable grades and departments to focus attention on reading in their respective content area.

Strategy Nine: Using Technology to Improve Reading

An abundance of reading technologies exist for today's students, and many of them are available for little or no cost. Assistive technologies can support accommodations for struggling readers and allow them to improve their reading skills (Berkeley and Lindstrom 2011). Whether students are struggling with a disability, need extra explicit instruction, or require more practice reading, technologies allow students to engage in learning and enable teachers to have another avenue for instruction and independent practice in teaching reading. Early primary students have benefited from sites such as Starfall (www.starfall.com), which provide learners the chance to interact with phonemes and vocabulary words in an age-appropriate manner.

Technology-based programs can also be used to enrich and extend reading instruction with tools that appeal to students and allow for sharing, archiving, and documenting student progress (Vasinda and McLeod 2011). Using Reader's Theatre along with podcasting, for instance, can allow students to showcase their talent while also practicing read-aloud skills. Interactive whiteboards provide young learners with opportunities to interact in a phonemic awareness activity or engage in sound identification.

At the middle and high school level, programs such as *READ 180* offer a component of computer-assisted instructional reading and incorporate related video segments (usually involving science or social studies content) with follow-up activities in comprehension, fluency, vocabulary, and word study (Slavin et al. 2008).

Strategy Ten: Emphasizing Writing Instruction

Research shows that effective writing instruction enhances the acquisition of reading skills, even in the primary setting (D'On Jones, Reutzel, and Fargo 2010). However, research also indicates that language arts teachers often fail to incorporate writing activities into their instruction (Stevens 2003).

Writing-to-learn strategies can bolster reading comprehension by help-ing students prepare for reading assignments as they search for meaning, work to summarize, and extend concepts learned (Knipper and Duggan 2006). By keeping learning logs and engaging in structured note-taking, students prepare for reading passages and assignments. Creating a mi-crotheme (where students piece together key ideas from the text), a text box that provides students with the opportunity to reflect on a portion of text, or perhaps a science lab diagram with corresponding thoughts and written reflection, students actively gain from their reading experiences (Knipper and Duggan 2006; Topping and McManus 2002).

Improving writing takes consistent, daily practice. Incorporating a daily activity, such as *Daily Grammar Practice* (http://www.dgppub-lishing.com/index.htm), can provide a consistent framework for having a daily "do now" introductory exercise that is grade-level appropriate and provides data for team discussions. By sharing a common writing prompt for students across a grade level, teachers similarly can work together to assess the impact of instruction.

SAMPLE READING OBJECTIVES

School planners must clearly identify objectives when seeking read-ing improvement. It is also important that specific strategies align with each objective. The examples at the end of the chapter address objectives and related strategies that might be found in School Im-provement Plans for elementary, middle, and high schools. An objec-tive to increase student achievement in reading through professional collaboration and community involvement in which 90 percent of students will either meet end-of-year benchmark standards or make one year's growth is outlined.

One strategy involves increasing student proficiency in sound recog-nition while a second strategy calls for strengthened student compre-hension and ability in retelling grade-level material. Other strategies address incorporating student-led assessments once per week while another focuses on teacher professional development. These examples provide an idea of how a plan might be structured to address possible objectives related to reading improvement.

CHAPTER REVIEW

Much has changed from the mid-eighteenth century when Sir William Curtis provided us with the "three R's," and yet reading instruction continues to be of utmost importance to practitioners and researchers alike. Today's school leaders have the opportunity to craft School Improvement Plans that provide a template for achieving results within the unique context of their school community. As noted in the first chapter, regardless of which strategies are ultimately chosen, planners should treat the School Improvement Plan as a "living document" that requires evaluation on an ongoing basis in order that necessary adjustments can be made when warranted.

Having a fundamental, working understanding of the five main areas of reading instruction is essential for school improvement teams concerned with literacy. Understanding student needs and knowing how to address them with proven, research-based strategies requires ongoing data analysis and professional development for team members as well as faculty in general.

REFERENCES

Allington, R. L. 2001. *What Really Matters for Struggling Readers: Designing Research-Based Programs.* New York: Addison Wesley Longman.
Allington, R. L. 2011. What at-risk readers need. *Educational Leadership*, 68(6), 40–45.
Armbruster, B. B., Lehr, F., and Osborn, J. 2001. *Put Reading First: The Research Building Blocks for Teaching Children to Read.* Center for the Improvement of Early Reading Achievement (CIERA) funded by the National Institute for Literacy (NIFL).
Bennett, S. 2007. *That Workshop Book.* Portsmouth, NH: Heinemann. Cited by Tovani.
Berkeley, S., and Lindstrom, J. H. 2011. Technology for the struggling reader: Free and easily accessible resources. *Teaching Exceptional Children*, 43(4), 48–55. Retrieved from EBSCO*host*.
Bromley, K. 2007. Nine things every teacher should know about words and vocabulary instruction. *Journal of Adolescent and Adult Literacy*, 50(7), 528–537. Retrieved from EBSCO*host*.

Buffum, A., Matto, M., and Weber, C. 2010. The WHY behind RTI. *Educational Leadership*, 68(2), 10. Retrieved from EBSCO*host*.

Castle, S., Deniz, C., and Tortora, M. 2005. Flexible grouping and student learning in a high-needs school. *Education and Urban Society*, 37(2), 139–150. doi:10.1177/0013124504270787.

Chall, J. S. 1983. *Stages of Reading Development*. New York: McGraw-Hill.

Cole, C., and McCann, S. 2009. Linking response to intervention and school improvement to sustain reading outcomes. *Sustaining Reading First*, 7, 1–12. Retrieved from http://www2.ed.gov/programs/readingfirst/support/linkinglores.pdf on September 6, 2011.

D'On Jones, C., Reutzel, D., and Fargo, J. D. 2010. Comparing two methods of writing instruction: Effects on kindergarten students' reading skills. *Journal of Educational Research*, 103(5), 327–341. Retrieved from EBSCO*host*.

Ediger, M. 2010. Which plan of reading instruction is best? *Reading Improvement*, 47(3), 138–141. Retrieved from EBSCO*host*.

Fisher, D., and Frey, N. 2009. Feed up, back, forward. *Educational Leadership*, 67(3), 20–25.

Fisher, D., and Frey, N. 2010. *Enhancing RTI: How to Ensure Success with Effective Classroom Instruction and Intervention*. Alexandria, VA: Association for Supervision and Curriculum Development.

Flood, J. J., and Lapp, D. D. 1992. Am I allowed to group? Using flexible patterns for effective instruction. *Reading Teacher*, 45(8), 608. Retrieved from EBSCO*host*.

Gersten, R., Compton, D., Connor, C. M., Dimino, J., Santoro, L., Linan-Thompson, S., and Tilly, W. D. 2008. *Assisting Students Struggling with Reading: Response to Intervention and Multi-Tier Intervention for Reading in the Primary Grades. A Practice Guide*. (NCEE 2009-4045). Washington, DC: National Center for Education Evaluation and Regional Assistance, Institute of Education Sciences, U.S. Department of Education. Retrieved from http://ies.ed.gov/ncee/wwc/publications/practiceguides/.

Grabe, W. 2010. Fluency in reading—thirty-five years later. *Reading in a Foreign Language*, 22(1), 71–83.

Ivey, G., and Fisher, D. 2006. When thinking skills trump reading skills. *Educational Leadership*, 64(2), 16. Retrieved from EBSCO*host*.

Jacobs, V. A. 2002. Reading, writing, and understanding. *Educational Leadership*, 60(3), 58–61.

Jalongo, M., and Sobolak, M. 2011. Supporting young children's vocabulary growth: The challenges, the benefits, and evidence-based strategies. *Early Childhood Education Journal*, 38(6), 421–429. doi:10.1007/s10643-010-0433-x.

Johnston, F. R., Ivernizzi, M., and Juel, C. 1998. *Book Buddies: Guidelines for Volunteer Tutors of Emergent and Early Readers*. New York: Guilford Press.

Kamil, M. L. 2005. Reading instruction for low-achieving and at-risk students. Laboratory for Student Success (LSS), The Mid-Atlantic regional Educational Laboratory. ERIC # ED508501.

Kendall, J. 2011. *Understanding Common Core State Standards*. Alexandria, VA: Association for Supervision and Curriculum Development.

Kelly, C. 2011. Personal communication.

Kelly, C. 2011. Reading intervention programs: A comparative chart. Retrieved from http://www.readingrockets.org/aRtIcle/42401/ on August 22, 2011.

Knipper, K. J., and Duggan, T. J. 2006. Writing to learn across the curriculum: Tools for comprehension in content area classes. *Reading Teacher*, 59(5), 462–470. doi:10.1598/RT.59.5.5.

Lauer, P. A., Akiba, M., Wilkerson, S. B., Apthorp, H. S., Snow, D., and Martin-Glenn, M. 2004. *The Effectiveness of Out-of-School-Time Strategies in Assisting Low-Achieving Students in Reading and Mathematics: A Research Synthesis*, updated ed. Aurora, CO: Mid-continent Research for Education and Learning.

Manning, M. 1999. Reading across the curriculum. *Teaching Pre K–8*, 29(5), 83. Retrieved from EBSCO*host*.

Meisinger, E. B., Bloom, J. S., and Hynd, G. W. 2010. Reading fluency: Implications for the assessment of children with reading disabilities. *Annals of Dyslexia*, 60(1), 1–17. doi:10.1007/s11881-009-0031-z.

National Governors Association Center for Best Practices, Council of Chief State School Officers. 2010. *Common Core State Standards for English/Language Arts*. Washington, DC: printed by author.

Ramsgate History. 2011. Sir William Curtis. Retrieved from http://ramsgate-history.com/information/sir_william_cuRtIs.pdf on August 7, 2011.

Rasinksi, T., Homan, S., and Biggs, M. 2009. Teaching reading fluency to struggling readers: Methods, materials, and evidence. *Reading and Writing Quarterly*, 25(2/3), 192–204.

Sanacore, J., and Palumbo, A. 2010. Middle school students need more opportunities to read across the curriculum. *Clearing House*, 83(5), 180–185.

Searle, M. 2010. *What Every School Leader Needs to Know about RTI*. Alexandria, VA: Association for Supervision and Curriculum Development.

Shagoury, R. 2010. Making reading meaningful. *Educational Leadership*, 67(6), 63–67.

Slavin, R. E., Cheung, A., Groff, C., and Lake, C. 2008. Effective reading programs for middle and high schools: A best-evidence synthesis. *Reading Research Quarterly*, July/August/September, 1–48.

Stevens, R. J. 2003. Student team reading and writing: A cooperative learning approach to middle school literacy instruction. *Educational Research and Evaluation*, 9(2), 137–160.

Tieso, C. L. 2003. Ability grouping is not just tracking anymore. *Roeper Review*, 26(1), 29–36. Retrieved from EBSCO*host*.

Tomlinson, C. A., and McTighe, J. 2006. *Integrating Differentiated Learning and Understanding by Design*. Alexandria, VA: Association for Supervision and Curriculum Development.

Topping, D., and McManus, R. 2002. A culture of literacy in science. *Educational Leadership*, 60(3), 30. Retrieved from EBSCO*host*.

Tovani, C. 2010. I got grouped. *Educational Leadership*, 67(6), 24–29.

Vasinda, S., and McLeod, J. 2011. Extending readers theatre: A powerful and purposeful match with podcasting. *Reading Teacher*, 64(7), 486–497. doi:10.1598/RT.64.7.2.

Wiggins, R. A. 1994. Large group lesson/small group follow-up: Flexible grouping in a basal reading program. *Reading Teacher*, 47(6), 450. Retrieved from EBSCO*host*.

SCHOOL IMPROVEMENT PLAN OBJECTIVE: Increase student achievement in reading through professional collaboration and community involvement. Ninety percent of students will either (1) meet end of year benchmark accountability standards or (2) make approximately one year's growth in reading achievement.

Improvement Strategies	Person(s) Responsible	Materials Needed and Costs	Time Line				In-Process Measures
			Check the projected quarter for implementing the strategy this school year.				
What we will do to achieve the objective	Person(s) who will monitor the strategy	What materials will be used to implement the strategy? What are the costs?	1st Qtr.	2nd Qtr.	3rd Qtr.	4th Qtr.	How we will monitor progress
K–6: Within Collaborative Learning Teams, identify area(s) of focus and achieve a SMART goal based on June and September data. Identify, share, and implement strategies to accomplish the goal.							
Kindergarten Increase student proficiency in sound recognition, resulting in at least 90 percent of kindergartners meeting or exceeding the kindergarten benchmark.	K teachers and related specialists	Basal text and supporting materials	✓	✓	✓	✓	Daily oral language informal observation Small-group guided reading anecdotal notes Biweekly classroom assessments
1st–2nd grades Strengthen student comprehension and ability to retell grade-level material through vocabulary and key ideas, resulting in at least 90 percent of first graders passing the Scholastic Reading Inventory (SRI) assessment.	1st and 2nd grade teachers and related specialists	1st and 2nd grade SRI materials, recommended resources	✓	✓	✓	✓	Quarterly common assessments scored with team-developed rubrics Quarterly progress report insert

1st–8th grades All students will incorporate the *Six Minute Solution* approach by completing an assessment (can be with a partner under general teacher administration/ supervision) and track their results. This will be done at least once per week.	Classroom teachers and specialists	*Six Minute Solution* materials Documentation logs	✓	✓	✓	Weekly data will be kept by teachers and submitted to reading specialist for review with administrator in PLC teams.
K–12 students All students will participate in a modified cloze technique in all content classes at least once per week to build up general knowledge base and exposure across the curriculum (all subject areas).	Classroom teachers and specialists	Documentation logs	✓	✓	✓	Weekly data will be kept by teachers and submitted to reading specialist for review with administrator in PLC teams.
All teachers Teachers (pre-K–12) will, at least twice weekly, model fluent reading by reading to students.	Classroom teachers and specialists	Documentation logs	✓	✓	✓	Weekly data will be kept by teachers and submitted to reading specialist for review with administrator in PLC teams.

(continued)

SCHOOL IMPROVEMENT PLAN OBJECTIVE: *(Continued)*

Improvement Strategies	Person(s) Responsible	Materials Needed and Costs	Time Line				In-Process Measures
All teachers All teachers will participate in monthly professional development to incorporate the *Daily Five* into their reading instruction.	All teachers	*Daily Five* book and workbook. Supporting video modules.	✓	✓			Teachers will complete modules and demonstrate competency in classroom observations.
All teachers Teachers (K–12) will complete a "crosswalk" and/or transition support document (see Kendall 2011) as a team that ensures alignment of their teaching with Common Core. This will be reviewed quarterly as a grade or department team.	All teachers	Common Core Standards guide, pacing guide, instructional materials. Additional professional development in targeted growth areas if needed.	✓	✓	✓	✓	"Crosswalk" documents will be submitted by team leaders quarterly and reviewed by administration.

Whole school	Teachers, administration	Stipends for teachers. Supporting materials for tutoring.				✓		✓	Attendance sheets from tutors. Completed coursework from students.
Extended-day tutoring will be incorporated and "at-risk" students (as defined by grade level teams) will achieve 90 percent attendance and completion of stated goals and objectives (fluency and comprehension targets). Tutoring will start in January and conclude by June.									

CHAPTER 5

Math Improvement
Overcoming the Middle School Math Dilemma

PREVIEW

A case study involving a middle school grappling with low math scores opens this chapter, followed by an overview of what experts say about effective math instruction. Ten strategies that will help improve student learning and engagement in math are examined. Sample objectives offer examples of ways to bolster student engagement and raise overall math achievement across the grade levels.

The School Improvement Team of Mason Middle School sat around the tables in the library examining the data that was only days old. Boxes of new books, newly bared walls, and rolled reading mats indicated that the school year was in its waning days. The last day of school was on Friday, yet the final Wednesday meeting of the year for the School Improvement Plan team had a somber feel to it.

Over the past three years, Principal Holly Paez had successfully rebuilt a culture of trust and accountability in the suburban school of eight hundred students and sixty-five instructional staff members. Reading scores had improved; and school climate surveys gathered from students, staff, and parents showed significant improvements in perceptions regarding safety, belonging, and overall satisfaction.

Improving academic achievement lacked one element, however: students still struggled in math. Sixth graders new to the schedule based on ninety-minute math blocks often fought to stay engaged in learning, and teachers were at their wits end on how to reach them effectively. All math teachers (there were either two or three per grade level) were

Table 5.1.   End-of-Year Math Exam Pass Rates by Grade Level and Ethnicity

	Student Pass Rate by Cohort (%)*
Sixth Grade—All Students	65
Sixth Grade—Students of Color	54
Sixth Grade—Caucasian	69
Seventh Grade—All Students	72
Seventh Grade—Students of Color	62
Seventh Grade—Caucasian	75
Eighth Grade—All Students	76
Eighth Grade—Students of Color	62
Eighth Grade—Caucasian	80

*88 percent needed to make proficiency targets

deemed "highly qualified," and Paez had not placed any of them on a formal improvement plan.

Paez had devoted much of her instructional leadership efforts to seeing that math scores improved. She recently adopted a textbook aligned to the Common Core, which provided a hybrid of hands-on investigative materials as well as a more traditional workbook format. Paez also introduced professional development opportunities that emphasized math instruction in department and grade-level meetings. Yet, the data indicated that much work was still to be done.

Despite the data, Paez was optimistic about the potential for significant improvement. A federal grant provided funding for a math specialist position for three years. Teachers were supportive of the newly implemented curriculum and were willing—even *hungry*, as one teacher characterized it—for professional growth opportunities in math. Parents were in favor of the changes and looking for ways to help, and after three years, Paez knew she had earned valuable support from stakeholders. She realized, however, that Mason was at a critical point, and she did not want to squander the energy and goodwill that were present. Although many believed Mason to be a good school, they wanted to see it become *great*, and overcoming the math challenge was job number one.

MASON'S MATH DILEMMA

Principal Paez and her team at Mason Middle are not alone in facing the middle school math dilemma. Student achievement in math often drops in the middle school years (typically defined as grades 6–8), as table 5.2 indicates, with sixth grade being particularly challenging for students (Virginia Department of Education 2011).

During a time of transition for students, the middle school instructional format presents new challenges in terms of structure, schedules, expectations, and even delivery of instruction when compared to the elementary format. Researchers offer a variety of reasons for low math achievement. Student anxiety often presents a problem around the middle school years. The National Mathematics Advisory Panel ([NMAP] 2008) noted a few potential risk factors for mathematics anxiety:

- Low mathematics aptitude,
- Low working memory capacity,
- Vulnerability to public embarrassment, and
- Negative teacher and parent attitudes (p. 31).

These problems in middle school years are compounded by the transitional challenges and developmental changes middle schoolers experience.

Another important issue involves teachers' unfamiliarity with rising middle school students. Teachers do not know the students well in terms of their math achievement level and may have difficulty placing them in an appropriate class section and targeting learning objectives that are reasonable. Finally, the mathematics to which students are exposed becomes more complex and abstract in middle school.

Table 5.2.   Pass Rates of Math Students in Virginia in 2011

End-of-Grade Math Assessment: Virginia Statewide Pass Rate	
Grade Level (or Subject Area)	Percentage of Students Passing
4th	89
5th	89
6th	73
7th	77
8th	82
9th (Algebra 1)	94
10th (Geometry)	87

KEY ISSUES: IDENTIFYING SCHOOL IMPROVEMENT PLAN GOALS AND OBJECTIVES FOR INCREASING MATH ACHIEVEMENT

Addressing math achievement requires an understanding of student learning. Teachers and school leaders from early childhood through postsecondary education can learn from what experts say about math achievement and adopt proven strategies to address school improvement plan objectives. Principal Paez must confront an all-too-common challenge: many of her students are failing in math. By ensuring that her team works together to understand what must be learned in math and how students learn math, they can begin to align objectives, and the subsequent strategies, to ensure that more students succeed in math.

Students arrive at middle school with varying levels of math readiness. Understanding how students learn and how to overcome common challenges, such as math anxiety and abstract concepts such as inverse elements and associativity, will enable the school improvement team to specify appropriate objectives and ensure that students have the tools that they need to succeed. Incorporating strategies that help engage students and maximize instructional time in the math classroom can serve as a critical catalyst for improved achievement.

WHAT EXPERTS SAY ABOUT MATH ACHIEVEMENT

The National Research Council's Mathematics Learning Study Committee in 2001 identified five strands of mathematical proficiency that are "interwoven and interdependent" and crucial to achievement in mathematics:

1. Conceptual Understanding—comprehension of mathematical concepts, operations, and relations
2. Procedural Fluency—skill in carrying out procedures flexibly, accurately, efficiently, and appropriately
3. Strategic Competence—ability to formulate, represent, and solve mathematical problems
4. Adaptive Reasoning—capacity for logical thought, reflection, explanation, and justification

5. Productive Disposition—habitual inclination to see mathematics as sensible, useful, and worthwhile, coupled with a belief in diligence and one's own efficacy (Kilpatrick, Swafford, and Findell 2001, p. 5)

And as the Common Core has increasingly been adopted, there has been both a renewed emphasis on the "conceptual understanding of key ideas" and a "returning to organizing principles such as place value or the properties of operations" to help promote a more focused, consistent, and coherent approach to learning math (National Governors Association Center for Best Practices 2010, p. 4). The Common Core State Standards (CCSS) for Mathematics consist of Standards for Mathematical Practice and also Standards for Mathematical Content for each grade level (p. 2).

The Common Core Standards for Mathematical Practice include eight focus areas for math educators at all levels:

1. Make sense of problems and persevere in solving them (being able to analyze a problem and reflect on their approach);
2. Reason abstractly and quantitatively (being able to both decontextualize and contextualize a problem as well as being able to decide flexibly how to represent and solve a problem);
3. Construct viable arguments and critique the reasoning of others (applying logic to determine if an argument is plausible);
4. Model with mathematics (applying math to solve everyday problems);
5. Use appropriate tools strategically (such as a ruler, protractor, spreadsheet, or pencil and paper);
6. Attend to precision (specifying careful formulas or definitions);
7. Look for and make use of structure (being able to discern a pattern or structure); and
8. Look for and express regularity in repeated reasoning (looking for general methods and shortcuts to solve problems) (pp. 6–8).

These eight practice standards are then connected to the content standards. Each grade-level content standard focuses on procedure and understanding. Grade-level standards are organized as follows:

I. Standards—what students should be able to do;

II. Cluster—groups of related standards that are connected; and

III. Domains—a larger group of related standards (National Governors Association Center for Best Practices 2010, p. 5).

These grade-level standards do not prescribe specific teaching methods, lessons, or curriculum. Therefore, continued planning and monitoring of instruction is important. Professional organizations, such as the National Council of Teachers of Mathematics, offer collections of tools, sample lessons, and tips for aligning math instruction to the Common Core (http://www.nctm.org/).

Students enter school with varying levels of number sense. Thus, early instruction and exposure to math concepts is important. The mathematical knowledge and skills that students have prior to entering kindergarten shape their math learning for many years to come. Students from lower socioeconomic backgrounds may bring to school less of a foundational understanding of math than their more-advantaged peers (NMAP 2008). Strategies and programs, however, that have been designed for elementary programs have resulted in success for at-risk students. Researchers have identified four methods of instruction that are beneficial for young students who have trouble learning math:

1. Systematic and Explicit Instruction—students regularly applying strategies through a guided and defined instructional sequence

2. Self-Instruction—students managing their own learning with specific prompting or solution-oriented questions

3. Peer Tutoring—pairing students to learn or practice an academic task

4. Visual Representations—using manipulatives, pictures, number lines, and graphs of functions and relationships to teach mathematical concepts (Steedly et al. 2008, p. 3)

Effectively teaching math, like reading, requires both a fundamental understanding of how students learn and also a systematic approach to engage diverse learners in the classroom. Students need a sound diet of fluency, problem solving and application, and independent practice. Several specific challenges also must be considered.

Algebraic Reasoning and Rational Numbers

Researchers agree that American students often struggle with fractions and algebraic reasoning. The NMAP (2008) notes that difficulty with fractions is "pervasive" and recommends that to prepare students for algebra, math curriculum "must simultaneously develop conceptual understanding, computational fluency, and problem solving skills" (p. xix). Teaching algebraic concepts actually can begin before kindergarten. For instance, having preschool students create and predict patterns using a repeated unit (such as "red, green, green; red, green, green," can be incorporated into a learning center (Schwartz and Copeland 2010). By familiarizing young students with key math concepts early in their schooling, the groundwork is laid for success in algebra and subsequent math courses.

Overcoming Math Anxiety

Researchers have studied math anxiety and found it can impact students when they work on problems that have larger numbers or multiple steps (Cavanaugh 2007). The National Mathematics Advisory Panel noted "anxiety about mathematics performance is related to low mathematics grades, failure to enroll in advanced mathematics courses, and poor scores on standardized tests" (2008, p. 31). The goals, perceptions, and beliefs of students regarding their math performance also can be affected by the levels of support and encouragement they receive from their parents and teachers.

The NMAP notes that many students give up on math because of the erroneous notion that math performance is based purely on innate ability rather than effort. Math anxiety can be addressed by focusing on improving the process of problem solving rather than simply getting the right answer (Sparks 2011a). Instead of focusing on getting a certain number of problems in a set correct, for example, teachers should concentrate on the process of problem solving and following the logic within each step. For example, students can be taught how to use a problem-solving model such as *4MALITY* to identify problem-solving steps; next, work through a multistep process to first understand the question and what it is asking; and, finally, to identify what is known and what needs to be solved (Maloy, Edwards, and Anderson 2010).

Math Specialists

Some schools have begun using math specialists to bolster math instruction. As with reading specialists, math specialists are not assigned to "fix" students who are struggling, but instead to work with teachers to better understand math teaching and learning. Math specialists must, first and foremost, be fundamentally sound teachers. They must understand what is needed to engage learners and enable all students to improve their learning.

The role of the math specialist is to improve math instruction. This requires enabling colleagues to become more effective at teaching math in a variety of ways to a variety of students. Math specialists can model an effective pedagogical approach by preplanning a lesson with teachers, co-teaching lessons, and observing teachers conducting the lessons and providing feedback afterward. The math specialist can also work with grade-level (or department) teams to ensure proper pacing and alignment of curriculum, monitor student achievement, and make needed adjustments along the way. The availability of math specialists is often determined by budgetary considerations. However, their role is a vitally important one, particularly given the importance of teachers seeing themselves as successful math teachers who are capable of engaging all math learners.

TEN STRATEGIES FOR IMPROVING MATH

A variety of strategies can be used by educators to bolster math teaching and learning. Some of these can be effectively implemented by individual teachers, whereas others are best adopted by grade-level teams or departments. These strategies can strengthen a School Improvement Plan that targets improving math achievement.

1. Breaking Up the Math Block by Differentiating Math Instruction
2. Incorporating Hands-On Materials
3. Using Visual Representations
4. Applying Formative Assessment Probes

5. Adopting the "Flip Model"
6. Integrating Math and Science
7. Initiating Peer and Cross-Age Tutoring
8. Using Open-Ended Questions
9. Introducing Math Games
10. Scaffolding Math Instruction

Strategy One: Breaking Up the Math Block by Differentiating Instruction

Teachers sometimes struggle with how to format a math lesson. Well-designed math instruction might include memory exercises and strategy steps that prompt students to properly order their approach to solving math problems (Steedly et al. 2008). Because students learn differently, teachers also should consider the benefits of differentiated instruction. Tomlinson (1999) offers an example of what differentiated math instruction might look like in a fourth-grade classroom where students are focusing on computation of whole numbers. She points out (2000, p. 6) that differentiation is more a philosophy regarding teaching and learning than it is a strategy. Here is how this approach might be incorporated in the math classroom.

In Tomlinson's scenario, differentiation takes place at five different stations. Station 1 involves the teacher directly instructing a small group of students; Station 2 entails students working with manipulatives to prove their work and have a partner check their understanding; and Station 3 involves either independent worksheets or a computer simulation to provide practice and gain speed. Station 4 calls for a problem-solving simulation in which students consider a predicament and write down their approach to solving the case. Station 5 involves small-group work to complete a long-term project (Tomlinson 1999, pp. 63–64). This variety of activities takes careful planning, but it can be effective in addressing the needs of different students.

Strategy Two: Incorporating Hands-On Materials

Using hands-on materials is effective in both elementary and secondary settings. These materials enable students to connect objects and ideas and reduce anxiety in math learning. They also can promote student collaboration in small groups.

Although educators typically align manipulatives to a particular objective, there is also value in allowing students the opportunity to explore independently and become familiar with the materials. From learning time with Judy Clocks to exploring programming games on an iPad, involving students in hands-on learning increases engagement. Though many textbook companies offer packages of manipulatives kits, common classroom supplies such as paper clips and everyday items such as pennies can also be used to demonstrate concepts.

Hands-on materials lead to learning experiences that are unpredictable and engaging for both the educator and the learner. Using physical objects to better understand abstract mathematical concepts helps students change the way they think about mathematics in general and problem solving in particular.

Strategy Three: Using Visual Representations

Students who use visual representations can learn abstract concepts more readily. NMAP (2008) notes that using a number line to represent fractions can help students link conceptual and procedural knowledge and that "instruction focusing on conceptual knowledge of fractions is likely to have the broadest and largest impact on problem-solving performance" (p. xix). Technology applications increasingly provide the means to accomplish this task.

A second-grade class might review "ten-frames" by using a Smartboard in which students come to the front of the classroom and "click and drag" elements on the interactive board and receive feedback from the teacher and classmates. Or, a high school student might work through a formula using a geometry sketch pad connected to a graphic calculator and projector that allows the class to see the various steps involved.

Using visual representations such as diagrams assists problem solving in math and related areas such as science (Zahner and Corter 2010). Teachers can model, teach, and encourage students to draw and create visual representations as a part of a daily "Do Now" activity, for example, to help make meaning of abstract concepts and reinforce student learning.

Strategy Four: Applying Formative Assessment Probes

Mathematical formative assessment probes help teachers "uncover student understandings and misunderstandings" and then make instructional adjustments (Rose, Minton, and Arline 2007, p. 2). Rather than waiting for end-of-course or even end-of-the-week assessment data, teachers should regularly use probes to determine students' conceptual and procedural understandings. Formative assessment, according to one researcher, "can effectively double the speed of student learning" (Wiliam 2007, p. 36) when it is implemented.

Understanding what needs to be learned is of fundamental importance when implementing formative assessment. The formative assessment probe, at any level of mathematics, should be designed to determine what the student understands and does not understand, thereby helping teachers plan for next steps. Using math exit slips as a standard routine to end class, for example, provides the teachers with valuable information on how students are progressing, enabling them to plan for the next day's math assignments. Exit slips also can be compiled into a list that provides a longitudinal record of how students are achieving and a basis for grade-level discussions of student progress (Sterrett and Fiddner 2007).

Strategy Five: Adopting the "Flip Model"

The "flip model" of instruction enables students to watch a lecture-formatted video clip of traditional "chalkboard" teaching *outside the classroom* and then use class time to apply learned material by solving problems with an instructor present (Sparks 2011b). Websites such as the Khan Academy (www.khanacademy.org) have given teachers access to online lessons and sources of content in an age of competing priorities for limited instructional time. The flip model enables students to learn content and strategies in an outside-the-class setting while allowing the instructor to focus more attention on application of the strategies in a more supervised format.

Instructors will need to consider summarizing and note-taking strategies that can help maximize learning from an online lecture or video-based format (Marzano, Pickering, and Pollock 2001). Educators should not rely solely on remote instruction, however, as the method for introducing concepts or explaining hard-to-understand strategies. A teacher might videotape solving a math problem and use technology to have added features such as on-screen pictorials of solving the equation with the teacher addressing commonly asked questions.

For an example of this interactive format, see a science teacher's reflections and demonstrations in the short YouTube video titled *The "Flipped" Classroom*: http://ddeubel.edublogs.org/2011/05/03/the-flipped-classroom/ (Deubelbeiss 2011). Socol (2011), however, cautions against the flipped approach, as disparities in home environments and available resources in such a "homework dependent" approach could potentially increase achievement gaps.

Teachers might vary the flipped format to include, perhaps on alternate days, in-class video lectures in order to demonstrate how best to learn from them. Pausing the video lecture at a key point and then leading a discussion and problem-solving session enables the teacher to model best practice to the class and get the most out of the flipped format.

Strategy Six: Integrating Math and Science

In most schools, from elementary on, math and science are taught as two separate subjects. Integrating them, however, helps connect abstract skills with concrete issues and address the complaint, "When are we ever going to use this?" (Coulter 2004, p. 16). Due to assessment and teacher licensure issues, the two subjects are likely to remain in separate "silos," but educators can work to infuse math concepts into science classes, and vice versa.

In the upper elementary grades and middle school, for example, measuring density requires an understanding of mass and volume. Rather than assuming that students bring those skill sets to class, science teachers either can co-teach a short unit with math teachers or offer to teach the math content in exchange for the math teacher infusing science review strands with math word problem assignments.

Strategy Seven: Peer and Cross-Age Tutoring

Researchers have found that peer and cross-age tutoring in math positively impacts both the tutor and tutee (Robinson, Schofield, and

Steers-Wentzell 2005). Peer tutoring, in which one student tutors a student of comparable age and cross-age tutoring, where an older student tutors a younger student, provide opportunities to address the needs of students who struggle with math.

A fourth-grade class, for example, can "adopt" a first-grade class and engage in peer tutoring once every two weeks, with fourth-grade students providing a short overview of a lesson, modeling a problem, and then working closely with the first graders to go through a sequence of practice problems. For tutoring to be effective, teachers need to ensure that expectations are clear for both the tutor and the tutee. Materials and sample problems should be readily available, and teachers should closely model how to tutor and monitor tutoring once it begins.

Strategy Eight: Using Open-Ended Questions

The use of open-ended questions by math teachers provides a sense of "uncomfortable ambiguity" that helps students recognize that math is more than a matter of precise answers and singular solutions (Small 2010). This strategy also provides another opportunity to infuse writing, as discussed in the previous chapter, into the math classroom.

An open-ended problem might entail having students generate a baseball team roster that has, over two games, a team batting average of .303. Asking students how many possible ways they can give change from a dollar for a purchase of 44 cents is another example. Rubrics can be developed that emphasize the process rather than one specific answer.

Students need to see the importance of working through problems, clarifying the ambiguous ones, and realizing they can successfully use math in any context. Open-ended questions provide rich opportunities for students to transfer knowledge into application and connect math concepts with solutions to problems.

Strategy Nine: The Use of Games

All students like to have fun, but many students do not view math as fun. The incorporation of games, as a whole class or in independent stations, makes learning about mathematics interesting and engaging. Games are useful for developing problem-solving skills and mathematical thinking in engaging and practical ways. Using the block game Qwirkle at a math station, for instance, promotes logic, sorting, and use of patterns.

Burns (2009) offers some tips to teachers on how to incorporate games into math lessons. Games that require reasoning and chance, for instance, promote strategic thinking. Holton et al. define mathematical play as "that part of the process used to solve mathematical problems, which involves both experimentation and creativity to generate ideas, and using the formal rules of mathematics to follow any ideas to some sort of a conclusion" (2001, p. 403). Some "five-minute activities" that can be used as a class opener or in-class activity might include allowing students to keep track of wins and losses during the "March Madness" basketball tournament, demonstrating fractions by determining horse "length" in the Kentucky Derby, or taking turns calculating batting averages using a roll of a die (Math games for every sport 2007).

Online math games that have been in existence for more than a decade and reviewed in terms of their form, function, and fun include A+ Math (www.aplusmath.com), FunBrain.com (www.funbrain.com), and CoolMath4Kids (www.coolmath4kids.com) (Keith 2001).

Strategy Ten: Scaffolding Math Instruction

As noted earlier in the chapter, math anxiety can deter students from learning math. Incorporating a scaffolded approach to teaching math provides the structure needed to overcome anxiety and gain confidence. Scaffolding involves teaching or modeling a strategy and then progressively shifting responsibility for applying that strategy to the student while monitoring the student's progress. Teachers can boost student self-efficacy by building on what the student knows and then "reviewing and restructuring" math instruction to promote greater independence (Anghileri 2006, p. 38).

Three levels of scaffolding can be considered in teaching mathematics, according to Anghileri (2006). Level 1 includes setting up "environmental provisions" such as wall displays, number lines on each student's desk, and manipulatives, as well as structuring the overall pacing and sequence of the lesson (p. 39). Level 2 involves direct interactions between the teacher and students in math instruction, including "explaining, reviewing and restructuring" (p. 41). Level 3 calls for "developing conceptual thinking" and supporting students as they make connections to what they have learned and transfer that understanding to applying what they have learned (p. 47).

SAMPLE MATH OBJECTIVES

When planning for math improvement, planners should consider incorporating the above strategies. In addressing a School Improvement Plan objective of "achieving a minimum of 90 percent pass rates in end-of-year benchmark assessments," a comprehensive approach is needed. The planning document at the end of the chapter first focuses on improving primary students' counting ability. Ensuring that students are proficient in counting and sequencing is fundamental to progressing in math. Strategies that are employed in realizing this growth include forward and backward counting and sequencing (for kindergarten students) and student fluency in counting by fives and tens in first- and second-grade classrooms.

At the middle school level, using "do now" activities to incorporate visual representations as a daily practice item allows teachers to reinforce relevant content while also empowering the students to build on what they know about solving the problem. A high school instructional strategy involves planning to teach at least one lesson a week using a "flip model" approach that allows the student to learn the content outside of class and then apply that work with the support of the teacher during the next class meeting.

All of these objectives depend on teachers collaborating to ensure that the strategies make a difference for students. Improving math instruction and student learning is possible, but it requires careful planning and monitoring to ensure that progress is being realized and that the objectives are being met (see table 5.3).

CHAPTER REVIEW

Teaching and learning math require an integrated and balanced approach to all five strands of mathematical proficiency (Kilpatrick et al.

2001). Today's school improvement teams can impact math achievement for all students by carefully addressing improvement objectives that are aligned to the needs of the school. By choosing strategies that engage students, foster collaboration, and challenge all students appropriately, planners can ensure that students overcome challenges such as math anxiety and are ready to understand the necessary fundamentals. Strategies can be accomplished by individual teachers, but a collaborative effort is preferable. By considering data trends, schedules and resources, and available support staff and collaborative opportunities, planners ensure that objectives are realized in an effective and efficient manner. Whether it involves introducing algebraic concepts to primary students or tackling a middle school math dilemma, success in math is attainable with careful planning and execution.

REFERENCES

Anghileri, J. 2006. Scaffolding practices that enhance mathematics learning. *Journal of Mathematics Teacher Education*, 9, 33–52.

Burns, M. 2009. 4 win-win math games. *Instructor*, 118(5), 23–29.

Cavanaugh, S. 2007. 'Math anxiety' confuses the equation for students. *Education Week*, 26(24), 12. Retrieved from EBSCO*host*.

Corbett, S. 2010. Learning by playing: Video games in the classroom. *The New York Times*, September 15. Retrieved from http://www.nytimes.com/2010/09/19/magazine/19video-t.html?_r=1andemc=eta1&agewanted=print on October 3, 2011.

Coulter, B. 2004. Bringing math and science back together. *Connect Magazine*, 17(4), 16–17.

Deubelbeiss, D. 2011. The "flipped" classroom [blog post]. http://ddeubel.edublogs.org/2011/05/03/the-flipped-classroom/.

Hawkins, J. 2011. Countdown to the games. *Mathematics Teaching*, (223), 28.

Holton, D., Ahmed, A., Williams, H., and Hill, C. 2001. On the importance of mathematical play. *International Journal of Mathematical Education in Science and Technology*, 32(3), 401–415. doi:10.1080/00207390010022158.

Honeycutt, B. B., and Pierce, B. A. 2007. Illustrating probability in genetics with hands-on learning: Making the math real. *American Biology Teacher*, 69(9), 544–551.

Keith, J. 2001. Math game web sites. *Library Talk*, 14(4), 25. Retrieved from EBSCO*host*.

Kilpatrick, J., Swafford, J., and Findell, B. (eds.). 2001. Executive summary of *Adding it up: Helping children learn mathematics*. Retrieved from http:// www.nap.edu/catalog.php?record_id=9822 on September 20, 2011.

Maloy, R. W., Edwards, S. A., and Anderson, G. 2010. Teaching math problem solving using a Web-based tutoring system, learning games, and students' writing. *Journal of STEM Education: Innovations and Research*, 11(1), 82–90. Retrieved from EBSCO*host*.

Marzano, R. J., Pickering, D. J., and Pollock, J. E. 2001. *Classroom Instruction That Works: Research Based Strategies for Increasing Student Achievement*. Alexandria, VA: Association for Supervision and Curriculum Development.

Math games for every sport. 2007. *Instructor*, 116(6), 60–62. Retrieved from EBSCO*host*.

National Governors Association Center for Best Practices, Council of Chief State School Officers. 2010. *Common Core State Standards for English/ Language Arts*. Washington, DC: printed by author.

National Mathematics Advisory Panel. 2008. *Foundations for Success: The Final Report of the National Mathematics Advisory Panel*. Washington, DC: U.S. Department of Education.

Robinson, D. R., Schofield, J., and Steers-Wentzell, K. L. 2005. Peer and cross-age tutoring in math: Outcomes and their design implications. *Educational Psychology Review*, 17(4), 327–362. doi:10.1007/s10648-005-8137-2.

Rose, C. M., Minton, L., and Airline, C. (2007). *Uncovering Student Thinking in Mathematics: 25 Formative Assessment Probes*. Thousand Oaks, CA: Corwin Press.

Schwartz, S. L., and Copeland, S. M. 2010. *Connecting Emergent Curriculum and Standards in the Early Childhood Classroom: Strengthening Content and Teaching Practice*. New York: Teachers College Press.

Small, M. 2010. Beyond one right answer. *Educational Leadership*, 68(1), 28–32.

Socol, I. 2011. Changing gears 2012: Rejecting the "flip." *SpeEdChange* blog. Retrieved from http://speedchange.blogspot.com/2012/01/changing-gears-2012-rejecting-flip.html on July 17, 2012.

Sparks, S. P. 2011a. 'Math anxiety' explored in studies. *Education Week*, 30(31), 1–16.

Sparks, S. P. 2011b. Lectures are homework in schools following Khan Academy lead. *Education Week*, 5(31), 1, 14.

Steedly, K., Dragoo, K., Arafeh, S., and Luke, S. D. 2008. Effective mathematics instruction. *Evidence for Education*, 3(1), 1–12. Retrieved from: http://nichcy.org/wp-content/uploads/docs/eemath.pdf on November 27, 2012.

Sterrett, W., and Fiddner, P. 2007. *Snapshot Portraits of Math Achievement: The Vital Role of Math Exit Slips in the Elementary Setting*. VAASCD Publications: Virginia Educational Leadership, 5(1), 94–97.

Tomlinson, C. A. 1999. *The Differentiated Classroom: Responding to the Needs of All Learners*. Alexandria, VA: Association for Supervision and Curriculum Development.

Tomlinson, C. 2000. Reconcilable differences? Standards-based teaching and differentiation. *Educational Leadership*, 58(1), 6.

Virginia Department of Education. 2011. School, school division, and state report cards. Retrieved from https://p1pe.doe.virginia.gov/reportcard/ on September 22, 2011.

Wiliam, D. 2007. Changing classroom practice. *Educational Leadership*, 65(4), 36–47.

Zahner, D., and Corter, J. E. 2010. The process of probability problem solving: Use of external visual representations. *Mathematical Thinking and Learning*, 12(2), 177–204. doi:10.1080/10986061003654240.

SCHOOL IMPROVEMENT PLAN OBJECTIVE: Students will achieve a minimum of 90 percent pass rates in end-of-year benchmark accountability assessments. Ninety percent of subgroups will meet end-of-year benchmark accountability standards.

Strategies	Person(s) Responsible	Materials Needed and Costs	Time Line				In-Process Measures
What we will do to achieve the objective	Person(s) who will monitor the strategy	What materials will be used to implement the strategy? What are the costs?	Check the projected quarter for implementing the strategy this school year.				How we will monitor progress
			1st Qtr.	2nd Qtr.	3rd Qtr.	4th Qtr.	
K–5: Within Collaborative Learning Teams, identify area(s) of focus to bolster student math achievement and develop a related goal based on June and September data. Identify, share, and implement strategies to accomplish the goal.							
Kindergarten Increase student proficiency counting and sequencing (forward to 100 and backward from 30). • Daily practice at learning stations • Providing home practice at least once a week as needed • Working with math specialist to monitor ongoing strategies	K teachers	Curriculum and supporting materials Stations within the class for individualized, differentiated instruction time with teacher (Instructional assistant leading this also an option)	✓	✓	✓	✓	Daily practice and informal observation Small-group guided practice notes Biweekly formative assessments

(continued)

SCHOOL IMPROVEMENT PLAN OBJECTIVE: (Continued)

Strategies	Person(s) Responsible	Materials Needed and Costs	Time Line				In-Process Measures
1st–2nd grades Strengthen student fluency in counting by 5s and 10s forward and backward. • Daily practice at learning stations • Providing home practice at least once a week as needed • Working with math specialist to monitor ongoing strategies	1st and 2nd grade teachers, math specialist	1st and 2nd grade curriculum and supporting materials Stations within the class for individualized, differentiated instruction time with teacher (Instructional assistant leading this also an option)	✓	✓		✓	Daily practice and informal observation. Small-group guided practice notes Math formative assessment probes
3rd–5th grades All students will strengthen problem-solving skills by correctly answering a weekly open-ended problem.	Grade-level teachers and math specialist	Open-ended problems aligned to curriculum map	✓	✓		✓	Weekly data will be kept by teachers and submitted to math specialist for review with administrator.

6th–8th grades: Within department teams, identify area(s) of focus to bolster student math achievement and develop a related goal based on June and September data. Identify, share, and implement strategies to accomplish the goal.

6th–8th grades All students will be given the opportunity to use visual representations in solving an opening "do now" problem at the beginning of each math class. The teacher will review the problem and encourage student leadership and demonstration in solving the problem.	Classroom teachers, math specialist	Daily "Do Now" problems and document camera Ensure that "Do Nows" are aligned with curriculum map.	✓	✓	✓	✓	Weekly data will be kept by teachers and submitted to math specialist for review with administrator.
6th–8th grades All students will complete at least two formative assessment probes that are aligned with curriculum guide.	All teachers (including specialists)	Documentation log Aligned formative assessment probes	✓	✓	✓	✓	Weekly data will be kept by teachers and submitted to math specialist for review with administrator.

(continued)

SCHOOL IMPROVEMENT PLAN OBJECTIVE: *(Continued)*

9th–12th grades: Within Collaborative Learning Teams, identify area(s) of focus and develop a goal based on June and September data. Identify, share, and implement strategies to accomplish the goal.

Strategies	Person(s) Responsible	Materials Needed and Costs	Time Line			In-Process Measures
All teachers Teachers in grades 9–12 will incorporate at least one "flip model" lesson per week in which the students are provided, in advance, a link to an instructed standard to review outside of class. The following day will be used as a "practice and problem-solving" session.	All teachers (including specialists)	Documentation log	✓	✓	✓	Weekly plans and attached curriculum map will be kept by teachers and submitted to math specialist for review with administrator.

CHAPTER 6

Improving School Culture

A New Principal, A New Culture

PREVIEW

A 7–12 school entrenched in a toxic culture has narrowly survived a takeover due to high administrator turnover, poor achievement data, and an apathetic environment. Drastic measures need to be taken. Ten strategies that will help improve school climate as well as shift the present culture to a healthy environment are shared. Sample objectives offer examples of how to shift the values and beliefs of a system to focus on student achievement.

"What was I thinking?" was the first question that echoed in the mind of Kelly Smail, first-time administrator of Peterstown High School; other questions followed. "How can I fix such a broken school, and where should I begin?" Changing the culture of a school can be the most challenging task administrators will ever face.

Peterstown High School is a 7–12 rural school with approximately six hundred students. There is little diversity; only 8 percent of the students are nonwhite. The majority of the staff lives locally, travels little outside of the area, and is deeply entrenched in the local culture. The county has a high unemployment rate. The school system is second only to a local hospital in job opportunities.

Peterstown High School is one of two high schools in the county, but it is the largest. Administrators are not promoted from within due to lack of qualified candidates, so external applicants typically are hired. The result is a revolving door nightmare. This leadership merry-go-round results in an unstable and uninviting environment for students and staff. The school has had four different administrators in the past five years. Each of the administrators sought alternative employment within months after beginning administrative service at the school.

Principal Smail was told when she interviewed that there were some cultural problems in the school she might want to address. She accepted the job with reservations. Three weeks into the job, Principal Smail is struggling and already laments that she neglected to ask the right questions.

The teachers bicker with each other publicly and without remorse, interactions often witnessed by students and community members. Students are herded through the corridors like cattle; excessive noise levels and altercations between the students are ignored by teachers assigned to monitor the hallways between classes. The general tone of the school environment is one of disdain and disgust. Even Principal Smail's own assistant is distrusting of her and is more of an obstacle than a source of support. Inconsiderate gestures and public comments indicate that the more influential staff want Smail gone as quickly as possible. There is little evidence of any focus on student learning in the classroom environment, and standardized tests confirm a sustained lack of effort by staff and students.

As a starting point, Principal Smail reviews the prior year's School Improvement Plan for evidence of prior planning and action. The Peterstown High School Improvement Plan does not follow a district-designed template for School Improvement Plans, and there is no indication that any portions of the plan have been implemented. During conversations with staff members, it becomes apparent to Smail that teachers do not have any knowledge of the plan.

Smail quickly assembles a Positive School Improvement Brigade that has the primary task of creating a plan to change the school culture. She also begins organizing small groups within the school with the hope that teachers will learn to work together, solve problems, and demonstrate professional attitudes. Simultaneously, Smail distributes to staff, students, and community members a cultural assessment tool to begin gathering tangible data as a baseline for the brigade to begin its work; in turn, the brigade is expected to provide direction to the staff.

Some of the responses from the cultural assessment tool reveal the following attitudes for staff, students, and the community at large:

Table 6.1.   Cultural Assessment Tool Results

Survey Section	Affirmative Responses (%)		
	Staff	Students	Community
You feel safe in your school.	56	12	78
You feel there is an atmosphere of trust.	12	9	56
There is a sense of community in the school.	10	10	45
The school environment is clean and inviting.	10	6	45
My teachers care about me.	NA	8	12
Someone cares about me as an important part of the school.	12	4	56
There is a reward system.	5	8	34

The survey instrument provided a space for written statements. Comments of particular interest to Smail include the following:

"Leave me alone . . . I don't need you here."

"You are a woman . . . you can't handle our system."

"We have a great school and we need a strong leader."

"We need help, but there are people in the school who want to keep power so they are not going to let you take away their power."

"No one cares about us, and you are no different."

"We need help."

"I want to find a job somewhere else, but I have no way of getting out of here."

"This place is crazy, and so are the people in it."

"I am afraid to say anything because I know I will be punished later on, and you can't protect me."

"Go away!"

"I would like to be left alone."

"Don't need any help."

"Go to HELL" (actually written in bold red letters across the face of the document with the rest of the survey instrument incomplete).

From the survey instrument, Smail determines the culture is so fractured that the staff cannot even articulate their feelings beyond a general sense of overwhelming hopelessness, anger, and bitterness. Even the language suggests isolation, with pronouns like "I" and "you" instead of "us" and "we." She realizes that it is going to take an aggressive—yet patient—effort to build a healthy school culture.

KEY ISSUES: IDENTIFYING SCHOOL IMPROVEMENT PLAN GOALS AND OBJECTIVES FOR IMPROVING SCHOOL CULTURE

A school is a living, ever-changing, and complex system of interlocking subcultures and climates. These interlocking subcultures and climates collectively form the overarching culture (Carr 2011a). Culture is the massive umbrella of basic tenets and embedded beliefs that guide those who interact with and within an organization (Schein 1992). These tenets and beliefs influence the distribution of power, protocols, and procedures for functioning in the organization, and attitudes and behaviors of those within the system.

Culture consists of layers or frames representing relationships, entrenched beliefs and standards, symbols, traditions, rituals, storytelling, heroes, and ceremonies (Schein 1992; Bolman and Deal 1997). In more simplified terms, culture is the heartbeat or soul of the organization; it is everything that makes the system unique and functional. The culture of an organization is intricately tied to its overall success.

Schools, like any system, can be healthy or unhealthy. An unhealthy system ceases to function effectively as an organization. Characteristics of an unhealthy school are poor or declining achievement, high staff turnover, absenteeism, unresponsive staff and students, distrust, conflict between subgroups, and lack of leadership. Toxic cultures can become healthy, but the path for change is often lengthy and blocked by many obstacles.

Administrators can change the climate of a school rather quickly, but altering the culture may take years. Cultural change requires deep transformation within the organization (Quinn 1996). When the school culture changes, the core beliefs, attitudes, and behaviors of the teachers and students in the school also change. Trust replaces mistrust. A positive climate replaces hostility. Courtesy replaces divisiveness. The environment changes to a culture of action instead of reaction.

One method for changing culture has been the takeover of public school systems by state or outside agencies (Garland 2003). In other cases, turnaround teams are used to improve unhealthy school cultures. A shift in leadership is frequently the catalyst to change school culture.

Duke (2008) cautions that dramatic transformations of school systems are rare, but systemic change can occur under the right conditions. School Improvement Plans can be instrumental in setting a path for change. Some goals for changing school culture rely on teams to address specific areas for school improvement. School Improvement Plans may also include a monitoring plan to sustain cultural changes and avoid reverting to old practices.

Policies and procedures can be valuable tools for achieving and reinforcing cultural change. They provide schools with operational guidelines that can be used to initiate a new culture. Administrators can use policies and procedures to signal desired beliefs and behaviors. An example is a policy that establishes protocols for nightly homework and after-school services for students. Another example is an established procedure for recognizing and encouraging acceptable practices such as hallway monitoring during class changes and faculty presence at student performances.

WHAT EXPERTS SAY ABOUT SCHOOL CULTURE

Culture has been studied for decades, and even today continued efforts to learn more about shifting and reshaping the culture of an organization remain of high interest. Studies often contrast healthy and unhealthy systems.

Assessing School Culture

Haynes, Emmons, and Ben-Avie (1997) suggest a checklist for school administrators to consider when evaluating the success of a system. This checklist contains fifteen key components of a healthy, supportive school culture. These components are:

1. achievement motivation,
2. collaborative decision-making,

3. equity and fairness,

4. general school climate,

5. order and discipline,

6. parent involvement,

7. school-community relations,

8. staff dedication to student learning,

9. staff expectations,

10. leadership,

11. school building,

12. sharing of resources,

13. caring and sensitivity,

14. student interpersonal relations, and

15. student-teacher relations.

These components provide a starting point for gathering data. Often surveys and interviews are used for collecting this type of information. These methods, however, can present challenges. Schools, according to Sarason (1996), can be difficult systems to measure due to the closed culture and some educators' attitudes toward outsiders.

Although cultural data from surveys and interviews provide one perspective on schools, other school data and direct observation in schools are equally important (Matthews and Crow 2010). The following are examples that can offer cultural insights:

Students:

- Attendance data
- Discipline referrals
- Suspensions
- Student mobility data

Staff:

- Staff attendance data
- Staff retention
- Discipline referrals
- Meeting attendance

- Hallway monitoring practices
- Responsiveness to requests

Observations:

- Cleanliness of halls, central areas, building passages
- Classroom appearances
- Graffiti
- Parking lot late arrivals
- How school visitors are greeted

Deal and Peterson (1999) describe cultural assessment as sleuth-like in nature and suggest that it requires a bit of historical reflection to understand a system. Stories from the past, ceremonies, symbols, and signs that are significant, past and present heroes, and events of significance to the school and community can provide clues to a school's culture.

The true essence of culture only can be captured through multiple lenses (Matthews and Crow 2010). Teachers see the school through a classroom lens, custodians see the school through a facility lens, and students see the school through a learning lens. Dissecting culture requires not only acknowledging that these different lenses exist, but also actually viewing the school from these different lenses for a holistic understanding of the school's belief structure and embedded values.

Improving a Toxic Culture

When encountering a toxic or unhealthy school culture, the sources of this culture must be confronted in order for it to be altered. Deal and Peterson (1999) have suggested *antidotes* for cultural negativism. First, negativity needs to be challenged by giving people a chance to speak out. Second, individuals with positive attitudes should be shielded and supported. Third, energy has to be focused on recruiting, selecting, and maintaining a positive staff. Fourth, the positive should be celebrated. Finally, a conscious and direct focus needs to be placed on eradicating the negative while building on positive norms and beliefs.

Cultural change is an ongoing process. Fullan (2001) identifies four factors characteristic of change: need, clarity, complexity, and quality. First, there must be an identified need felt by those who will be impacted by the change. Second, there must be agreement that the change is needed. Third, those impacted by the change must understand the complexity in creating the change. Finally, there must be expectations concerning the quality of the change.

Educators are walking advertisements for the schools they serve. Every reaction to a student, situation, parent, or community member constitutes a cultural indicator. Daily modeling of desired behaviors is one example of how educators can begin to change a culture. Another example is keeping the focus on school goals through daily activities such as morning announcements about goal attainment, data walls for weekly monitoring of progress, and school Web page updates. Constant modeling of the beliefs and values that are foundational for a school serves to build a strong support system for cultural change.

TEN STRATEGIES FOR IMPROVING SCHOOL CULTURE

1. Using Staff Team-Building Activities
2. Building Professional Learning Communities
3. Integrating Celebrations and Ceremonies
4. Creating Symbols and Signs
5. Creating Architectural Details
6. Establishing Norms of Excellence
7. Monitoring the Culture
8. Planning for Technology
9. Engaging in Professional Development Activities
10. Incorporating Storytelling

Strategy One: Using Staff Team-Building Activities

Improving school culture requires changing patterns of behavior and attitudes of the staff. To provide opportunities for this type of growth, teams can be effective. The environment of an unhealthy school is often laden with power struggles, distrust, and autocratic decision-making. Teams can shift the focus from power dynamics to working collaboratively.

Team members share power by collaborating on topics, developing sustainable goals, and initiating school plans. Team building is an effective method of promoting trust, independence, and distributed leadership. Staff will work together when there is a reasonable distribution of power and opportunities for all members to participate in discussions and decision-making. It is an avenue for creating cultural change in an organization. Various teams, outlined in table 6.2, can be used to develop and maintain a healthy culture.

Building a school team requires assigning people with specific skills to particular roles. An example is assigning goal monitoring to a member of a team. This team member is responsible for providing an update on progress toward designated goals. Another example is a team member who has the duty of collecting data for the team to review. Regardless of the size of the team, roles need to be established. If the team is large, then several members may work together on a particular responsibility.

Strategy Two: Building Professional Learning Communities

Professional Learning Communities (PLCs), according to DuFour (2004), involve shifting the focus from teacher instruction to student learning. Teachers can focus on building strong PLCs once the culture is

Table 6.2. Examples of School Decision-Making Groups

School Improvement Team	This team is responsible for developing and monitoring the School Improvement Plan.
School-wide Curriculum Team	All curriculum decisions flow to this committee for final review and approval.
School Budget Committee	All budget approvals are made by this committee.
School Policy and Procedure Review Team	This committee is responsible for reviewing policies and suggesting new policies as well as communicating procedures to all staff and students.
Facilities and Safe Schools Committee	This committee recommends changes in the areas of facilities and school safety.
Student Support Team	This team serves as a liaison between students and staff to ensure that all students are treated fairly and receive the support they need to succeed.

no longer an obstacle to healthy thinking. With open minds and a desire to improve student learning, PLCs can be successfully implemented.

DuFour explains that a PLC is a process that cannot be purchased. PLCs require patience and time. A PLC requires leaders to be direct and define goals for the members of the PLC. In a PLC, teacher teams plan for enriching children's experiences. This planning is accomplished through different structures such as cross-grade team meetings and grade-level teacher meetings. The meetings also provide mentoring opportunities for beginning staff as they interact and work on solutions to pressing concerns.

DuFour gives an example of a teacher team addressing four common questions: 1) What are the students learning? 2) What are the students not learning? 3) Why are the students not learning? and 4) What can we do to improve student learning? (personal communication 2012).

One example of a PLC task is the review of student records. The records are filled with columns and rows labeled with student names and the achievement data for each student. Teachers work together to review and discuss student performance data as it relates to achievement goals. They share strategies regarding what is working in the classroom and how to engage struggling learners. "The teachers share and discuss student progress and data collaboratively and positively rather than blaming students or other conditions outside of their control" (Sterrett 2011, p. 24).

Strategy Three: Integrating Celebrations and Ceremonies

Schools celebrate successes in various ways—awards programs, recognitions, incentives, and public/private acknowledgments. Successes can include student, teacher, team, and community accomplishments.

Celebrations that support school culture go beyond the success of any one individual or small group to represent the success of the entire school. The celebration must be authentic. Staff and students should embrace the need to celebrate and have a vested interest in the event. The celebrations should align with a school goal, such as reaching a benchmark. Benchmarks can be improved student performance on state tests, attendance gains, and decreased dropout rates and disciplinary referrals. Small celebrations over the school year can lead to a larger, more visible event held annually to publicize a year of successful efforts.

Staff recognition is also an important cause for celebration. Staff can be recognized for helping a student, promoting positive culture, and performing a "random act of kindness." Celebrations serve to reinforce key values and beliefs in a school. Teachers especially appreciate being nominated by students for an award. Teacher awards bring pride to the teaching staff and students alike.

Ceremonies can also reinforce values and beliefs in a new culture. Similar to celebrations, repeated ceremonies become traditions in a school. An example is a community ice cream social held each year as a fundraiser. The event is not a celebration of any one accomplishment but an invitation to stakeholders to work together on a project to benefit the school and community.

Celebrations and ceremonies are events that hold the fabric of the school together. These do not need to be grandiose or expensive. Successful celebrations and ceremonies create a sense of pride and belonging, a feeling of being part of something larger than the individual.

Strategy Four: Creating Symbols and Signs

Signs and symbols are as important to schools as a logo to a large commercial business. The symbol can be a mascot for a sports team, a banner for a school award, a welcome sign donated by a graduating class, a tree planted as a memorial, or the name of a school building. These signs and symbols convey meaning to those associated with the school.

Signs and symbols are a vital component of school culture. There are various ways to create symbols and signs. A school lacking a school song can work with the music department to create a school song. A community contest can be held to create a school logo that appears on stationery and T-shirts worn by students on designated days. Unveiling the logo can be a good opportunity for a celebration or ceremony.

Strategy Five: Creating Architectural Details

Architectural details encompass elements of the physical plant as well as the setting in which it is located. Some examples include landscaping of the school grounds; proximity of various spaces; the cleanliness of the school entrance, hallways, and cafeteria; and the attractiveness and utility of instructional spaces. The appearance of the school facility says a great deal about its culture.

Creating a warm and welcoming environment can reinforce a cultural transformation. A parent lounge where visiting parents can hang up a coat, make a phone call, and hold a meeting with a teacher tells parents they are valued. Having a paint day or cleanup day where community, staff, and students work together to enhance the appearance of the school can be a powerful impetus for cultural change. Parent organizations will donate time and often funding when asked to support programs that enhance the school. Businesses often will contribute supplies to support facilities enhancement. Improvements to the physical plant of the school need to be celebrated. Ribbon cuttings for a new playground, an unveiling of a new classroom, and an open house to admire artwork are occasions that reinforce the dawn of a new culture.

Strategy Six: Establishing Norms of Excellence

When the focus of school improvement planning zeros in on reculturing a school, a useful objective can be for teachers and administrators to identify a set of norms they believe should govern how adults relate to other adults in the school, how adults and students relate to each other, and how students relate to other students. There is no reason why students cannot be a part of this discussion, but it is important that teachers and administrators provide appropriate parameters. The key to developing norms is to strive for exemplary conduct, not settle for typical behaviors.

Planners should consider the kinds of behaviors and interactions that currently present problems. Perhaps the office staff does not treat all visitors with kindness and understanding. Norms for conducting meetings may have been allowed to slip, creating feelings of frustration and futility. Teachers may not share a common commitment to helping students who are struggling. Agreeing to explore the expectations to which everyone in the school should be held can be a very meaningful step toward a new and improved school culture.

Strategy Seven: Monitoring the Culture

All schools require monitoring, but schools moving to a healthier culture require a stronger monitoring system. Cultural monitoring is a continuous process focusing on desired changes in norms, expectations, beliefs, and assumptions.

Planning for cultural monitoring can be an important component of many School Improvement Plans. Monitoring involves the regular collection of data and can be accomplished through observations, record reviews, minutes, walk-throughs, and interviews. An example of a monitoring plan for team meetings might entail the appointment of a process observer to provide feedback to team members. Hallway monitoring between classes could be accomplished by regular walk-throughs. Observation notes might address how students and teachers interact and how inappropriate behavior is handled.

Interviewing is another source of data for cultural monitoring. Students and teachers can be randomly selected during the year for informal discussions about the school. Regular assessments of how students and staff feel about the school environment reveal important insights concerning aspects of school culture. Valuing the voices of students and staff can constitute a cultural change in some schools.

Strategy Eight: Planning for Technology

Technology is used during classroom *instruction* as a strategy for engaging students, but technology can also be used to improve an unhealthy culture. Using technology as a communication tool is one such application.

Parents can receive daily text messages from the school through mobile phones. The news may cover high points of the day and updates on particular school goals. Blog sites, providing public access to parents and the community, can post different topics for discussion. Websites are designed to provide information but can also be used to gather data by incorporating survey sections.

Eric Sheninger serves as principal at New Milford High School in Bergen County, New Jersey, and has been lauded as an NASSP *Digital Principal Award* winner in 2012. Sheninger has capitalized on the use of cell phones as a cultural improvement strategy. For years, he grappled with how to appropriately empower students in today's digital age; beginning in 2011, he lifted the cell phone ban at New Milford and entered into a contract with his students. He states, "We have focused on learning over chaos. Students see our initiative as a privilege, and we have leveraged phone use as a tool to accomplish learning goals" (personal communication 2012a).

From creating QR codes to link to their art portfolios to tweeting a 140-character synopsis of a science lab, New Milford High students are engaged in learning through use of their phones (personal communication 2012a; Sheninger 2012b). Students can take notes using Evernote and use GoogleDocs or Dropbox to store documents. Sheninger offers some tips to implementing a cell phone use policy in schools:

- View phones as "mobile learning devices"—In lifting the ban on cell phones to allow phone use during noninstructional time, the staff refers to "mobile learning devices" as tools to use during appropriate related times. More than a dozen such strategies and examples are outlined in a recent blog post titled "A Commitment to Digital Learning" (Sheninger 2012b).
- Acceptable Use Policy—The AUP has been crafted to permit responsible cell phone use during designated times and in specified formats. The school addresses cell phone infractions as any other discipline issue.
- Set expectations within the learning environment. Assemblies and guest lectures target digital responsibility and digital citizenship. "We are better preparing our students for a society that has become very dependent on handheld technology," Sheninger states. Cyber bullying has decreased due to training and staff emphasis on the responsible use of technology.

According to Sheninger, "People cannot believe our high school cafeteria when they visit; students are engaged and communicating in a responsible manner. Sure, some students are playing games, but many are on-task, doing work during noninstructional hours. Before, our cafeteria was just chaos; now students are using their phones responsibly" (personal communication 2012a). Adapting to the realities of cell phone use has enabled a cultural shift at New Milford High.

Strategy Nine: Engaging in Professional Development Activities

When a school culture is in need of change, professional development can provide the impetus. Learning to work together productively is a worthy focus for professional development. Activities might address conflict resolution, decision-making skills, building consensus, and goal attainment.

One challenge in maintaining a healthy school culture is acclimating new staff. As new staff join the school, orientation training is important to socialize newcomers to core values and expectations. Assigning mentors to new staff is another way to introduce a school's culture.

Self-mentoring programs also can provide support to newcomers through self-directed learning opportunities (Carr 2011b). Self-mentoring provides opportunities for new staff to take the lead in their own professional growth. They become responsible for developing a plan that includes classroom observations, professional networking, and self-reflection. It can be difficult for newcomers to interpret the culture of a school upon arrival. One strategy supported through a self-mentoring program is early identification of core school values and beliefs.

Self-mentoring can also focus on student achievement. One example involves videotaping classroom instruction. Teachers observe their own instructional practice privately and note areas for possible improvement. These areas for improvement then become foci for professional development and coaching by more experienced teachers.

Strategy Ten: Storytelling

Storytelling is the art of sharing the history of an organization and using symbolic events to interpret the past for contemporary stakeholders. School leaders who use storytelling capture the essence of the school and portray events in a positive light that defines the values of the school. Storytelling is also a method of connecting people with events and achievements that elicit emotion. The importance of storytelling is the connection it provides between the past and present.

Storytelling can be woven into ceremonies and celebrations. A ceremony may begin with a story about how the people involved in a project worked to achieve a dream or how land was used in the past before being donated to the community for erecting a new high school. The school can showcase relics from the past to enhance its "story."

Storytelling does not have to be rooted in the past. Storytelling can relate to a current goal or vision. An example is a courtyard project for a middle school that is open for the community to use in the evenings and on weekends. Christening the courtyard might include invitations to the community for a parent-sponsored picnic. At this event, the community and school officials can share stories about the importance of the project and how it was accomplished through the cooperative efforts of community members.

SAMPLE CULTURE OBJECTIVES

Improving school culture is a long-term project, the success of which depends on carefully laying the groundwork. A collaborative culture that supports academic achievement cannot be dictated from above. The three strategies in the sample School Improvement Plan at the end of the chapter focus on the initial steps in re-culturing a school. To increase buy-in, the first step involves surveying the staff about their perceptions of the strengths and weaknesses of the existing school culture. The next step involves interdisciplinary teams of teachers analyzing the survey data. Each team proposes recommendations for improving school culture. These recommendations then are reviewed by the School Improvement Team, and a set of recommended improvements is developed for submission to the faculty for approval.

CHAPTER REVIEW

Changing school culture is a difficult task that requires deep change from within. There will be individuals in the school who will resist change and create obstacles that must be overcome in order to create a constructive culture. Planners must focus on recognizing and reinforcing desired norms, values, and expectations. The process of moving from a toxic to a healthy school culture is an incremental one requiring modeling, monitoring, and commitment by school leaders.

REFERENCES

Bolman, L. G., and Deal, T. E. 1997. *Reframing Organizations: Artistry, Choice, and Leadership.* San Francisco: Jossey Bass Publishers.

Carr, M. L. 2011a. *From Hostile Takeover to a Sustainable-Successful System.* LAP Academic Publishing (https://lap-publishing.com/).

Carr, M. L. 2011b. *Self-Mentoring: The Invisible Teacher.* NC: University of North Carolina at Wilmington.

Deal, T. E., and Peterson, K. D. 1999. *Shaping School Culture: The Heart of Leadership.* San Francisco: Jossey Bass Publications.

DuFour, R. 2004. What is a "professional learning community"? *Educational Leadership,* 61(8), 6–11.

Duke, D. 2008. *The Little System That Could.* New York: University of New York Press.

Fullan, M. 2001. *The New Meaning of Educational Change.* New York: Teachers College Press.

Garland, L. J. 2003. *Navigating Treacherous Waters: A State Takeover Book.* Lanham, MD: Scarecrow Press.

Haynes, N. M., Emmons, C., and Ben-Avie, M. 1997. School climate as a factor in student adjustment and achievement. *Journal of Educational & Psychological Consultation,* 8(3), 321–329.

Lezotte, L. W., and Jacoby, B. C. 1992. *Sustainable School Reform: The District Context for School Improvement.* Okemos, MI: Effective Schools Products, Ltd.

Lezotte, L. W., and McKee, K. M. 2002. *Assembly Required: A Continuous School Improvement System.* Okemos, MI: Effective Schools Products, Ltd.

Morgan, G. 1997. *Images of Organization.* Thousand Oaks, CA: Sage Publishers.

Odell, S. J., and Ferraro, D. P. 1992. Teacher mentoring and teacher retention. *Journal of Teacher Education,* 43, 200.

Quinn, R. E. 1996. *Deep Change: Discovering the Leader Within.* San Francisco: Jossey Bass Publishers.

Sarason, S. B. 1996. *Revisiting the Culture of the School and the Problem of Change.* New York: Teachers College Press.

Schein, E. H. 1992. *Organizational Culture and Leadership.* San Francisco: Jossey Bass Publications.

Schlechty, P. C. 1997. *Inventing Better Schools: An Action Plan for Educational Reform.* San Francisco: Jossey Bass Publishers.

Sheninger, E. 2012. Personal communication, February 24, 2012.

Sheninger, E. 2012b. A commitment to digital learning. *Connected Principals* blog. Retrieved from http://connectedprincipals.com/archives/5412 on February 24, 2012.

Sterrett, W. 2011. *Insights Into Action: Successful School Leaders Share What Works.* Alexandria, VA: Association for Supervision and Curriculum Development.

SCHOOL IMPROVEMENT PLAN OBJECTIVE: Improve the culture of the organization for a positive climate and focus on student achievement.

Strategies	Person(s) Responsible	Materials Needed and Costs	Time Line Check the projected quarter for implementing the strategy this school year.				In-Process Measures
What we will do to achieve the objective	Person(s) who will monitor the strategy	What materials will be used to implement the strategy? What are the costs?	1st Qtr.	2nd Qtr.	3rd Qtr.	4th Qtr.	How we will monitor progress
K–12 Instructional Staff: Select a cultural audit or climate instrument to survey the staff.							
Provide each staff person in the school with a survey instrument to gather affective data.	Principal	Reproduction costs unless use online process	✓	✓	✓	✓	Data will be collected and disaggregated for cross-sectional and various patterns. This survey will continue annually to constantly monitor the pulse of the system.
K–12 Instructional Staff: Within Collaborative Teams, incorporate team-building exercises to provide an opportunity for establishing trust and fostering shared decision-making.							
All instructional staff In small groups, focus on building trust through collaborative projects.	Principal, all instructional staff (within respective grade or department)	Incentives for successful team work	✓	✓	✓	✓	Observations and strategic decision-making progress Anonymous exit slips to principal for feedback Continual monitoring in faculty meetings

(continued)

SCHOOL IMPROVEMENT PLAN OBJECTIVE: *(Continued)*

Strategies	Person(s) Responsible	Materials Needed and Costs	Time Line			In-Process Measures
Pre-Week Leadership Retreat—As small groups begin working together, the small groups begin planning larger events for the full staff that focus on building trust and teaming.	Principal, planning team	Team-building facilitator who could lead this An "off-campus" site such as a ropes course	✓	✓	✓	Informal group discussion and feedback
Implementation of professional learning communities						
The principal engages team (or department) leaders in a trust-building exercise to "set the stage" for collaborative team-building exercises to follow throughout the year.	Classroom teachers, specialist, community members, outreach services	Meeting time built into scheduling, release time, and some substitute costs. Incentive programs.	✓	✓	✓	Weekly data will be kept by teachers and submitted for review with administrator in PLC teams.

CHAPTER 7

Improving Instruction:
Moving out of the Comfort Zone

PREVIEW

A suburban high school has met achievement objectives and faces no external pressures to change or improve. In examining observation data and reflecting on student perceptions, the leadership team realizes there is ample opportunity to grow. This comes during the proposal window for a federal grant initiative providing funds for schools that can demonstrate innovative practices that bolster student learning. Ten strategies that can lead to improved instruction are examined, and a sample plan is provided to meet the objective of better engaging students through effective instruction.

Assistant Principal Sam Ramirez exited the biology lab and hit "send" on his handheld device. Instantly, the science teacher received specific instructional feedback in her e-mail inbox; Sam wondered if she would respond to his reflective question regarding leading short discussion breaks between lab stations to better ascertain student progress. The Sandy Acres School District had implemented the new *Teach-Learn* walk-through software, and all administrators were equipped with the capability to routinely observe teachers in five-minute windows and immediately offer feedback. The intense two-day training for school leaders was helpful, and teachers seemed to appreciate the feedback provided.

Ramirez focused primarily, though not exclusively, on ninth- and tenth-grade instruction in the midsized suburban high school. His fellow school leaders were Beth Jameson, who—like Sam—was in her second year as assistant principal at Twin Rivers High; and Nigel Frank, the veteran principal who was near retirement and well-loved by the school community where he had served as principal for nineteen years. Sam and Beth relished the walk-throughs, and each logged at least ten a day as they had agreed to do in establishing their shared SMART goals. Nigel was supportive of their efforts and allowed them to facilitate discussions in faculty meetings to make the walk-through observations relevant to the teaching staff.

Two data points had recently grabbed Sam's attention. When he compiled the school-wide observation data, he first looked at two components of the walk-throughs—student engagement and Bloom's taxonomy. The engagement data was based on Phil Schlechty's (2002) model: authentic engagement, ritual engagement, passive compliance, retreatism, and rebellion. Using Bloom's taxonomy, the walk-through model addressed what students were doing in one of six categories of cognition: remembering, understanding, applying, analyzing, evaluating, and creating. As they consolidated and analyzed their observation data, Sam, Beth, and Nigel noticed that students were tending to be either "ritually engaged" or "passively compliant" (table 7.1) and participating mostly in lower-level learning exercises (table 7.2).

Table 7.1.   Observation Data on Student Engagement—Twin Rivers High (Fall Semester)

Level of Engagement (as defined by Schlechty 2002, pp. 10–11)	Engagement Levels Noted in Observations (%)
Authentic Engagement—Students "see meaning in what they are doing, and that meaning is connected to ends or results that truly matter to the students" (p. 10).	14
Ritual Engagement—"Students do the work and carry out the tasks," but for extrinsic reasons; the actual product is "unimportant to the student" (p. 10).	29
Passive Compliance—Defined as "acceptance and resignation more than enthusiasm and commitment" (p. 11).	34
Retreatism—Defined by disengagement. Students "simply withdraw—mentally and sometimes physically—from what is going on" in the learning environment (p. 11).	14
Rebellion—Defined by the student "overtly reject(ing) the task, refus(ing) to comply" (p. 11).	9

Table 7.2. Observation Data on Intellectual Behavior—Twin Rivers High (Fall Semester)

Level of Intellectual Behavior on the Revised Bloom's Taxonomy (as defined by Overbaugh & Schultz citing the work of Anderson & Krathwohl, 2001)	Taxonomy Levels Noted in Observations (%)
Creating—When a student creates a new product or point of view.	13
Evaluating—When a student justifies a stand or position.	8
Analyzing—When a student can distinguish between different parts.	11
Applying—When a student uses information in a new way.	20
Understanding—When a student explains an idea or concept.	22
Remembering—When a student recalls or remembers.	26

The Twin Rivers team knew they could maintain the status quo with little pushback from anyone. Scores were acceptable, the teaching staff was stable and competent, and because the school simply did not have much student diversity, achievement gaps were not a glaring concern. The school was solidly "good." Sam posed a question to the team. "Can we look at our student perception data while we have these observation data sheets handy?" Nigel nodded, and Beth clicked on the spreadsheet. Twin Rivers collected data from seniors and alums at the five-year reunion mark. Four statements on the Student Perception of Teaching (SPOT) survey (table 7.3) were glaringly relevant to their discussion. When compared to median survey data from similar schools, these data were distinctly lower.

Nigel jumped in: "Colleagues, I think our fall walk-through observation data lines up perfectly with what the students are telling us in this survey." Sam and Beth nodded as Nigel continued. "We have been

Table 7.3. Twin Rivers Student Perception of Teaching (SPOT) Survey Results

Selected Statements	Students Who Agree (%)
Relevant Instruction—"My teachers made sure that instruction is relevant to me as a student."	22
Relevant Instruction—"The level of instruction I received at Twin Rivers adequately prepared me for my next steps (college or occupation)."	24
Innovation—"My teachers taught in an innovative manner."	19
Innovation—"My teachers were open to new and current ideas and strategies in teaching and learning."	12

encouraged by our district chief financial officer to submit a proposal for the federal *Tech and Teach* grant that our district has received. But we need to show evidence that we are actively seeking to integrate innovative teaching methods in our building. To get—and keep—the funding, we will be required to show practices that bolster student engagement and effectively use technology. Our teachers are actually going to have to embrace and *own* these changes. While I have always been wary of applying for grants because of the strings attached, I think we need those strings in this case. I think we can make a strong case for change, and we will have the funds to support it this time. However, for this plan to work, it must be owned by our School Improvement Team. This cannot be a top-down initiative if it is going to succeed—and last."

Sam knew that Nigel was right. Earlier in the week, he had specifically looked to see how teachers were using the new whiteboards that had been installed in every classroom as part of the district technology upgrade cycle. Fewer than a quarter of all teachers were using the whiteboards in an interactive format with students. Most were using them simply to portray PowerPoints as they had done when they previously had only projectors and screens. One teacher actually used it as a bulletin board of sorts, taping student reports on the white surface. This was a classic case of "tech in a box" in which the school had received its allocation with no training, modeling, or supervision. Given their hectic schedules, most teachers simply did not have the time to investigate new ways of integrating whiteboards—or any new technologies—to improve teaching and learning.

INSTRUCTIONAL IMPROVEMENT TO INCREASE STUDENT ENGAGEMENT

Sam, Beth, and Nigel confront common problems facing many schools today: outdated modes of instruction, low student engagement, underused resources. It is rare, however, that a school such as Twin Rivers is able to focus on improving teaching simply for teaching's sake. Usually, improvement efforts center around a content area such as math or reading. Although test results are important in today's accountability era, so are the continuous improvement of instruction, student engagement, and student feedback.

KEY ISSUES: INSTRUCTIONAL IMPROVEMENT AND INNOVATION

Two opportunities await Twin Rivers: the opportunity to improve instruction and the opportunity to be innovative in the process. Myriad books, presentations, and professional development opportunities offer help on improving teaching and learning. The challenge for school planners involves, as noted in the first chapter, gathering relevant data and diagnosing the situation to determine which steps the planning team needs to address. Knowing that many students perceive teaching as nonengaging and irrelevant justifies a greater focus on instruction.

In today's increasingly "flat" world, innovation is key to staying relevant and ensuring students receive an education that prepares them for the realities of an increasingly competitive global marketplace. Bolstering engagement and student achievement are both important by-products of focusing on effective instruction. As Schmoker (2011) has emphasized, focusing on *what* we teach and *how* we teach are two important steps to realizing greater success in teaching and learning.

WHAT EXPERTS SAY ABOUT EFFECTIVE INSTRUCTION

The work of Marzano, Pickering, and Pollock (2001) is often cited when discussing monitoring, evaluating, and improving instruction. They identified nine teaching strategies and techniques that research indicates have positive effects on classroom learning, including the following:

1. Identifying similarities and differences;
2. Summarizing and note-taking;
3. Reinforcing effort and providing recognition;
4. Homework and practice;
5. Nonlinguistic representations;
6. Cooperative learning;
7. Setting objectives and providing feedback;
8. Generating and testing hypotheses; and
9. Cues, questions, and advance organizers.

This research has been updated (Dean, Stone, Hubbell, and Pitler 2012) to include further studies, examples, and related strategies as well as a framework for instructional planning. However, the authors of both editions stress the need for caution. Dean et al. note "teachers must bring to bear their knowledge of and skill with the instructional strategies, and they must exercise judgment and wisdom with regard to the use of the strategies" (p. xiii). Similarly, Marzano (2009) points out that educators can make three mistakes when relying too heavily on the list of nine strategies and actually impede progress:

1. Focusing on a narrow range of strategies. Marzano notes that the strategies must be considered as a whole, not solely in isolation.
2. Assuming that high-yield strategies must be used in every class. Marzano cautions against "fall(ing) into the trap of assuming that all strategies must be used in every classroom" (p. 32).
3. Assuming that high-yield strategies will always work. The educator must look for positive results rather than just focusing on the strategy itself. Not all strategies will always work.

One thing is clear in the research: one size does not fit all. Differentiated instruction provides an approach to answering the frequently asked question of "How do I divide time, resources, and myself so that I am an effective catalyst for maximizing talent in all my students?" (Tomlinson 1999, p. 1). Differentiated instruction has been discussed as a key strategy in earlier chapters, but it is worth mentioning again in light of today's increasingly diverse classrooms, which—due to budget cuts and staff reductions—are often growing in size. When considering differentiation as a means to improve instruction and student learning, Tomlinson (2000) notes, "(I)t is a way of thinking about teaching and learning. It is a philosophy" (p. 6). In this vein, Tomlinson and Javius (2012) offer seven principles to "teach up" to all students:

1. Accept that human differences are not only normal but desirable;
2. Develop a growth mind-set;

3. Work to understand students' cultures, interests, needs, and perspectives;
4. Create a base of rigorous learning opportunities;
5. Understand that students come to the classroom with varied points of entry into a curriculum and move through it at different rates;
6. Create flexible classroom routines and procedures that attend to learner needs; and
7. Be an analytical practitioner.

Components of an effective lesson plan should also be considered. In *The Art and Science of Teaching* (2007), Marzano argues that the "elements of (Madeline) Hunter's lesson design are well-articulated and still useful" (p. 180). Hunter (1984) articulated the seven elements of lesson design as follows:

1. Anticipatory Set—Causes students to focus on what will be learned.
2. Objective and Purpose—Students and teachers alike benefit from clarity.
3. Input—Teachers design and implement a plan to help students acquire new information.
4. Modeling—Showing students examples of the process or end product.
5. Checking for Understanding—Teachers should ensure students are equipped to begin work.
6. Guided Practice—Students practicing under the supervision of the teacher.
7. Independent Practice—Students work without supervision once the teacher affirms they are ready (Marzano 2007, citing Hunter 1984).

Innovation and technology can be used to bolster student engagement and, ultimately, learning. By infusing strategies that are focused on enhancing teaching and learning by infusing collaboration, incorporating new technologies, and giving students an active voice in their work, school planners will realize improvement.

TEN STRATEGIES FOR IMPROVING INSTRUCTION

Strategies for improving instruction provide opportunities for reflection, growth, and innovation. The ten strategies discussed in this section provide teachers and school leaders opportunities to rethink teaching and learning in practical, effective ways. From embracing new technologies to bolstering student research skills, these strategies can help the planning team to refocus their own lens on instruction—for the sake of learning.

1. Sharing Walk-Through Observation Data
2. Embracing Social Media as a Learning Tool
3. Planning for 1:1 Tech Instruction
4. Raising Learning Targets
5. Implementing an Instructional Coaching Model
6. Using Formative Assessment Frequently
7. Organizing Lessons into Cohesive Units
8. Using Instructional Rounds to Bolster Learning
9. Using Whiteboards Effectively
10. Bolstering Student Research Skills

Strategy One: Sharing Walk-Through Observation Data

School leaders are increasingly relying on short walk-through observations as a part of the supervision and evaluation process. Frequent walk-throughs provide a varied and ongoing glimpse of teaching and learning to go along with more formal—and less frequent—class observations that focus on one particular lesson for an extended period of time.

Administrators should consider how best to share walk-through observation data with teachers and teams. It is important to draw a distinction—if applicable—between the evaluative nature and the professional development nature of such a transaction. If designated as a focus for professional development, walk-through data on instruction can be shared openly with a department or grade-level team. Data then can be used to highlight effective practices and areas in need of development. An extension of this form of data collection and analysis would be to use handheld cameras to catch brief glimpses of teaching in a classroom to serve as a basis for a collaborative discussion in a faculty meeting (Sterrett, Williams, and Catlett 2010).

Strategy Two: Embracing Social Media as a Learning Tool

Chapter 6 addressed the importance of preparing for social media in a manner that promotes an academic culture for students. Principal Eric Sheninger allows the use of cell phones (he terms them "mobile learning devices") in his school because "students are already engaged and immersed in social media, so already, teachers do not have to work as hard to capture their attention because that is the world that they know" (personal communication 2012). Students, Sheninger adds, can apply tools of the twenty-first century to achieve a learning objective and apply, create, or evaluate learned content in the learning climate. He notes "it all comes down to essential skills—including communication, collaboration, media literacy, technological proficiency, global awareness, and most of all, creativity." Social media serve as powerful tools to help students realize learning targets. Students use cell phones to submit science data, research background information, and present findings (Sheninger 2012a).

The following tips are important to consider when incorporating social media in a school setting. Clear expectations regarding acceptable use must be shared, understood, and enforced. Sheninger (personal communication 2012) notes that the principal is in a unique position to lead by emphasizing the following:

1. Give teachers autonomy to be creative, innovative, and take risks.
   a. Model the variety of tools that are available. Sheninger provides examples of engaged digital learning (Sheninger 2012b) in school:
      - Using QR Codes in an art class scavenger hunt;
      - Using YouTube to critique Super Bowl commercials in a marketing class;
      - Using surveys via cell phones to capture students' prior knowledge in math class;
      - Creating travel brochures with PowerPoint technology about biome-specific trips for biology class; and

- Using GoogleDocs and search engine software to research period paintings for a European history class.
2. Provide targeted training on effective uses of social media. (Sheninger reduced nonessential duty times to allow for two to three extra periods per week embedded in the school day for teachers to pursue professional growth. He provides collaborative resources—such as *Teacher Learning Community*, *PD 360*, webinars, and other tutorials—and requires teachers to log their hours and demonstrate what they have incorporated into their growth plans).

Sheninger emphasizes that social learning tools are contagious. "We started with about three core teachers and now over a third of the staff actively uses social media tools in the classroom or are learning on their own" (personal communication 2012). Teachers working to provide opportunities for students to use their "mobile learning devices" plan to incorporate social media as an innovative strategy.

Strategy Three: Planning for 1:1 Tech Instruction

Schools are increasingly providing each student with a computer in order to promote a "1:1" learning environment. If used effectively, this arrangement can foster alignment between content delivery and learning objectives. Of course, planning is required. Nash (2012) suggests giving teachers adequate time to familiarize themselves with the devices before distributing them to students.

Thomas Taylor, principal of Charlottesville (VA) High School, led his school through a 1:1 implementation because he believed it would "give students a competitive advantage at the next level of their life after high school" (personal communication 2012). Taylor notes that the "geography of the classroom" has changed (teachers now often stand in the back of the classroom in order to monitor a Twitter feed, for example) as the learning environment is "instantly more collaborative" and everyone is considered a learner (including the teacher). Because there are always unintended consequences and challenges, Taylor offers the following tips:

- Invest in a high-quality wireless network that recognizes both personal devices and school devices;
- Invest heavily in a project manager at the building administration level as a "resident expert" to answer questions and serve as a communications hub; and
- Avoid calling it an "initiative" and instead focus on the work as a permanent means of promoting effective instruction.

These critical considerations can greatly reduce frustration and skepticism. Seen less as a "fad" and more as a complementary instructional addition, 1:1 learning bolsters student engagement in a profound manner and re-energizes teaching and learning.

Strategy Four: Raising Learning Targets

James Raths (2002) notes there are a variety of ways to improve instruction. He suggests raising learning targets "on increasingly more complex cognitive processes, particularly *Analyze, Evaluate*, and *Create*" to enable students to build on their learning and prepare for new learning experiences (p. 235). Raths argues that instead of writing narrow behavioral objectives, teachers should strive to cognitively challenge students. This key point has not been lost on recent policy makers; the Common Core State Standards Initiative (2011) embodies standards that "include rigorous content and application of knowledge through high-order skills" (para. 5).

More than a posted objective on the classroom whiteboard, "a learning target should convey to . . . students what today's lesson should mean for them" (Moss, Brookhart, and Long 2011, p. 68). For example, when teaching about the planets in our solar system, instead of asking students to *list* the eight planets and *identify* qualities of each, the teacher should instead have students *argue*, as "Chief Travel Agent" for a particular planet, why their particular planet would be more interesting to visit and *evaluate* the various considerations that would be necessary in preparing for such a visit. Students then have a sense of ownership regarding "their" choice while also studying other planets in order to ensure that they can make a sound argument.

Students, Raths argues, often reflexively work to "push down" targets for a more comfortable low-level cognitive approach. By proactively planning to have at least one high-level learning target per lesson, teachers can take steps to continually challenge students to achieve higher levels of engagement and success.

Strategy Five: Implementing an Instructional Coaching Model for All Teachers

Instructional coaching often serves as a component of teacher induction programs, but it holds promise for all teachers—regardless of experience level. Coaching helps teachers to be more reflective about their practice and to identify and pursue growth areas in their teaching. As Tschannen-Moran and Tschannen-Moran (2011) note, "coaching has become a vital tool of professionalism" (p. 12).

There are different applications of coaching. Cognitive coaching, for example, is a model that is comprised of a pre-conference planning meeting, an observation, and a post-conference. Cognitive coaching emphasizes understanding one's self as a lifelong learner and identifying key growth areas in self-assessing one's own effectiveness and development as a teacher. Other forms of coaching address expanding teacher's effectiveness in a certain area, such as reaching ELL students or preparing to teach an Advanced Placement class. *Tools for Coaches* (2011) notes a "trove of literacy coaching tools" through the Literacy Coaching Clearinghouse Archive (www.literacycoachingonline.org) (p. 15). Coaching is a *process* that enables teachers to "strengthen professional performance by enhancing one's ability to examine familiar patterns of practice and reconsider underlying assumptions that guide and direct action" (Costa and Garmston 2002, p. 5). Coaching allows teachers to be more reflective in their work by working with a fellow educator to examine data (e.g., the number of times they call on a student, the way they use proximity to maximize engagement, or the level of questions they ask) and determine targets for improvement.

Coaching can be a useful strategy for various school improvement goals and objectives. For example, if asking higher-order questions is an improvement goal, coaching can center on collecting data on the type of question teachers are asking, reviewing what the data indicate, and considering ways to increase the use of relevant, higher-order questions. Similarly, in Year One of a 1:1 implementation in science, coaches can focus on the pacing of a lesson as a teacher leads a lab through a computerized simulation. In this case, coaching is intended to help experienced teachers better implement new technology while ensuring that students are engaged and progressing.

Strategy Six: Using Formative Assessment Frequently

Checking for student understanding is vitally important because it enables teachers to make important adjustments in order to improve student learning (Fisher and Frey 2007). Stiggins (2007) emphasizes that "we need to move from exclusive reliance on assessments that verify learning to the use of assessments that support learning—that is, assessments *for* learning" (p. 22). This approach can provide students with confidence and a desire to continue to take appropriate risks in learning. School planners should consider ways of balancing benchmark assessments—such as quarterly assessments for the purpose of trying to predict a high-stakes end-of-course score—with thoughtful formative assessments that provide students with timely and nonthreatening feedback.

Schmoker (2011) offers the following examples of formative assessments:

- Circulating, observing, and listening as students work in pairs;
- Calling on a sampling of students randomly between each step (not on students who raise their hands);
- Having students signal their understanding: thumbs up or down; red, green, or yellow Popsicle sticks; and
- Having students hold up dry-erase boards with answers/solutions (p. 54).

Considering how students can demonstrate their learning by responding to formative assessments enables teachers to maximize instructional time. Wiliam (2007a) notes "when implemented well, formative assessment can effectively double the speed of student learning" (pp. 36–37, citing Wiliam 2007b). Checking for understanding on a regular basis reduces the time spent on assessments and enriches instructional time.

Strategy Seven: Organizing Lessons into Cohesive Units

Marzano (2007, pp. 174–188) describes a series of five action steps for creating a unit, beginning with identifying the focus of instruction, planning for routine lesson segments that build familiarity for students, planning for content-specific lesson segments, planning for "on-the-spot" action segments to engage students and maintain high expectations, and developing a draft of daily activities for a unit.

Too often, teachers use favorite lessons that lack alignment with current content strands or target improvement areas. Within the context of unit design, teachers should pause and ask themselves the following important questions to ensure that they continue to reach their students:

• How does this work ensure that students have access to the entire curriculum?
• What data will I use to ensure students are learning?
• How will I know that students are engaged?
• What procedures are in place to build a sense of consistency and affirm students' success?
• How will I adjust my teaching and my overall plan for this unit when students are losing focus, lacking engagement, or not succeeding?

Due to hectic schedules and increased demands, many teachers may feel they are in a survival mode of day-to-day planning. A comprehensive approach that incorporates a unit-long perspective can promote curriculum coherence and greater student engagement.

Strategy Eight: Using Instructional Rounds to Bolster Learning

Teachers often teach in isolation. Instructional rounds provide a systematic, consistent framework for visiting colleagues' classrooms. The instructional rounds model for improving instruction is based on medical rounds and involves "three common elements of improvement: classroom observation, an improvement strategy, and a network of educators" (City 2011, p. 36). Seen as an inquiry process rather than an evaluative process, instructional rounds enable teachers to form networks of colleagues, determine improvement targets, visit classrooms in small groups, debrief after the observations, reflect and identify next steps, and then repeat the process (p. 38).

A team of middle school science teachers looking to better incorporate effective transitions between lab stations, for example, can visit two art teachers who similarly rotate students throughout art lesson activities to accomplish different objectives. After observing, the science team debriefs and discusses what comparable steps, if any, might be useful in teaching science. Later, they follow up with either the art teacher or each other to reflect on what they have learned.

Strategy Nine: Using Whiteboards Effectively

Interactive whiteboards provide an opportunity to engage students at any level. These systems include a mounted screen (usually the size of a dry-erase whiteboard or chalkboard), a projector (that is usually mounted from the ceiling); and accompanying hardware and software. Teachers and students can touch the screen and move, manipulate, and interact with text, pictures, scaled objects, and drawings. This innovative technology captures the interest of learners, allows for student movement and participation, and refocuses teaching on student learning. Using an interactive whiteboard, for example, first-grade students learning about states of matter can drag an element of heat to a pan of water and watch the state of water transform into steam.

Quillen (2012) notes that nearly 60 percent of teachers in the United States report whiteboard availability in their schools. Effective implementation, however, is essential to ensure that instruction is improved and learning is maximized.

School planners should consider the following when implementing whiteboard technology (Rabidoux 2012, personal communication):

• Vision for Implementation—The principal must articulate why this implementation is essential for the school's mission. Ownership of this work must be clarified; it should be established that this is a school-wide (or only specific grade or subject-area teams) implementation.

- Emphasize Quality over Price—Whiteboard technology involves significant cost for the initial purchase as well as maintenance and support. The School Improvement Plan team must consider the instructional needs first rather than seeking the lowest price. When the quality is compromised, teachers are less likely to embrace the innovation.
- Initial Training—Each staff member should receive an agreed-upon minimum baseline of training in order to ensure proficiency. Clearly established procedures (for resources, technical support, questions) must be communicated.
- Differentiated Training—Following the initial training, targeted training will benefit teachers with specific subject area needs and different levels of proficiency.
- Management Preparation—Teachers should consider the student perspective in determining placement of the whiteboard (where students can easily access it, see it, etc.) and in considering the flow of the instructional process.
- Engaged Professional Development—The principal should model and actively engage in professional development efforts. Principals spend significant time observing teachers and can connect needs to resources. Playing an active role in implementation, management, and continued innovation is critical as successful implementation can take between three and five years.

Investing in whiteboard technology is a significant commitment, but it can yield powerful results. November (2010) notes that in many ways, teachers are "digital immigrants" who are learning and adapting in a new world of innovation (p. 48). He contends the "real bottleneck to the creative use of technology is staff development" (p. 48). With careful planning and an articulated vision, school planners and leaders can minimize impediments to successful innovation in schools.

Strategy Ten: Bolstering Student Research Skills

When research skills are taught correctly, they provide a basis for student inquiry, problem solving, and active, engaged learning. Consequently, strategies associated with the teaching of research strategies not only enhance the curriculum, they can serve as an impetus for instructional improvement. Research skills are clearly emphasized in the reading and writing strands of the Common Core Standards (National Governors Association Center for Best Practices 2010).

Teachers should be striving to build student autonomy and confidence in using research skills effectively. November (2010) advocates promoting student responsibility for learning, noting that teachers "can help shape a problem and identify resources and tools" (p. 59) and then allow students to engage in the activities to enhance skills such as communication, critical thinking, and collaboration. Focusing on research skills does not have to lead to dull instruction. Creating a lesson to allow students to gather flora samples from the school grounds, identify the plants through use of a dichotomous key, and then produce a short "museum narrative" that is one-minute long using a handheld camera, for example, focuses on higher-order research skills while providing an opportunity for active learning.

Key personnel can help showcase new methods for teaching research skills in faculty meetings and focused trainings. School media specialists, for example, are uniquely positioned to serve as key staff developers and curriculum coordinators when it comes to strategies for teaching research skills. Previewing a few helpful apps that are research-related for faculty can lead to productive discussions about how to use technology to enhance the teaching of research skills.

SAMPLE OBJECTIVES

The School Improvement Plan at the end of the chapter includes three objectives intended to promote instructional improvement. Increasing student engagement as evidenced by walk-through observation data and student survey responses is addressed by three overarching strategies: involving all teachers in the coaching cycle process, using formative assessment data in a systematic manner, and implementing whiteboard strategies in instruction. Each strategy involves a series of steps to ensure it will be used effectively (see table 7.4).

CHAPTER REVIEW

It is difficult to imagine a School Improvement Plan without at least one objective associated with instructional improvement. Teaching is a very complex enterprise, one that is subject to changes in content, expectations, technology, and students. Efforts to raise student achievement and address related issues almost always require adjustments in how teachers work with students. This chapter presented a variety of strategies designed to enhance educators' understandings of the instructional process and produce more effective teaching.

REFERENCES

Anderson, L.W., and Krathwohl, D. R. (eds.). 2001. *A Taxonomy for Learning, Teaching, and Assessing: A Revision of Bloom's Taxonomy of Educational Objectives.* New York: Addison Wesley Longman. Cited by R. C. Overbaugh and L. Schultz at "Bloom's Taxonomy." Retrieved from http://www.odu.edu/educ/roverbau/Bloom/blooms_taxonomy.htm on January 3, 2012.

City, E. A. 2011. Learning from instructional rounds. *Educational Leadership,* 69(2), 36.

Costa, A. L., and Garmston, R. J. 2002. *Cognitive Coaching: A Foundation for Renaissance Schools* (rev. ed.). Norwood, MA: Christopher-Gordon.

Dean, C. B., Stone, B., Hubbell, E., and Pitler, H. 2012. *Classroom Instruction That Works: Research-Based Strategies for Increasing Student Achievement* (2nd ed.). Alexandria, VA: Association for Supervision and Curriculum Development.

Fisher, D., and Frey, N. 2007. *Checking for Understanding: Formative Assessment Techniques for Your Classroom.* Alexandria, VA: Association for Supervision and Curriculum Development.

Hunter, M. 1984. Knowing, teaching, and supervising. In P. Hosford (ed.), *Using What We Know about Teaching* (pp. 169–192). Alexandria, VA: Association for Supervision and Curriculum Development.

Marcoux, E. 2012. Common core and technology. *Teacher Librarian*, 39(3), 68–69.

Marzano, R. J. 2007. *The Art and Science of Teaching: A Comprehensive Framework for Effective Instruction*. Alexandria, VA: Association for Supervision and Curriculum. Development.

Marzano, R. J. 2009. Setting the record straight on "high-yield" strategies. *Phi Delta Kappan*, 91(1), 30–37.

Marzano, R. J., Pickering, D. J., and Pollock, J. E. 2001. *Classroom Instruction That Works: Research-Based Strategies for Increasing Student Achievement*. Alexandria, VA: Association for Supervision and Curriculum Development.

Moss, C. A., Brookhart, S. M., and Long, B. A. 2011. Knowing your learning target. *Educational Leadership*, 68(6), 66.

Nash, J. 2012. No laptop for you! (Until you set goals). Retrieved from http://bigthink.com/education-recoded/no-laptop-for-you-until-you-set-your-goals on February 29, 2012.

National Governors Association Center for Best Practices, Council of Chief State School Officers. 2010. *Common Core State Standards for English/Language Arts*. Washington, DC: printed by author.

November, A. 2010. *Empowering Students with Technology* (2nd ed.). Thousand Oaks, CA: Corwin.

Quillen, I. 2012. Battle for whiteboard-market supremacy heats up. *Education Week*, 5(2), 31, 33–34.

Rabidoux, S. 2012. Personal communication, February 29.

Raths, J. 2002. Improving instruction. *Theory Into Practice*, 41(4), 233–237.

Schlechty, P. C. 2002. *Working on the Work: An Action Plan for Teachers, Principals, and Superintendents*. San Francisco: Jossey-Bass.

Schmoker, M. J. 2011. *Focus: Elevating the Essentials to Radically Improve Student Learning*. Alexandria, VA: Association for Supervision and Curriculum Development.

Sheninger, E. 2012. Personal communication, February 24.

Sheninger, E. 2012a. *Eric Sheninger website*. Retrieved from http://ericsheninger.com/esheninger on May 16, 2012.

Sheninger, E. 2012b. A commitment to digital learning. *ASCD Edge* blog post. Retrieved from http://edge.ascd.org/_A-Commitment-to-Digital-Learning/blog/5771003/127586.html on February 24, 2012.

Sterrett, W., Williams, B., and Catlett, J. 2010. Using technology and teamwork to enhance peer observations. *Virginia Educational Leadership* 7(1), 65–71.

Stiggins, R. 2007. Assessment through the student's eyes. *Educational Leadership*, 64(8), 22.

Taylor, T. 2012. Personal communication, March 4, 2012.

Tomlinson, C. A. 1999. *The Differentiated Classroom: Responding to the Needs of All Learners*. Alexandria, VA: Association for Supervision and Curriculum Development.

Tomlinson, C. A. 2000. Reconcilable differences? Standards-based teaching and differentiation. *Educational Leadership*, 58(1), 6.

Tomlinson, C., and Javius, E. L. 2012. Teach up for excellence. *Educational Leadership*, 69(5), 28.

Tools for coaches. 2011. *Educational Leadership*, 69(2), 9.

Tschannen-Moran, B., and Tschannen-Moran, M. 2011. The coach and the evaluator. *Educational Leadership*, 69(2), 10.

Wiliam, D. 2007a. Changing classroom practice. *Educational Leadership*, 65(4), 36.

Wiliam, D. 2007b. Content then process: Teacher learning communities in the service of formative assessment. In D. B. Reeves (ed.), *Ahead of the Curve: The Power of Assessment to Transform Teaching and Learning* (pp. 183–204). Bloomington, IN: Solution Tree.

SCHOOL IMPROVEMENT PLAN OBJECTIVE: Increase student engagement as evidenced by walk-through observation data and student survey responses. Walk-through data will indicate at least 70 percent student engagement. Seventy percent of students will indicate affirmation of "relevant instruction" and "innovation" on student survey data.

Strategies	Person(s) Responsible	Materials Needed and Costs	Time Line				In-Process Measures
What we will do to achieve the objective	Person(s) who will monitor the strategy	What materials will be used to implement the strategy? What are the costs?	Check the projected quarter for implementing the strategy this school year.				How we will monitor progress
			1st Qtr.	2nd Qtr.	3rd Qtr.	4th Qtr.	
K–12: All teachers will conduct a full coaching cycle (pre-observation conference, observation, and post-observation conference) as both a mentor and a mentee each semester and identify one data point as a growth target.							
Identify a coaching partner. If you are having difficulty, contact your administrator for assistance. Complete the "coaching essentials" training. Plan and conduct the coaching cycle. Keep and reflect upon your data reflection sheet. Turn in "reflections on coaching and growth" sheet to administrator.	Teacher	Release time granted by administrator. Administrator will ensure coverage during the observation time for the teacher in the mentoring role.	✓	✓	✓	✓	Informal feedback via exit slips in faculty meeting. End-of-year survey (complied online). Teacher reflections sheet included in their performance review.

(continued)

SCHOOL IMPROVEMENT PLAN OBJECTIVE: (Continued)

K–12: All teachers will use formative assessment data to improve instruction. At least two formative assessment strategies per week will be documented longitudinally to inform instruction. Biweekly benchmark assessments are no longer required.

Strategies	Person(s) Responsible	Materials Needed and Costs	Time Line				In-Process Measures
Complete the "formative assessment basics" introductory module. Create and assess two formative assessment strategies per week that are aligned to the core standard that is being taught. Each week—in extended planning time—evaluate student performance (by student, by strand, and by cohort). Discuss as a team. Identify growth areas and conference with students. Determine extended learning time (ELT) needs if appropriate. Complete the assessment roster and file student progress in folder. Give a copy of data to your instructional contact every three weeks.	Teacher as a member of the professional learning community team, instructional leader (department head, grade-level chair, or administrator), principal	Curriculum guides, assessment items, ongoing training, release time for team discussion	✓	✓	✓	✓	Continued review of three-week data compilation Participation in assessment modules Review of final student summative data Review of student engagement indicators

K–12: All teachers will use one whiteboard strategy per week and involve all students at least once (per week) in an interactive whiteboard instructional exercise.

	Teachers, administrators, tech integration specialist	Whiteboard technology and related support				
Complete "whiteboard basics" module.			√	√	√	√	Completed module training documentation sheets
Complete quarterly "instructional strategies" module in their respective grade/subject area.						
Identify a minimum of nine different whiteboard strategies per quarter.						Weekly logs
Document the specific strategy and related standard in weekly log.						
Model one strategy in monthly faculty meeting.						Monthly faculty meeting demonstrations
Survey students at the end of each quarter regarding whiteboard instructional integration.						Student survey data

CHAPTER 8

Reaching English Language Learners
Ensuring Academic Achievement for All

PREVIEW

A case study involving an elementary teaching staff striving to meet the challenges of a growing English Language Learner (ELL) population opens this chapter. An overview of what experts say about ELL instruction is anchored in reading and relationships. Ten strategies that are centered on improving academic achievement and engagement for ELL students offer proven practices such as using graphic organizers and tutors effectively. Sample objectives include strategies for teachers in both elementary and secondary schools.

Assistant Principal Wayne Goshen waved enthusiastically as the buses left the school premises. *What a week*, he thought to himself. Nottingham Elementary School, in a suburban midwestern town situated just outside an ever-expanding urban ring, had just completed the first week of school. With the usual influx of new families, new teachers, new schedules, and new surprises, the first week's adrenaline rush had carried Goshen and his staff through the early days, and he finally had some quiet moments in which to reflect.

Nottingham had officially become a "majority minority" school in which more than half of the students were considered to be members of a racial minority. Though the school had grown increasingly diverse over time, the difference, when considered over the past six years, was significant. Hispanic students had more than tripled in total percentage of the student population in just six years. Table 8.1 shows the changing demographics at Nottingham Elementary from 2006 to 2012.

Table 8.1.   Demographics at Nottingham Elementary by Total Percentage (%) of Student Population

	2006–2007	2007–2008	2008–2009	2009–2010	2010–2011	2011–2012
White	65	59	56	52	50	42
Black	11	13	14	14	15	14
Hispanic	10	14	17	22	25	33
Other	14	14	13	12	10	11
Designated English language learners (ELL)	13	15	19	21	24	31

As a result of the growth in the Hispanic population, Nottingham had the "subgroup scrutiny" to consider in terms of meeting federal accountability benchmarks. The federal government has designated students, such as English Language Learners (ELL), a "subgroup" (Department of Education 2004, p. 27). And although Nottingham's total scores had remained above average for the past few years, the increase in student subgroups coincided with a decrease in some of the overall pass rates.

Although the teachers were, as a group, dedicated to the notion of "teaching all students," in reality, many struggled to meet the needs of a growing, diverse student population. Many, though not all, of the Hispanic students spoke Spanish as the sole language at home. Teachers focused primarily on welcoming the non-English speakers to their classroom and doing their best to instruct them in learning how to read, but having four or five ELL students in a kindergarten or first-grade classroom presented a new challenge to many of Nottingham's successful veteran teachers.

Fortunately, Nottingham had a full-time English as a Second Language (ESL) teacher, Ms. Julie Prince, who was fluent in Spanish but, more importantly, extremely effective at communicating with parents and teachers alike. She translated correspondence, came to the office to translate whenever she could, and attended many school events to connect with families. Though her job description did not involve translating and other such tasks, she often picked these up by default.

Assistant Principal Goshen and the veteran principal, Lorry Conners, were grateful for Ms. Prince but worried that she was stretched too thin. More than one hundred of the four hundred Nottingham students worked with Ms. Prince to some degree, depending on their need for services. And though Nottingham was slated to receive a second ESL teacher in the middle of the year (a budget freeze had delayed the start date), a growing air of frustration was evident to the administrative team as teachers were working very hard but struggling to meet the needs of the ELL students, particularly in reading and language acquisition.

Principal Conners and Assistant Principal Goshen met with Ms. Prince to discuss the projections for incoming students, needs of students, and possibilities for addressing the growing concern regarding ELL academic achievement. Ms. Prince's indefatigable enthusiasm glowed as she spoke: "Lorry and Wayne, I may sound crazy, but I honestly think all of our students can make great gains, and many will meet their year-end targets," she said, referring to the federal benchmarks. "I've seen a handful of small successes in a few classrooms when teachers 'get it' and use some strategies that we all know work. It will be great to have more support, but I think we can approach this wholesale as a school and really see some growth this year," she added. She rattled off a few strategies and a book that had helped her, and then left to meet a parent in the office.

Assistant Principal Goshen looked at Principal Conners. "If only all our teachers held that belief," he said admiringly. "Yes, and spoke Spanish too," chuckled Conners. "Ms. Prince is 'Exhibit A' in how one teacher can make a difference in a school. Without her, our ELL scores would be toast, but many of our families, students, and staff would be struggling as well and we all know it," she stated. "Well," said Goshen, "we only have one Ms. Prince. We have over one hundred ELL students and more are coming. What do we need to do next?"

KEY ISSUES: IDENTIFYING SCHOOL IMPROVEMENT PLAN GOALS AND OBJECTIVES FOR INCREASING THE ACHIEVEMENT OF ENGLISH LANGUAGE LEARNERS

Two "R's" that are at the forefront of ELL success are *reading* and *relationships*. Learning a new language and being able to interact with text is a challenge to the new student who may not even be able to read in his or her native language. Furthermore, the relational component's importance cannot be understated as students must feel welcomed and supported in their learning environment in order to succeed. Welcoming ELL students into the classroom can be difficult simply because of the language barrier. Similarly, teaching reading when concepts of text, reading, and language acquisition are new to students can prove to be difficult.

Schools must strive to teach all students. In this case, all includes ELL students. Too often, teachers rely heavily on "expert" staff such as reading specialists, math intervention teachers, and ESL teachers. It is important that all grade-level and subject-area teachers see ELL students as their responsibility. Focusing on reading and relationships should be the overarching goals as school planners look to bolster student achievement.

WHAT EXPERTS SAY ABOUT THE ACHIEVEMENT OF ENGLISH LANGUAGE LEARNERS

In studying national student population trends, it is clear that English language learners represent the "fastest-growing subset of the K–12 student population" (Short and Echevarria 2004, p. 9). In today's high-stakes testing environment, ELL students' academic performance "is measured by tests that were designed for English-speaking students and, as such, may be culturally and linguistically inappropriate for ELLs," causing a dilemma for educators who are striving to meet accountability requirements and also provide a welcoming learning environment for all students (Honigsfeld and Giouroukakis 2011, p. 8).

Some researchers and educators have advocated for a "dual-language" approach where programs are bilingual and focus, for example, on both English and Spanish rather than English alone. The reasoning here is to allow students to focus on skills such as learning to read first in their native language before learning another language (Estrada, Gomez, and Ruiz-Escalante 2009; Slavin and Cheung 2004).

Eleni Pappamihiel notes, "Students are able to progress in their content knowledge while learning English. Dual language programs are designed for both native English speakers and nonnative English speakers. Results from many studies show that kids who exit these programs outscore almost every group on achievement tests" (personal communication 2012). Yet the fact remains that most ELL students stay in the "regular" or "mainstream" classroom and depend heavily on teachers who do not have formal training in teaching ELL students. As Karathanos (2010) observes, the diverse needs of many ELL students fall on the grade-level mainstream teacher who must ensure that content is aligned with standards while also ensuring that the students can read proficiently. The World-Class Instructional Design and Assessment (WIDA) organization defines six performance levels of English language proficiency covering how learners process, understand, produce, and use content in the English language (WIDA 2007). Level 1 (Entering), Level 2 (Beginning), Level 3 (Developing), Level 4 (Expanding), Level 5 (Bridging), and Level 6 (Reaching) are performance levels that "define the expectations of students at each proficiency level" (p. ii) and encompass the following three criteria:

1. Linguistic complexity—the amount and quality of speech or writing for a given situation;
2. Vocabulary usage—the specificity of words or phrases for a given context; and
3. Language control—the comprehensibility of the communication based on the amount and types of errors (p. ii).

The U.S. Department of Education's Institute of Education Sciences offers a guide for practitioners who are targeting effective literacy instruction for elementary students. The report is geared to shaping practice and policy in schools with the "one major theme [of] intensive, interactive English language development instruction for all English learners" that develops academic language such as "the decontextualized language of the schools, the language of academic discourse, of texts, and of formal argument" (Gersten et al. 2007, p. 5). Five recommendations emerge from the report's findings:

1. Screen for reading problems and monitor progress;
2. Provide intensive small-group reading interventions;
3. Provide extensive and varied vocabulary instruction;
4. Develop academic English; and
5. Schedule regular peer-assisted learning opportunities (pp. 6–7).

Clearly, strategies must be employed to engage this growing body of learners in today's schools. Research shows that carefully chosen strategies can do much to help students succeed. School improvement planners can ensure that their objectives are met by aligning these relevant strategies with their efforts to help all ELL students succeed.

TEN STRATEGIES FOR IMPROVING THE ACHIEVEMENT OF ENGLISH LANGUAGE LEARNERS

1. Infusing Culturally Responsive Practices
2. Targeting Parental Involvement
3. Learning a New Language as Staff Development
4. Focusing on Language in the Classroom
5. Planning for Language Objectives in Lessons
6. Emphasizing Content Strands as Learning Foci
7. Using Graphic Organizers
8. Rotating Stations to Allow for Individualized Instruction
9. Implementing Collaborative Tutoring Led by ESL Staff
10. Using Service Learning

Strategy One: Infusing Culturally Responsive Practices

Students in a new learning environment need to feel that they are supported and that they can succeed. Honigsfeld and Giouroukakis (2011) note that by using culturally responsive practices, teachers can build upon what is familiar to them and then introduce new, local, and current events and ideas with which students can engage as they learn. They recommend that teachers expand "ongoing, formative assessments to include authentic, performance-based, project-based, or task-based assessment tools" to allow students various opportunities to demonstrate what they have learned in terms of content and language (p. 9). This scaffold-like approach will allow students to recognize their ability to succeed and strive to meet new learning targets.

A teacher immersed in a unit in measurement can invite her third-grade students to bring in their favorite recipes to discuss making entrées of their choice. After discussing the various entrées, the class chooses several for a class meal. Discussing where to find the ingredients, how to prepare and serve the food, and times of the year (or day) the meal is typically enjoyed engages the learners in making connections to their previous experiences. Actually making, serving, and enjoying the dishes together serves as an opportunity to share cultural experiences while accomplishing learning targets.

Ferlazzo (2010) emphasizes focusing on accessing prior knowledge (through activities such as stories, family trees, K-W-L exercises, and digital storytelling, to name a few) in order to engage students. Deeper conversations prompted by such questions as "Why do you miss your grandmother so much?" and "Why do you consider her to be a role model?" also provide opportunities to better understand cultural beliefs and philosophies (Pappamihiel, personal communication 2012).

Engaging students requires that educators first understand them. Infusing culturally responsive approaches in classrooms ensures that efforts are made to welcome and affirm *who* students are while also emphasizing *what* is expected of them. This approach strengthens the underlying relational dynamic of trust and promotes learning.

Strategy Two: Targeting Parental Involvement

Parental involvement is fundamentally important in nearly every facet of school improvement. When addressing the needs of ELL students, however, targeted parental involvement serves as a critical catalyst for improving that important "R"—*relationships*. ELL families often have little or no means of communicating with the school, or they have different cultural expectations regarding how to be involved with their child's school; thus carefully targeted efforts are needed (Gray 2004). Building on the previous strategy of infusing culturally responsive approaches, efforts to connect parents to the work in the classroom can enhance student learning.

Teachers, for example, can organize a "Heritage Night" where students and their families showcase meals, dress, music, and other manifestations of culture in science fair–like displays that are geared toward introducing their particular national heritage to other students. To reach a deeper understanding of culture, separate meetings can be arranged to get to know students in smaller, homogenous groups (Pappamihiel, personal communication 2012).

These efforts can be enhanced by serving a meal. Providing meals often boosts attendance and participation. Keeping a communications and activities log that includes face-to-face meetings, phone calls, and e-mails helps teachers monitor steps taken to ensure that parents are connected to their students' learning.

Home visits provide opportunities to engage ELL families, especially, as Campos, Delgado, and Soto Huerta (2011) advise, when there is a clear objective for the visit and the child's academic progress is discussed. The language barrier often presents an initial challenge, but drawing on available bilingual staff and taking deliberate steps to coordinate communications (for instance, making it a habit to translate the weekly class news bulletin or other take-home flyers or notices) increases the likelihood of reaching the families of ELL students.

Strategy Three: Learning a New Language as Staff Development

Educators are required to accrue professional development credits regularly in order to maintain their credentials. Earning points by learning another language is an attractive option. Districts can give points to principals and teachers for time spent using a computer-based software program (these programs are increasingly online and can document user time) or for completing a second language course (many universities offer courses such as "Spanish for Educators").

When an educator strives to learn another language, it serves several purposes. First, it allows the educator to better communicate with the learners in his or her own class. Second, it can boost empathy for the challenge of learning a new language and also encourage the educator to take risks and perhaps interact with students in new ways. Third, it shows ELL parents that the teacher is willing to work to understand a new language, thus helping to bridge the communication gap.

Two barriers to learning a new language are *time* and *cost*, but both can be addressed. Grants at both the district level (in the form of professional development funds) and external level (funds for innovation) are available to cover the cost of acquiring a site license for an online language learning program for the school staff (and perhaps families as well). Similarly, tuition credits exist at the division and, in many cases, at the university level for school staff taking courses. In some cases, teachers can study a new language on-site from school-based foreign language teachers.

Strategy Four: Focusing on Language in the Classroom

The British Columbia Ministry of Education (1999) issued a publication titled *ESL Learners: A Guide for Classroom Teachers* in which the agency stressed the importance of "the teacher's use of language" (p. 18), particularly in allowing for additional "wait time" as students translate the answer from their native language, formulate and solve a problem, and then translate it back into English. These measures take considerable time, but they can be very helpful to the student in encouraging participation. Other tips in the publication include the following:

- Be conscious of vocabulary—Pay special attention to word roots to build familiarity.
- Teach the language of the subject—This is particularly helpful in content-specific areas. A "cloze exercise" where students fill in missing blanks in a sentence can be an effective instructional technique.
- Simplify sentence structures—Reducing negatives and repeating sentences verbatim gives students an extra opportunity to process what is being said.
- Clearly mark transitions—Using explicit directions such as, "First, let us move here . . ." allows for clearer understanding of what is expected of the student.
- Periodically check for understanding—Watching for active listening behaviors and "checking in" on students to ensure they are understanding (pp. 18–19).

Honigsfeld and Giouroukakis (2011) emphasize the importance of "linguistically responsive practices" such as modifying reading assignments and worksheets to reduce complexity and offering step-by-step linguistic modeling through think-alouds, read-alouds, and write-alouds to build students' skills in tackling challenging academic tasks.

Strategy Five: Planning for Language Objectives in Lessons

Building upon the previous strategy of teacher use of language involves deliberate planning for specific language objectives. Short and Echevarria (2004) note that while "most teachers address content objectives in their lessons, they rarely discuss language objectives—a crucial area for English language learners" (pp. 11–12). The authors note that "pre-reading" strategies, such as discussing headings and key, boldfaced words enable English language learners to read with meaning.

Teachers can introduce a passage before independent reading time and then closely work with ELL students to highlight key words prior to having them read the passage. Focused professional development ensures that all teachers are equipped with a few fundamental strategies to help "pre-read" and "pre-write" with ELL students and thus boost their confidence in completing a new task or assignment. Setting common expectations in regard to this practice ensures continuity and collaboration as teachers work to infuse planned language objectives in all lessons.

Strategy Six: Emphasizing Content Strands as Learning Foci

Teachers often labor under the misconception that they have to create separate lesson plans for ELL students (Pappamihiel, personal communication 2011). Instead, teachers can build in content strands—specific defined elements within a subject area that students must learn to master that particular subject—with targeted support in order to help English language learners.

For instance, in a math exercise focusing on describing the difference between two stacks of coins, the teacher would provide extra assistance to ELL learners in the *describe* component of the problem while expecting all students to address the issue of the two different coin stacks. Focusing on the verb *and* the activity involved allows proper adjustments to be made for the specific level of the ELL student. This provides teachers, across the content areas, the opportunity to address key terms with all learners in a consistent manner while focusing the differentiation on the action verbs associated in the work.

Keeping the content strands intact ensures that all levels of ELL students maintain access to important grade-level concepts while receiving specific, individualized attention in regard to what is expected of them. Doing so results in targeted interventions that are manageable for the teachers and helpful for the students.

Strategy Seven: Using Graphic Organizers

The Alliance for Excellent Education, citing work by the New Teacher Center, stresses the importance of "the use of modeling, graphic organizers, and visuals" (2005, p. 3) to help ELL students recognize important information and make connections to what they are learning in class. Although graphic organizers as a strategy are helpful for all students, ELL students can particularly benefit from their use as they make connections to various concepts and key terms they are learning.

Using and modifying graphic organizers in daily instruction to ensure that learning is at the appropriate level helps make new concepts and vocabulary meaningful (Gallavan and Kottler 2007; Gill 2007). When teaching about the seasons and related weather events, for example, students can use an ordered graphic organizer that has four points with spaces to draw the season and related weather events (Gallavan and Kottler 2007). In elementary science, teachers can incorporate a computer program such as *Kidspiration* to draw a word cluster that describes photosynthesis and related key terms (Gill 2007).

Students of any language can express themselves with pictures, sketches, and diagrams. Using graphic organizers allows students to feel they can convey their thoughts while processing a new language and understanding new concepts, regardless of their level of language learning.

Strategy Eight: Rotating Stations to Allow for Individualized Instruction

The use of learning stations is a means for targeted teaching to the ELL student's specific level of need as well as an opportunity to maximize explicit instruction. Learning stations enable students to focus on key concepts by working in a smaller, targeted group (or independently) on a specific task.

In a middle school science class that is learning about the concept of density, for instance, the teacher might work at the first station with several ELL students and a few English-speaking peers. Emphasizing the key terms *density*, *mass*, and *volume*, the teacher uses manipulatives such as small lead weights, a scale, a cup of water, and different sized marbles to demonstrate the principles of density. The teacher should ensure that the students have knowledge of each of the words while emphasizing action verbs (such as *weigh*) that relate to the terms.

A second station calls for the students to map out a graphic organizer that connects the key terms in a pictorial involving two different plastic bottles—each with a different mass—either floating or sinking in an aquarium. The concept of density, mass, and volume are again emphasized. Having hands-on stations encourages engagement and working together in ways that transcend language gaps, and all learners benefit from the extra reinforcement and extension opportunities that learning stations provide.

Strategy Nine: Implementing Collaborative Tutoring Led by ESL Staff

The role of ESL teachers as collaborators is very important in ensuring that all teachers are equipped to meet the needs of their ELL students. In addition to teachers, tutors—either part-time or extended staff or volunteers—effectively build language skills and enhance content knowledge during extended learning time. Tutoring sessions that are scheduled after school enable English language learners to have additional instruction time. Tutoring can also be used during the instructional day in a targeted manner.

ESL teachers readily pinpoint their students' needs in regard to language acquisition and content knowledge. Tutors might be drawn from the ranks of parent volunteers, community members, university students, or even student peers. They should be trained by certified ESL teachers to address these needs and reinforce instruction in regular classes.

Strategy Ten: Using Service Learning

Relationships are important to sustaining the success of ELL students. Service learning that involves teachers working specifically in practical ways to help the ELL community can foster a better understanding of the unique needs of ELL learners and build constructive relationships in the process. Whereas researchers have emphasized the use of service learning approaches for preparing preservice teachers as multicultural educators (Bollin 2007), it is also worth noting that schools can similarly engage in authentic service learning projects to reach out to the families of ELL students.

Parents of ELL students often face daunting challenges such as poverty, language barriers, and unfamiliarity with American schools (Bollin 2007). Finding ways to help them with practical issues such as a holiday "Santa Fund" drive where teachers work with local stores to provide gifts for families can go far toward building a sense of community. Serving as a mentor for ELL students over an extended period helps foster a sense of connection between students and staff. Teachers often feel overburdened with extra responsibilities, so it is important that school planners balance these service-learning initiatives in a thoughtful manner so as not to impose too many additional responsibilities on teachers.

SAMPLE OBJECTIVES

Sample strategies are provided (at the end of the chapter) that are aligned to the overarching school improvement goal of improving academic achievement in ELL students so that 90 percent are meeting grade-level benchmarks in both reading/language arts and math by the end of the school year. Strategies include enabling the K–12 instructional staff to infuse cultural responsive practices into lessons and promoting greater parental involvement. A K–12 instructional strategy emphasizes content strand objectives in lessons. A K–8 instructional strategy calls for helping teachers to use graphic organizers in all core courses. Finally, a secondary-level strategy targets tutoring by drawing upon the expertise of ESL staff and using the energies and capabilities of volunteers and peers who have gone through an extensive training process (see table 8.2).

CHAPTER REVIEW

With a growing number of ELL students in today's classrooms, it is essential that school leaders, staff, and planning teams are knowledgeable about and ready to work with these students and their families. ELL students provide an opportunity for schools to embrace school-community relational work while focusing on effective instructional practices as well. This must be a shared approach; having designated ELL teachers or staff targeting ELL efforts will not alone transform a school. Continued and sustained success must be a focus of school planners and a shared effort among staff members. ELL students can become successful learners who bolster the success of the school community.

REFERENCES

Alliance for Excellent Education. 2005. *Six key strategies for teachers of English-language learners.* Retrieved from http://www.all4ed.org/files/archive/publications/SixKeyStrategies.pdf on October 18, 2011.

Bollin, G. G. 2007. Preparing teachers for Hispanic immigrant children: A service learning approach. *Journal of Latinos and Education*, 6(2), 177–189. doi:10.1080/15348430701305028.

British Columbia Ministry of Education 1999. English as a second language learners: A guide for classroom teachers. Retrieved from http://www.bced.gov.bc.ca/esl/policy/classroom.pdf on October 13, 2011.

Campos, D., Delgado, R., and Soto Huerta, M. E. 2011. *Reaching out to Latino Families of English Language Learners.* Alexandria, VA: Association for Supervision and Curriculum. Development.

Estrada, V. L., Gomez, L., and Ruiz-Escalante, J. A. 2009. Let's make dual language the norm. *Educational Leadership*, 66(7), 54.

Ferlazzo, L. 2010. *English Language Learners: Teaching Strategies That Work.* Santa Barbara, CA: Linworth.

Gallavan, N. P., and Kottler, E. 2007. Eight types of graphic organizers for empowering social studies students and teachers. *Social Studies*, 98(3), 117–128. Retrieved from EBSCO*host.*

Gersten, R., Baker, S. K., Shanahan, T., Linnan-Thompson, S., Collins, P., and Scarcella, R. 2007. *Effective Literacy and English Language Instruction for English Learners in the Elementary Grades: A Practice Guide* (NCEE 2007-4011). Washington, DC: National Center for Education Evaluation and Regional Assistance, Institute of Education Sciences, U.S. Department of Education. Retrieved from http://ies.ed.gov/ncee/wwc/publications/practiceguides on October 7, 2011.

Gill, S. 2007. Learning about word parts with *kidspiration*. *Reading Teacher*, 61(1), 79–84. doi:10.1598/RT.61.1.8.

Gray, T. 2004. Successful strategies for English language learners. *Educational Leadership*, 62(4), 84. Retrieved from EBSCO*host*.

Honigsfeld, A., and Giouroukakis, V. 2011. High-stakes assessments and English language learners. *Delta Kappa Gamma Bulletin*, 77(4), 6–10. Retrieved from EBSCO*host*.

Karathanos, K. A. 2010. Teaching English language learner students in US mainstream schools: intersections of language, pedagogy, and power. *International Journal of Inclusive Education*, 14(1), 49–65. doi:10.1080/13603110802504127.

Pappamihiel, E. 2012. Personal communication, January 25.

Public Law No. 107-110. 2002. An act to close the achievement gap with accountability, flexibility, and choice, so that no child is left behind. Retrieved from http://www.gpo.gov/fdsys/pkg/PLAW-107publ110/content-detail.html on October 7, 2011.

Short, D., and Echevarria, J. 2004. Teacher skills to support English language learners. *Educational Leadership*, 62(4), 8. Retrieved from EBSCO*host*.

Slavin, R., and Cheung, A. 2004. How do English language learners learn to read?. *Educational Leadership*, 61(6), 52.

Sterrett, W., Murray, B., and Sclater, K. 2011. Preemptive relationships: Teacher leadership in strengthening a school community. *Virginia Educational Leadership*, 8(1), 17–26.

U.S. Department of Education. 2004. No child left behind: A toolkit for teachers. Retrieved from http://www2.ed.gov/teachers/nclbguide/nclb-teachers-toolkit.pdf on October 7, 2011.

WIDA. 2007. English language proficiency standards prekindergarten through grade 5. Retrieved from http://www.wida.us/get.aspx?id=7 on October 18, 2011.

WIDA. 2010. The cornerstone of WIDA's standards: Guiding principles of language development. Retrieved from http://www.wida.us/aboutUs/Academic Language/ on October 18, 2011.

WIDA. 2012. 2012 edition overview tutorial. Retrieved from http://www.wida.us/standards/elp.aspx on October 18, 2011.

SCHOOL IMPROVEMENT PLAN GOAL: To improve the academic achievement in ELL students so that 90 percent are meeting grade-level benchmarks (or applicable ELL level-equivalent) in reading/language arts and by the end of the school year.

Strategies	Person(s) Responsible	Materials Needed and Costs	Time Line				In-Process Measures
			Check the projected quarter for implementing the strategy this school year.				
What we will do to achieve the objective	Person(s) who will monitor the strategy	What materials will be used to implement the strategy? What are the costs?	1st Qtr.	2nd Qtr.	3rd Qtr.	4th Qtr.	How we will monitor progress
K–12 Instructional Staff: Infusing culturally responsive practices into the learning environment.							
Identify at least two culturally responsive practices to implement each semester. These will be identified at the beginning of each semester and self-evaluated at the end of the year. During the school year pre-week, a workshop led by the ESL coordinator will allow opportunities for ideas and resources to be shared and collected.	Principal, planning team, ESL coordinator, teachers	Pre-week workshop offering will allow for sharing and collecting of resources and ideas.	√		√		Self-evaluation

K–12 Instructional Staff: Targeted parental involvement.								
Teachers will submit all important school-home correspondence to ESL teacher one week in advance for translation of key items. Essential should include the following: quarterly newsletters, progress reports, report card comments, and any concerns. Release time will also be granted to any teachers wishing to coordinate a home visit with the presence of the principal, ESL teacher, ESL liaison, or school social worker.	Principal, planning team	Release time supplemental records. Supplemental pay for translation if necessary/applicable.	✓	✓	✓	✓	✓	Anonymous exit slips to principal for feedback Continual monitoring in faculty meetings
K–12 Instructional Strategy: Emphasizing content strand objectives in lessons.								
All ELL students will be given the opportunity to complete grade-level content-specific assignments with consistent adherence to key content-specific terms (see WIDA 2012).	Teachers, ESL teacher, ESL coordinator	WIDA overview and workshop	✓	✓	✓	✓	✓	Quarterly evidence logs will be kept by the ESL teacher in coordination with teachers (monthly PLC times will be scheduled to facilitate this work).

(continued)

SCHOOL IMPROVEMENT PLAN GOAL: (Continued)

Strategies	Person(s) Responsible	Materials Needed and Costs	Time Line			In-Process Measures

K–8 Instructional Strategy: Using graphic organizers in all core courses.

Strategies	Person(s) Responsible	Materials Needed and Costs	Time Line			In-Process Measures
Teachers will incorporate, at least once per week, a learning activity that involves using a graphic organizer.	Teachers, ESL teacher, ESL coordinator	*Kidspiration* software. "Graphic organizers" workshop and supporting materials	✓	✓	✓	Quarterly samples will be shared in faculty meetings to generate ideas and foster discussion.

Grades 6–12 Instructional Strategy: Targeted tutoring will emphasize pre-teaching, reteaching, reading comprehension practice, and completion of projects.

Strategies	Person(s) Responsible	Materials Needed and Costs	Time Line			In-Process Measures
All ELL students will be given the opportunity to be tutored in the extended learning block (or study hall) by either a trained volunteer or peer in a manner that is consistent with course expectations.	Volunteers, administration, peer tutors Teachers will complete "tutoring log request" for students enrolled to align work to expectations.	"How to tutor" overview and workshop Volunteer orientation and clearance (administration) Weekly evidence logs	✓	✓	✓	Daily tutoring logs maintained by office staff and tutors will be submitted monthly to administration.

CHAPTER 9

Addressing the Special Needs of At-Risk Students

At-Risk Student Intervention

PREVIEW

This chapter opens with a case study involving an elementary school grappling with a struggling subgroup of students, followed by an overview of what experts say about identified at-risk students, specifically addressing dropout prevention. Ten strategies that will help improve student engagement and promote academic success are examined. Sample objectives offer examples of early intervention for students identified as at risk.

By most accounts, Sandy Brook Elementary is a successful school. Recently awarded the "Title of Distinction" for surpassing 90 percent pass rates in all areas, the school is highly regarded as a successful, positive learning community. However, the school's principal, Dr. Herbert Hammonds, is aware of a growing concern that he has noticed over the three years he has served.

Though only a fraction (15 percent) of his students fall into an at-risk "subgroup" (either by ethnicity and/or socioeconomic status), they are disproportionately failing. They tend to be brought up quickly for "child study," and some teachers admit they do not know how to teach them.

"He is more than two grade levels behind; how can I teach him?" was a remark Hammonds recently heard in the teacher's lounge. Concerned at the perception that "those kids are hard to teach," Hammonds is determined to work collaboratively to address the needs of his small but significant at-risk population.

Early intervention seems to be the key; therefore, Hammonds begins to examine programs for school-wide implementation that target teacher interventions. Assembling a representative from each grade level, Hammonds sets the stage through a distribution of evidence and research-based practices. He leads conversations about continuums of help and multitier approaches. With the teachers on board, the wheels begin to turn. A plan for implementation emerges.

THE AT-RISK STUDENT DILEMMA

With more than 1.2 million students dropping out annually, the United States loses an estimated $320 billion in potential earnings, according to CNN.com (2010). At-risk students are a national concern, one not easily dismissed. At-risk students must be identified and programs developed to assist them. There are multiple reasons why students do not meet standards and eventually quit school.

IDENTIFYING AT-RISK STUDENTS

Experts vacillate on methods for identifying students who are at risk. At-risk students are those not meeting standards, according to Gavigan and Kurtts (2010). A review of school achievement data is one means of identifying these students, but Janna Robertson, co-coordinator of the South East North Carolina Dropout Prevention Coalition, contends that effective identification is more complex. Robertson suggests that educators should consider two primary sets of identifying factors for students who are at risk of failing or dropping out of schoo (see table 9.1):

Robertson cautions that the most common mistake when reviewing only at-risk characteristics is the omission of students who do not fit neatly within conventional parameters. Students with high resiliency may be at risk but not identifiable from an at-risk checklist.

Resiliency factors such as "a caring adult in the home, a person at the school who connects with the student, having a mentor, and having a strong self-esteem or work ethic" are important considerations, according to Robertson. "Often a student, who excels in one area related to school, such as athletics or the arts, will stay in school since they have motivation beyond just academics. Other students who appear to have

Table 9.1.   At-Risk Factors

Individual Factors
Has a learning disability or emotional disturbance
High number of work hours
Parenthood
High-risk peer group
High-risk social behavior
Highly socially active outside of school
Low achievement
Retention/overage for grade
Poor attendance
Low educational expectations
Lack of effort
Low commitment to school
No extracurricular participation
Misbehavior
Early aggression

Family Factors
Low socioeconomic status
High family mobility
Low education level of parents
Large number of siblings
Not living with both natural parents
Family disruption
Low educational expectations
Sibling(s) has dropped out
Low contact with school
Lack of conversations about school

Source: Hammond, C., Smink, J., and Drew, S. 2007. Dropout Risk Factors and Exemplary Programs: A Technical Report. National Dropout Prevention Center. D. Linton: Communities In Schools, Inc. May 2007. http://www.dropoutprevention.org/major-research-reports/dropout-risk-factors-exemplary-programs-technical-report.

it all, meanwhile, experience a disconnect from the school and drop out despite high achievement" (Robertson, personal communication 2012).

When students are grouped by labels such as high risk and low socioeconomic status, educators may be too quick to accept these labels and ignore the real problem solving that should be occurring during instruction. Labels often lead to lower expectations and hinder the provision of appropriate support services. Educators must raise expectations for serving at-risk students and preventing dropouts. They must believe all students are capable.

National reports indicate that almost half of the dropouts in the United States are Latino and African American students. Other predictors include low socioeconomic status, unfamiliarity with the English language, disabilities, single-parent households, pregnancy, habitual drug use, one or more years of grade retention, poor reading skills, and loss of interest in school.

Educators should use caution when considering race and ethnicity in the identification of at-risk students. Diversity and deficiency are not synonymous. Although some foreign-born at-risk students struggle to learn a new language, once the language barrier is removed, they achieve well academically. Ethnicity also is not an automatic indicator of being at risk nor is lower socioeconomic status. If students have little or no support outside of the school, then they may be at risk, regardless of their other characteristics.

KEY ISSUES: IDENTIFYING SCHOOL IMPROVEMENT PLAN GOALS AND OBJECTIVES FOR AT-RISK POPULATIONS

School Improvement Plan goals and objectives should incorporate strategies that address the varied needs of at-risk students. Early identification is crucial. Interventions can be implemented for students as early as kindergarten. Interventions can be school-wide, course or grade-level oriented, or customized for individual students.

Multitiered approaches encompass a combination of programs and strategies. The approaches should align closely with school improvement goals. If the school is working to reduce student dropouts or decrease the number of at-risk students, then programs that have proven to be successful in meeting these goals should be considered. Programs and strategies that are no longer effective need to be eliminated. All programs and interventions should be evaluated on a regular basis to ensure they are meeting student needs.

WHAT EXPERTS SAY ABOUT AT-RISK POPULATIONS

At-risk students have been a focus of concern for years. Often at-risk students are youngsters with severe or chronic behavioral concerns. The population of at-risk students in schools has grown as a broader range of at-risk factors has been recognized. Zweig (2003) argues that mainstream education does not adequately meet the needs of many at-risk students.

The National Dropout Prevention Center/Network serves as a clearinghouse on issues related to dropout prevention and solutions for student success. The center has identified fifteen strategies that have been found to have a significant impact on reducing the dropout rate. The strategies are grouped into four categories: 1) School and Community Perspective, 2) Early Interventions, 3) Basic Core Strategies, and 4) Making the Most of Instruction.

School and Community Perspective includes systemic renewal, school-community collaboration, and a safe learning environment. Early Interventions include family engagement, early childhood education, and early literacy development. Basic Core Strategies are mentoring/tutoring, service-learning, alternative schooling, and after-school opportunities. Finally, Making the Most of Instruction comprises professional development, active learning, educational technology, individualized instruction, and career and technology education.

Students who fail to graduate face a bleak future. A high school diploma provides access to economic opportunity. Students who drop out are more likely to become involved with the justice system and earn lower wages (Sweeney 2010).

Other chapters in section II have presented a variety of strategies aimed at helping planners address the needs of at-risk students. These strategies range from programs that target struggling readers to initiatives that focus on raising student attendance. The fact is, though, that no single strategy, even a relatively comprehensive one such as Response to Intervention, can meet the needs of all at-risk students.

It also should be noted that no strategy, however well designed, is likely to succeed without the involvement of highly qualified educators. This last point must not be taken lightly. It has been estimated, for example, that only a quarter of primary grade teachers are prepared to teach at-risk children (Pianta, Belsky, Houts, and Morrison 2007; Scharlach 2008).

Meeting the academic and developmental needs of at-risk students requires processes for diagnosing needs and prescribing interventions, systematic monitoring of student progress, and adjustment of interventions when evidence indicates they are not working (Duke 2010). Making sure these measures are in place and working effectively requires capable leadership and ongoing professional development.

TEN STRATEGIES FOR HELPING AT-RISK STUDENTS

It is impossible to cover all the possible strategies for helping at-risk students in one chapter or one book, for that matter. The particular needs of students vary significantly, depending on their age, experiences, and past performance in school. What can be accomplished in this part of the chapter is to present some general strategies that school improvement planners may want to adapt to the needs of their school's at-risk students.

1. Identifying Needs Early
2. Targeting Interventions
3. Designing Discussion Groups
4. Building Trust
5. Providing Culturally Responsive Instruction
6. Promoting Community Cooperation
7. Mentoring Students
8. Teaching for Engagement
9. Individualizing Instruction
10. Implementing Universal Design for Learning

Strategy One: Identifying Needs Early

Intervention programs depend on accurate and timely screening. Diagnosing student needs can begin as early as kindergarten, though educators must exercise caution when reaching conclusions about very young students. Data concerning academic achievement, attendance, behavior, interactions with peers, interests, and extracurricular activities can help in the identification of students at risk of school failure. Parental input and teacher observations are especially important in the screening process.

School improvement planners should conduct an inventory of existing screening practices and assessment tools to determine whether changes or adjustments are needed. It may be helpful to identify a sample of students who "slipped through the cracks" and failed to receive timely interventions. Planners need to determine how these missed opportunities could have been avoided.

Schools where students in need of help are identified in a timely manner typically have established processes for the regular review of student progress by teams of teachers and specialists. Where such reviews are not occurring or where they are not being conducted effectively, planners should consider providing training and monitoring team meetings to ensure that screening is accurate and timely.

Strategy Two: Targeting Interventions

Aligning interventions with the needs of the students requires constant planning and openness to new ways to organize instruction. In a study conducted by Scanlon and colleagues (2010), for example, researchers found that 50 thirty-minute tutorial sessions for at-risk kindergarten learners and 75–150 thirty-minute tutorials or very small group sessions for at-risk first graders coupled with ninety minutes of high-quality classroom reading lessons resulted in 98 percent of all first graders reading on level.

One early intervention program receiving a lot of attention is the Response to Intervention (RtI) initiative. RtI provides intensive focused instruction to students who are experiencing academic or behavioral problems.

The standard RtI program involves three tiers of intervention. Tier 1 involves primary prevention efforts for all students. If Tier 1 efforts are not effective for certain students, they move to Tier 2 where assistance is provided in small, specialized groups. Tier 3, the final step in RtI, calls for specialized assistance for individual students. This help can be provided in the classroom or elsewhere. RtI requires the careful and continuous monitoring of student progress. Students who fail to benefit from the RtI assistance continuum may be eligible for special education services.

Strategy Three: Designing Discussion Groups

Discussion groups can be designed for academic or nonacademic purposes. They can be held in or outside of the classroom. In-class discussion groups include all students but take into account each student's learning style. All students are of equal importance to the discussion. An example of an in-class differentiated discussion group is a focus circle where students each contribute to a particular topic.

If the topic is the world's tallest mountains, for example, then each student would have an assignment that matches his own learning style. One student might read a book and share what was read with the group. Another student might watch a video. A third student might work on detailed sketches of different mountain ranges. As each student contributes in the group, the contributions are woven into a full report.

Cooperative learning strategies frequently involve grouping arrangements that enable high-achieving and struggling students to work together productively. Some of these strategies call for heterogeneous groups to review new material in preparation for classroom contests. When contestants are drawn from each group, the teacher is careful to choose students of comparable ability. Handicapping systems are used so that struggling students can make greater contributions to their team's score than high-achieving students. These handicapping systems ensure that high-achieving students help their teammates learn the material on which they will be quizzed.

Discussion groups can also be conducted outside of class. This approach is beneficial for gathering students from different grade levels. A multigrade group can be used to discuss school problems for at-risk students with a counselor leading the discussion. Topics can range from academic challenges to dealing with bullies. Differentiated discussion groups provide opportunities for at-risk students to reach out and make connections, build relationships, feel engaged in learning, and develop a sense of belonging, all of which decrease the chances of students dropping out.

Strategy Four: Building Trust

Building trust is crucial to cultivating relationships with at-risk students. Trust building consists of multiple steps. Brown and Skinner propose a model involving five recommendations: 1) listen, 2) validate, 3) problem-solve, 4) positive regard, and 5) hope.

The first step in building a trusting relationship is listening, which "requires conscious effort and continued practice" (Brown and Skinner 2007, p. 2). Not listening signals a lack of concern or a non-caring attitude. The second step involves validating and respecting student feelings. Step three is a series of questioning techniques to guide students through problem solving. Questioning opens the line of communication with a student, according to Brown and Skinner. Positive regard, the fourth step, allows the student to recognize and acknowledge acceptable behaviors in and out of the classroom. Adult interactions focus on modeling appropriate conduct. The fifth step is hope. Hope is fostered when all four of the previous steps have been successfully achieved.

At-risk students often act out as a result of their personal situations. This negative behavior can be a manifestation of personal struggles. Once these students connect in an authentic relationship, they can begin to cope with and work through "emotional roadblocks" in their daily lives that sabotage their chances for success.

Strategy Five: Providing Culturally Responsive Instruction

Students at risk can battle cultural differences. A Culturally Responsive Instructional (CRI) program helps level the playing field for these students (Gay 2000). Gay defines culturally responsive teaching thusly:

- Acknowledging the legitimacy of the cultural heritages of different ethnic groups that affect students' dispositions, attitudes, and approaches to learning and as worthy content to be taught in the formal curriculum;
- Building meaningful bridges between home and school experiences as well as between academic abstractions and lived sociocultural realities;
- Using a wide array of instructional strategies that are connected to different learning styles; and
- Incorporating multicultural information and materials in all subjects and skills routinely taught in schools (p. 29).

One way to legitimize diverse cultures is by using storytelling to teach writing skills. Another approach is to create culturally diverse study groups. Teachers have a responsibility to make authentic knowledge about ethnic groups accessible to all students. Students can be assigned to study different cultures in their local communities. What are the various cultures that make up the community? What do they have in common? What are their differences? What is valued by the different communities? As students begin to see commonalities and learn to respect differences, social tolerance develops. By promoting cross-cultural understanding, teachers address one of the concerns associated with students being at risk.

Strategy Six: Promoting Community Cooperation

The National Dropout Prevention Center/Network suggests that all groups in a community should partner to provide collaborative support in order to sustain caring and supportive school environments. Collaborative community initiatives have sponsored tobacco cessation programs, neighborhood watch groups, shelters for the homeless, after-school centers, and sports programs. These kinds of projects provide much-needed assistance to young people from disadvantaged homes and build local social capital.

One example of a community-wide effort to help at-risk students is Achievable Dream Schools, a model program in Newport News, Virginia, that focuses on students from poor homes. The model adheres to the basic tenet that all students, regardless of socioeconomic status, can achieve if provided the right conditions. Components of this program include relationship building between educators and parents, positive peer activities, constructive social norms, and rewards for pro-social behavior.

James Comer's *School Development Program* (Comer 2004) focuses on improving the educational experiences of poor minority students through building supportive bonds among students, parents, and school staff. The mission of the program is to create a positive attitude about school in poor communities. The Comer program operates with three teams: 1) the School Planning and Management Team, 2) the Mental Health Team, and 3) the Parents' Group. Each group has a specific set of goals and operating procedures. Together, the teams strive to improve the learning experience for all students.

Another successful community-based program is the Harlem Children's Zone (HCZ). The HCZ seeks to end the cycle of generational poverty by addressing the needs of an entire neighborhood. There are five dimensions to the program referred to as the HCZ Project Pipeline: early childhood, elementary school, middle school, high school, and college bound. Early childhood programs, for example, include Baby College, the Three Year Old Journey, and Harlem Gems and focus on ensuring that preschoolers get off to a good start. Family, community, and health services components support HCZ's education mission. A high percentage of HCZ participants go on to college.

Strategy Seven: Mentoring Students

Mentoring typically involves an older mentor with a younger mentee or a more experienced mentor with a less experienced mentee. The mentor guides the mentee and offers support when needed. At-risk students benefit from mentoring programs.

After School Matters is a Chicago-based nonprofit organization that provides high school students with after-school opportunities for work-based and project-based learning. The projects are in the arts, technology, communications, and extracurricular areas. Students serve as paid interns and are assigned mentors.

Another example is a dropout prevention program that assigns peer mentors to students at the beginning of the ninth grade and extends through graduation. The mentors work at building long-lasting relationships of trust and respect over the years. Mentors can be in the same grade level or one grade level above the mentee. Teacher mentors also can be assigned to at-risk students in order to help them face academic and other challenges (Sterrett, Murray, and Sclater 2011).

Mentors also play key roles in drop-back-in intervention programs for students who have exited school and decided to reenter. Transitioning back into a school setting after leaving can be challenging for an at-risk student. Assigning mentors to students as they reenter school provides support to prevent the student from becoming a dropout again.

Strategy Eight: Teaching for Engagement

Lessons that are boring and noninteractive fail to engage students, especially those who are struggling. Project YES (Youth Engagement for Success) is a participatory action research project headed by Martin Wasserberg, coauthor of the *Incredible Work of the Elementary School*. Wasserberg had students describe fun math lessons, distinguish between boring and exciting teaching strategies, and develop games for classroom learning. Getting students to play an active role in making learning more engaging is a useful strategy for increasing motivation.

Lessons that call for students to solve real-world problems can be especially engaging for at-risk students. Problem-based learning is particularly meaningful when the problems are drawn from the communities in which students live and when the solutions to problems lead to community improvement.

Strategy Nine: Individualizing Instruction

Some at-risk students are unable or unwilling to benefit from instruction in conventional classrooms. These students can benefit under certain circumstances from various forms of individualized instruction. Technology has made it possible for students to complete coursework on their own as long as they have access to assistance when they encounter difficult material.

Individualizing instruction also can be a useful option for students who need to repeat a course or recover credits in order to graduate. There are side benefits to requiring repeaters to re-take courses on their own. Having repeaters in classes with first-timers can have negative consequences. Repeaters are not good role models for first-timers, and they can be disruptive.

Strategy Ten: Implementing Universal Design for Learning

Universal Design for Learning (UDL) provides at-risk students with multiple and flexible opportunities to make curricular goals accessible (Gavigan and Kurtts 2010). Instead of altering a preexisting lesson or instructional practice, UDL transforms instruction from the onset. For at-risk students, the curriculum can be transformed to "broaden the definition of the learners who are expected to succeed in the general education environment" (p. 11). Three principles make up the framework for UDL: Principle 1 supports multiple methods of presentation. Principle 2 embraces various methods of expression and apprenticeship. The final principle calls for a variety of options for engagement. The key to all three principles is greater options for students, especially those who have struggled academically.

An example of a UDL reading assignment might involve the study of a country. Some students may prefer a hard copy of a book to research the country. Other students may prefer a digital copy. Students also can be given assignments in multiple formats. Consider how students present reports. One student creates a YouTube video about the assigned content. Another student uses animation software with characters that act out or speak about the topic. Yet another student designs an actual performance. Students choose the delivery system that aligns with their learning style and expertise level. Flexibility is the key to UDL. When ability and interest are aligned, students are more likely to be engaged, and engagement increases student learning.

SAMPLE OBJECTIVES

Addressing the special needs of at-risk students requires a deliberate approach to identifying students' needs, determining effective strategies to meet those needs, and allocating resources to ensure the needs are met in an efficient and effective manner as early as possible. Three strategies for helping at-risk students succeed are included in the sample School Improvement Plan at the end of the chapter. They include targeted interventions, mentoring, and teaching for engagement.

CHAPTER REVIEW

There are many reasons why students are considered to be at risk. The first step in helping at-risk students succeed is determining why they are at risk and assessing their needs. Once students' needs are identified, interventions can be selected. The earlier interventions are implemented, the greater the likelihood they will succeed. Interventions that have proven effective with at-risk students range from strategies for boosting engagement to mentoring and individualized instruction.

REFERENCES

Allington, R. L. 2011. What at-risk readers need. *Educational Leadership*, 68(6), 40. Retrieved from http://0-ehis.ebscohost.com.uncclc.coast.uncwil. edu/ehost/pdfviewer/pdfviewer?sid=7cb7c6bb-f663-4451-8677-24cad1647 560%40sessionmgr110andvid=27andhid=120.

Brown, D., and Skinner, D. A. 2007. Brown-Skinner model for building trust with at-risk students. Retrieved from http://www.eric.ed.gov/PDFS/ ED495498.pdf.

Browning, A. D. January 1, 2010. The use of a reading intervention program with students at risk of reading failure. *ProQuest LLC*. Retrieved from http://0-gateway.proquest.com.uncclc.coast.uncwil.edu/openurl?url_ ver=Z39.88-2004andrft_val_fmt=info:ofi/fmt:kev:mtx:dissertationandres_ dat=xri:pqdissandrft_dat=xri:pqdiss:3397426.

Byers, T. 2009. The BASICS intervention mathematics program for at-risk students. *Australian Mathematics Teacher*, 65(1), 6–11. Retrieved from http://www.eric.ed.gov/PDFS/EJ853820.pdf.

Capelouto, S. October 9, 2006. Georgia employs high school 'graduation coaches.' Georgia Public Broadcasting, GA, http://www.npr.org/templates/ story/story.php?storyId=6223902.

CNN.com. June 10, 2010. Obama highlights federal funds to lower high school dropout rate. http://www.cnn.com/2010/POLITICS/03/01/obama. education/index.html.

Comer J. P. 2004. *Leave No Child Behind*. New Haven, CT: Yale University Press.

Comer J. P. 1968. Comer School Development Program Website: http://www .schooldevelopmentprogram.org/about/people/faculty/comer.aspx.

Duke, D. L. 2010. *Differentiating School Leadership*. Thousand Oaks. CA: Corwin.

Fairbrother, A. 2008. "They might need a little extra hand, you know": Latino students in at-risk programs. *Urban Education*, 43(5), 587–611.

Gavigan, K., and Kurtts, S. (2010). Together we can: Collaborating to meet the needs of at-risk students. *Library Media Connection*, 29(3), 10–12.

Gay, G. (2000). *Culturally Responsive Teaching: Theory, Research, and Practice*. New York: Teachers College Press.

Hammond, C., Smink, J., and Drew, S. 2007. Dropout Risk Factors and Exemplary Programs: A Technical Report. National Dropout Prevention Center. D. Linton: Communities In Schools, Inc. May 2007. Retrieved from http://www.dropoutprevention.org/major-research-reports/dropout-risk-factors-exemplary-programs-technical-report.

Harlem Children's Zone. http://www.hcz.org/.

Jones, J. L. 2006. "The numbers are astounding? The role of the media specialist in dropout prevention." *Library Media Connection*, 25(2), 10–13.

Menzies, H. M., and Lane, K. 2011. Using self-regulation strategies and functional assessment-based interventions to provide academic and behavioral support to students at risk within three-tiered models of prevention. *Preventing School Failure*, 55(4), 181–191.

Morehouse, L. November 12, 2007. Can "The Wire" tell us how to reach the unreachable?: Putting the focus on at-risk kids. http://www.edutopia.org/the-wire-troubled-students.

Munoz, M. A. 2002. Facing the challenges of at-risk students in urban school districts: The impact of an attendance and dropout prevention program in a non-traditional school. Retrieved from http://www.eric.ed.gov/PDFS/ED463364.pdf.

National Dropout Prevention Center/Network. http://www.dropoutprevention.org/effective-strategies.

Office of Research Education Consumer Guide. September 1993. Comer School Development Program. http://www2.ed.gov/pubs/OR/ConsumerGuides/comer.html.

Pianta, R. C., Belsky, J., Houts, R., and Morrison, F. 2007. Opportunities to learn in American's elementary classroom. *Science*, 315(5820), 1795–1796.

Robertson, Janna. 2012. Personal communication, April 21, 2012.

Scanlon, D. M., Gelzheiser, L. M., Vellutino, F. R., Schatschneider, C., and Sweeney, J. M. 2010. Reducing the incidence of early reading difficulties: Professional development for classroom teachers versus direct interventions for children. In P. H. Johnston (ed.), *RTI in Literacy: Responsive and Comprehensive* (pp. 257–291). Newark, DE: International Reading Association.

Scharlach, T. D. 2008. These kids just aren't motivated to read: The influence of pre-service teachers' beliefs on their expectations, instruction, and evaluation of struggling readers. *Literacy Research and Instruction*, 47(3), 158–173.

Shirley, D. G. December 1, 2009. Evaluation of at-risk students' needs in public alternative schools. Retrieved from http://www.eric.ed.gov/PDFS/ED508752.pdf.

Sterrett, W., Murray, B., and Sclater, K. 2011. Preemptive relationships: Teacher leadership in strengthening a school community. *Virginia Educational Leadership*, 8(1), 17–26. Retrieved from www.catstonepress.com/vascd-spring-2011.

Sterrett, W. L., Williams, B., and Catlett, J. 2010. Using technology and teamwork to enhance peer observations. *Virginia Educational Leadership*, 7(1), 65–71. Available at http://www.catstonepress.com/vascd-spring-2010.

Sweeney, H. January 1, 2010. Academically at-risk students' perceptions of a constructivist high school biology pedagogy. *ProQuest LLC*. Retrieved from http://0-search.proquest.com.uncclc.coast.uncwil.edu/docview/839314572.

Teaching Every Student. 2012. *Universal Design for Learning.* http://www.cast.org/teachingeverystudent/.

Vellutino, F. R., Scanlon, D. M., Zhang, H., and Schatschneider, C. 2008. Using response to kindergarten and first grade intervention to identify children at-risk for long-term reading difficulties. *Reading and Writing*, 21(4), 437–480.

Walker, B. L., and Wasserberg, M. 2011. *The Incredible Work of the Elementary School.* Dubuque, IA: Kendall Hunt Publishing Company.

Zweig, J. M. 2003. *Vulnerable Youth: Identifying Their Need for Alternative Educational Settings.* Washington, DC: Urban Institute.

SCHOOL IMPROVEMENT PLAN OBJECTIVE: Improve the school's approach in addressing the special needs of at-risk learners.

Strategies	Person(s) Responsible	Materials Needed and Costs	Time Line				In-Process Measures
What we will do to achieve the objective	Person(s) who will monitor the strategy	What materials will be used to implement the strategy? What are the costs?	Check the projected quarter for implementing the strategy this school year.				How we will monitor progress
			1st Qtr.	2nd Qtr.	3rd Qtr.	4th Qtr.	

K–12 Instructional Staff: Implement targeted interventions in a collaborative, systemic manner.

Provide each staff person with an overview training of the identification process, available intervention resources, and monitoring procedures.	Principal	Materials reproduction, training release time, trainer fees	√	√	√	√	Data will be collected and disaggregated by student subgroup. A staff survey will continue annually to monitor the effectiveness of the intervention process.

(continued)

SCHOOL IMPROVEMENT PLAN OBJECTIVE: (Continued)

K-12 Instructional Staff: Infuse a school-wide mentoring process.

Strategies	Person(s) Responsible	Materials Needed and Costs	Time Line			In-Process Measures
All instructional staff will work in a collaborative team (grade level or department) to identify students in need of targeted mentoring. Students who are not already receiving individualized attention should be prioritized. Students matched with available mentors (either staff or volunteer) who will check in with the students at least once a week. Quarterly activities will be scheduled with all mentors and mentees (such as a field trip to local bowling alley).	Principal, teachers, team leaders, chairs, school planners	Incentives for successful teamwork, release time Scheduled activities (for example, a field trip for all mentors and mentees)	√	√	√ √	Documentation of students identified, time spent mentoring. Pre- and post-surveys of mentors and mentees will examine perceptions of the mentoring process. Review of documentation and survey data by the planning team.

K–12 Instructional Staff: Teach with relevance.

The principal will engage team (or department) leaders in an overview of teaching with relevance. The principal and team leaders will lead session during school year pre-week on relevant teaching. Teams (grade level or department) will preplan for relevant teaching strategies that include movement, reducing worksheet-type tasks, and fostering creativity. At the beginning of each faculty meeting, the principal will work with team leaders to highlight cases of relevant teaching using video footage of teaching and learning from within the building. Teachers will lead discussion on relevant teaching and learning.	Classroom teachers, specialist, community members, outreach services	Meeting time built into scheduling, release time, and some substitute costs. Incentive programs. Curriculum materials as needed. Handheld video cameras for principal and team leader.	√	√	√	√	Weekly data will be kept by teachers and submitted for review with administrator in PLC teams. A video library will be maintained of relevant teaching and learning from within the building.

CHAPTER 10

Improving Attendance

Achievement Gaps Due to Absenteeism

PREVIEW

A case study involving a middle school struggling to meet state benchmarks opens this chapter, followed by an overview of what experts say about the impact of absenteeism on achievement. Ten strategies for improving student attendance are examined through the lens of current research and best practices. Sample objectives offer examples of how to plan for reduced absenteeism.

Looking around the room at the members of the Garfield Middle School Improvement Council, Principal Rosey Walker spoke with candor and sincerity. "If we want to improve our state achievement ranking, then we are going to have to talk about school-wide absenteeism." Present at the table were all ten members of the school's council. The membership represented the community, including businesses, partnerships, civic organizations, and parents as well as faculty representation from the school.

Edward Martinez, a parent representative, looked bewildered and asked, "I don't understand, how is this a school-wide problem? Isn't it just an issue of several families not getting their kids to school? What can we do to change a family that has no respect for education or concern about their child?"

Principal Walker had assumed the principalship of Garfield Middle School as it was facing its second year of improvement status. Achievement gaps persisted among students, and staff morale was poor. As Principal Walker scrutinized the data, one statistic in particular caught her attention: there was an 88 percent attendance rate, which was 6 percent lower than the district (and state) average. Absenteeism, in Walker's judgment, would need to be an immediate area of focus for the team as they framed their improvement goals.

Affirmative nods indicated that members of the School Improvement Council were in agreement with Martinez's assessment of the situation; however, Principal Walker spoke with conviction to the council, "I think it is naive of us to see absenteeism only as a problem of certain families. Research suggests that absenteeism is a school-wide and a community problem. There are direct links between student attendance and achievement." A low murmur was heard in the room as Walker gave the group time to absorb her comments. Walker then stood and began to talk about her plan.

THE ATTENDANCE DILEMMA

High absenteeism by even one student is a school-wide problem. A student cannot perform well academically when he is frequently absent. And when many students have low attendance, this behavior undermines the capacity of all students and teachers to pursue high-quality education. When a school-wide problem exists, solutions must be sought. Absenteeism is a leading cause of low achievement. Schools where absenteeism contributes to decreased achievement need to identify and address the causes of frequent absences and how to overcome them.

An individual student's frequent absenteeism is often a symptom of disengagement and academic difficulties. Some reasons for student disengagement include a lack of meaningful content, poor classroom instruction, and negative peer pressure. A review of instructional content coupled with classroom observations may provide valuable clues to why some students are missing school. The problem may not be isolated to one classroom but may derive from practices school-wide. A school-wide plan then becomes necessary. Addressing absenteeism requires targeted professional development and cultural change. Parental and community involvement can also be critical.

Chronic absenteeism impacts school resources. "Absenteeism is believed to affect a range of concomitant elements from the budget to truancy and crime to daily lunchroom planning" (Strickland 1998, p. 2). Because attendance rates often are a common basis for school funding, lost funds due to absenteeism can be a major problem for school administrators. Fewer resources for schools are likely to impact academic achievement and perhaps lead to additional absences.

KEY ISSUES: IDENTIFYING SCHOOL IMPROVEMENT PLAN GOALS AND OBJECTIVES FOR IMPROVING STUDENT ATTENDANCE

Reducing school absenteeism is critical for schools. A frequent goal in school improvement planning involves greater student engagement. Engaged students want to attend and will maneuver through various obstacles to be part of the school. The strategies to improve student attendance need to focus on classroom instruction as well as parental and community involvement. Improvement plans also can address student absenteeism indirectly through shifts in the school culture.

The first step for a School Improvement Team involves collecting data about absenteeism at the school. School Improvement Teams need to explore two questions when tackling high absenteeism: 1) *What is causing absenteeism at the school?* 2) *What strategies can be put in place to reduce excessive absences*? (Adelman and Taylor 2010). The first question leads to additional questions about student absenteeism, such as: *Do students come to school and then cut class? Do students arrive late? Do students leave early? Are some students consistently tardy at specific times? Does one class have higher absenteeism than another? What types of parental involvement does the school encourage? How is the community involved in school activities? Is there consistently high absenteeism from particular neighborhoods?*

The second question also leads to additional questions, such as: *What strategies or programs are presently used at the school to reduce absenteeism? What is working and not working?* School Improvement Teams can collect responses to these questions as a starting point to evaluate the present status of school efforts as well as a springboard to design new programs to improve attendance.

WHAT EXPERTS SAY ABOUT ATTENDANCE AND ACHIEVEMENT

Research indicates a strong link between attendance and student achievement. Students who attend school between 85 and 100 percent of the time pass state tests in reading and math at much higher rates than students who attend school less than 85 percent of the time, according to the Center for Mental Health at UCLA (Adelman and Taylor 2010).

The Center's student support initiative states that ultimately schools must "develop a comprehensive system of student and learning supports to address barriers to learning and teaching and re-engage disconnected students" (p. 2). Such a system includes a range of supports for transitions and classroom and school-wide programs designed "to re-engage students who have become actively disengaged from schooling" (p. 2).

The report (Adelman and Taylor 2010) identifies common contributors that make school attendance difficult for children:

- Teen motherhood,
- Single motherhood,
- Low maternal education,
- Welfare,
- Unemployment,
- Food insecurity,
- Poor maternal health,
- Having multiple siblings,
- Other serious family concerns (e.g., mental illness, homelessness, child or domestic abuse, incarceration of a parent).

Schools develop various attendance policies in hopes of reducing absenteeism. Schools also hire truant officers to decrease tardiness and absenteeism. Yet, school policies and truant officers often have little impact on improving student absenteeism and reducing tardiness. Reardon (2008) conducted a study to determine the impact of school attendance policies on improving absenteeism. The study found that school attendance policies rarely result in improved attendance.

This is not to advocate against having attendance policies but only to emphasize the need to look beyond these measures for additional strategies. If absenteeism is to be decreased, then improvement efforts need to focus on changing the school environment. One key to this type of change is parental and community involvement.

Absenteeism cannot be ignored. Chronic absenteeism not only creates problems at the school level, it is also a major factor leading to delinquency (Puzzanchera 1999). Greater attention is needed to designing potent interventions to ensure students are welcomed at school and connected with ongoing social supports. Although special attention is needed for students identified as at risk, all students have the potential to be at risk if programs are not in place to provide ongoing support.

Absenteeism is especially prevalent during times when students move from elementary to middle school and middle school to high school. Other transition points can also lead to missing school:

* Entry into school at kindergarten
* Moving to a new home and entry into a new school
* Beginning a new year in a new class
* Beginning the first year in a new school
* Reentry from suspensions, expulsions, juvenile detention
* Transferring from a self-contained special education class to general education classes
* Returning to school after prolonged illness
* Returning to school after the death or illness of a relative or a caregiver

During transition times, parental involvement is important as a support for students. If home support is not available, then efforts to support students through alternative resources are necessary. The community can play an important role. Structured programs that offer student support are available in most communities. Improvement plans need to address available local resources for student transitioning as well as school-based sources of assistance.

TEN STRATEGIES FOR IMPROVING ATTENDANCE

When absenteeism prevents students from learning, School Improvement Plans need to include strategies to improve attendance. The ten strategies described in this section can make a difference.

1. Establishing Personal Contact with Parents
2. Providing Counseling Services
3. Implementing Academic Assistance
4. Building Social Supports
5. Undertaking Creative Renewal
6. Working with Community Youth Development Programs
7. Recognizing Special Needs
8. Designing Transition Programs
9. Creating Alternatives
10. Celebrating Good Attendance

Strategy One: Establishing Personal Contact with Parents

School environments should be designed so they contribute to student attendance. Communication is a key element of effective environments. The goal of communication is to make positive personal contact with all students and their parents or caregivers. The California Department of Education hosts a website with school attendance improvement strategies that have a positive effect on decreasing absenteeism. These strategies include how to establish personal contact with parents.

According to the website, phone calls should be made, when possible, within the first hour of the start of the school day when students are absent. Recorded messages should be avoided. Telephone answering devices that allow parents to report excused absences also are helpful.

Contacting parents is only one form of personal contact. Telephone hotlines can be established for community reporting of students suspected of skipping school and truancy. Home visits are another way to build school-home ties. These visits allow educators to gain insight into home conditions as well as determine appropriate support and resources to assist families.

Strategy Two: Providing Counseling Services

Counseling services are typically provided to students in all public schools. To improve attendance, the counseling services may need to be expanded to assist students who are frequently absent. Counselors should focus on conversations about attendance with students who are frequently absent. Root cause issues such as lack of sleep, inadequate support structures, safety concerns, and lack of transportation could be focus areas for discussion and setting goals. When students are encouraged to talk about their absenteeism, schools can begin to develop strategies and implement plans to improve attendance. Counselors also can serve as liaisons between home and school, conducting scheduled meetings with parents and home visits, and making phone calls to let parents know when their children are not at school.

Students who miss a certain number of days might also be required to attend counseling meetings to discuss the reasons for their absences. Counselors can analyze student reasons for absenteeism and seek resources in the community to help improve attendance. Resources include Big Brother/Big Sister programs, the YMCA and YWCA, Boy and Girl Scouts, and local churches and synagogues.

Strategy Three: Implementing Academic Assistance Programs

Students who fall behind in classes often miss school due to academic frustration and discouragement. Remedial services should be provided to all students, particularly those exhibiting high rates of absenteeism. Discussions about tardiness and absenteeism should be a component of student assistance efforts. School Improvement Plans should focus on identifying appropriate remediation services for chronically absent students.

One example of a remediation service is a tutorial during or after school with a teacher or specialist. During the tutorial, the teacher works to determine the causes of disengagement and develops a plan of action for the student. It is possible, for instance, that a student does not get along with a particular teacher or struggles with a particular subject. An individualized plan of assistance including ongoing support should be created for each student. It may be necessary to alter the schedules of students who have difficulty achieving with particular teachers. Matching students with teachers is not always easy but must be considered.

Giving students a voice in designing assistance programs can lead to innovative thinking. An example of how to effectively use student feedback in designing remedial programs comes from Fort Worth's South Hills High School (Duke and Jacobson 2011). A student advisory group led the charge to alter the traditional after-school tutorial program. Students argued that after-school tutorials were not well attended because students were exhausted or had after-school commitments. They suggested offering tutoring on Monday evenings from 6:30 to 8:30 p.m. The principal agreed and provided pizza. "Monday Madness" became a success because students had a voice in determining when tutoring should be scheduled.

Strategy Four: Building Social Supports

Social supports may be needed for students who frequently miss school. Some social services are available outside of school. For example, there are community services that provide family support, transportation, and interpreters when language is a barrier. Schools provide counseling, after-school programs, tutoring, and extracurricular activities to help students.

To improve attendance, one social support to be considered is a peer mentoring program. Chronically absent students can be paired with older students who share similar interests and are of the same gender. Peer mentoring programs should operate with prescribed guidelines and provide training for the peer helpers.

Another support involves social media. Students may be assigned a Text Buddy, for example. Text Buddy is a form of technology that allows students to have immediate support. Text Buddies are especially helpful for students who are frequently absent. They have access to another student who cares and will respond to text messages regarding assignments and missed coursework. Training students to be supportive and helpful to classmates who are frequently absent promotes responsibility and compassion. Students who are frequently absent need to know that someone cares about them. Programs that provide emotional support to students who miss school can make a difference.

Strategy Five: Undertaking Creative Renewal

A school that sets a goal to improve attendance needs to focus on strategies that promote and support attendance. Creative renewal is a comprehensive approach that calls for redesigning a school to develop a totally different learning environment. Such an approach may be necessary when school-wide student disengagement is evident. In a renewal process, the "schoolscape" is changed dramatically. There can be changes to physical space, schedules, assignments, and roles. The goal of creative renewal is to alter students' perceptions of school.

Once students become disengaged, it is difficult to reengage them in the "same old environment." Dramatic environmental change signals a new opportunity for students. Planners need to consider ways teachers can develop and sustain constructive relationships with students.

An example of creative renewal comes from a Texas high school where the newly hired principal was charged with turning around the chronically low-performing school. Nancy Weisskopf, the principal, encouraged the development and implementation of "several high-profile, high-interest academic majors, including Culinary Arts, Digital Arts and Gaming, and Green Engineering" (Duke and Jacobson 2011, p. 37). She also launched a dynamic student leadership council, redefined the role of guidance counselors, and created a bold new credit recovery program.

To signal the dramatic changes, a new school mascot and new school colors were chosen. Weisskopf's plan was to assist struggling students without overcorrecting and losing capable students. Creative renewal served to establish balance in the school environment so that all students felt valued.

Strategy Six: Working with Community Youth Development Programs

Most communities support one or more nonschool-based organizations devoted to youth development and welfare. In some cases these organizations focus on one type of youth-related problem. In other cases, they provide a comprehensive set of services, often referred to as wrap-around services. One of the most comprehensive initiatives of this kind is the Harlem Children's Zone in New York City. The HCZ serves as a coordinating body for health and mental health services, welfare assistance, and parent education. School authorities work with the HCZ and its cooperating agencies to ensure that young people receive the help they need.

Positive Youth Development (PYD) is another comprehensive approach that has proven beneficial for young people who confront challenges to succeeding in school and elsewhere (Butts, Mayer, and Ruth 2005). PYD stresses the need for partnerships between schools, neighborhoods, community organizations, social programs, and employers. Three assumptions undergird PYD: 1) strengths and assets are a better focus than deficits and problems, 2) strengths and assets are usually acquired through positive relationships, and 3) development of youth assets occurs in multiple contexts.

When a school faces high rates of absenteeism, it is likely that community assistance must be enlisted in order to address the problem successfully. School planners should consider comprehensive approaches such as HCZ and PYD that bring together resources from across communities.

Strategy Seven: Recognizing Special Needs

Some students have preexisting conditions or face situations outside of school that prevent them from being in school on a regular basis. Examples include students who are injured in an accident. These students probably will be assigned tutors or home instructors, but they can become disengaged from classroom instruction. Accidents and injuries are not the only circumstances when a student may be absent from school for a long time. Students who are chronically ill experience frequent excused absences. A student with severe allergic reactions, for example, may miss school frequently during certain times of the year.

Students who are injured or ill can still feel a part of the classroom through the use of distance learning technology. Home and hospital computers can be provided to students so they can "attend" classes using Internet options such as Skype. When technology will not work, learning communities consisting of parents or caregivers, medical providers, and educators can be created.

Strategy Eight: Designing Transition Programs

Some students do not transition well from grade level to grade level. The change can be devastating to a child entering school and even greater for students shifting from elementary to middle or middle to high school. Creating special programs for transitioning students has proven to be beneficial for many young people.

One example of a transition program involves creating a student support team to monitor student progress during the first three months of transition. The identification of students likely to need one-on-one support is done prior to the transition.

Another strategy to consider involves developing student safe zones. Often overlooked as a transitional strategy, a safe zone is a place where students can go at any time they feel anxious, uncomfortable, or threatened. A safe zone provides a setting in the school where students can seek assistance without fear of being ridiculed by other students.

Some of the most effective transition programs take place during the summer before students enter a new school. These programs familiarize incoming students with their new school and provide them opportunities to meet teachers and other staff members. Some summer programs also assign older students to serve as guides and helpers for newcomers. Having a fellow student to turn to for help can make a tremendous difference for a new student.

Strategy Nine: Creating Alternatives

Sometimes a regular school setting, for whatever reason, is not appropriate for certain students. Perhaps the students require an alternative schedule because they are parents or caregivers for relatives. Perhaps they do not function well in large classes where they get into trouble easily. These students are more likely to attend school if they have access to an alternative program designed to address their specific needs.

Alternative programs come in a variety of forms. Some function as schools-within-schools; others occupy separate facilities. Some operate schedules similar to regular schools; others run abbreviated schedules or in the evening. A growing number of alternative programs provide individualized instruction using computer-based curriculums. A few of these programs allow students to complete one course at a time. An alternative program may help some students get through a crisis, thereby enabling them to return to their regular school. In other cases, students need to continue in the alternative program until they graduate.

Strategy Ten: Celebrating Good Attendance

Another strategy for improving attendance involves the public sharing of school attendance data and recognition of students who attend school regularly. Celebrations can be planned so that grade levels, classes, and individual students are recognized for meeting attendance targets. The names of students who meet school attendance goals should be displayed in a prominent location. Letters of commendation can be mailed home for students with high attendance and significantly improved attendance. This strategy also presents an opportunity for School Improvement Team members to solicit help from community partners. By canvassing local businesses, planners can enlist merchants to provide prizes as a means to encourage student attendance.

SAMPLE ATTENDANCE OBJECTIVES

When preparing to improve student attendance, planners should consider incorporating strategies that are clearly understood, consistent, and proactive in nature. In addressing the goal of "improving student attendance so that overall student attendance will meet or exceed 95 percent," a comprehensive approach that engages all stakeholders is desirable.

The planning document at the end of the chapter first addresses clearly communicating policies regarding attendance to the school community. School staff are expected to monitor attendance carefully and determine why some students are chronically absent. As attendance goals are met or exceeded, individual, class, and school-wide recognition affirms the collective work of stakeholders. Some forms of recognition are underwritten by local businesses.

CHAPTER REVIEW

To facilitate academic progress, School Improvement Teams need to identify strategies for addressing poor attendance. In order to do so, School Improvement Teams should understand what is causing frequent absenteeism. Common reasons for frequent absenteeism include academic difficulties in the classroom setting, fear of bullying, and nonschool obligations.

Because there are various reasons for absenteeism, School Improvement Teams are advised to consider a continuum of strategies for increasing attendance. Among the strategies discussed in the chapter are special counseling services, academic assistance programs, transition initiatives, and recognition programs.

REFERENCES

Adelman, H., and Taylor, L. 2010. Center for Mental Health at UCLA. Los Angeles: School Mental Health Project in the Department of Psychology at University of California LA.

Butts, J., Mayer, S., and Ruth, G. October 2005. Focusing juvenile justice on positive youth development. Chicago: Chaplin Hall Center for Children at the University of Chicago.

California Department of Education. 2012. School attendance improvement strategies. Retrieved from http://www.cde.ca.gov/ls/ai/cw/attendstrategy.asp.

Duke, D. L., and Jacobson, M. February 2011. Tackling the toughest turnaround—Low-performing high schools. *Kappan*, 92(5), 36–37. Retrieved from kappanmagazine.org.

Puzzanchera, C. 1999. Detention in Delinquency Cases, 1990–1999. National Center for Juvenile Justice. Office of Juvenile Justice and Delinquency Prevention, July 2003.

Reardon, R. T. May 2008. *An Analysis of Florida's School Districts Attendance Policies and Their Relationship to High School Attendance Rates.* Boca Raton: Florida Atlantic University.

Roby, D. 2004. Research on school attendance and student achievement: A study of Ohio schools. *Educational Research Quarterly*, 28(1), 3–14.

Strickland, V. P. 1998. *Attendance and Grade Point Average: A Study.* Chicago: ERIC.

SCHOOL IMPROVEMENT PLAN OBJECTIVE: Improve student attendance so that overall student attendance will meet or exceed 95 percent. Students demonstrating past poor attendance as defined by local and/or state policy will increase attendance rate to at least 93 percent.

Strategies	Person(s) Responsible	Materials Needed and Costs	Time Line				In-Process Measures
What we will do to achieve the objective	Person(s) who will monitor the strategy	What materials will be used to implement the strategy? What are the costs?	Check the projected quarter for implementing the strategy this school year.				How we will monitor progress
			1st Qtr.	2nd Qtr.	3rd Qtr.	4th Qtr.	

K–12: The principal will identify student attendance as a school issue and clearly define policy and expectations. Office staff will take a lead role in personally contacting parents/guardians of tardy and absent students. These personal contacts will be logged as documentation.

Strategies	Person(s) Responsible	Materials Needed and Costs	1st Qtr.	2nd Qtr.	3rd Qtr.	4th Qtr.	In-Process Measures
The school principal, in start-of-school Open House nights, initial meetings, and in other communication efforts, will clearly define policy and expectations regarding attendance. Ensure alignment of student records and request at least three phone numbers when compiling registration documentation.	Office administrative staff, principal, central office liaison	Newsletters and mailings that reference policy and expectations in a consistent manner. Updated registration and record-keeping software that allows efficient and effective retrieval of student contact information.	✓	✓	✓	✓	Clearly defined district and/or state policy made relevant to all stakeholders including students, parents/guardians, and staff. Logged documentation of student tardies/ absences will be reviewed weekly by administrative team and quarterly by School Improvement Plan team.

After five tardies and/or unexcused absences have been documented, the principal will sign and send letter requesting meeting with the student, parent/ guardian, counselor, and administrator. At this meeting, district attendance policy will be reviewed and attendance improvement plan will be developed and signed by all parties. After ten tardies and/or unexcused absences, principal will document with district liaison (if applicable) and with parent via signed letter. As applicable to district policy, the principal will initiate proceedings with local magistrate.

Clearly defined district and/ or state policy made relevant to all stakeholders including students, parents/ guardians, and staff.

Absences will be noted in student file.

(continued)

SCHOOL IMPROVEMENT PLAN OBJECTIVE: (Continued)

K-12: Counseling services will be provided in targeted manner to students falling below target attendance rate. Once the "five absences/ tardies" trigger is activated as noted previously, the counselor will participate in initial attendance improvement plan meeting with all parties and follow up with meetings with the student as applicable. The counselor will work to ascertain if special needs are a potential issue with the relevant classroom teacher and Response to Intervention (RtI) team.

Strategies	Person(s) Responsible	Materials Needed and Costs	Time Line				In-Process Measures
Counselor will participate in initial attendance improvement plan meeting.	School counselor, classroom teachers, RtI team	Allocated time in school counselor's schedule and calendar to facilitate the check-in meetings and related calls.	✓	✓	✓	✓	Documentation of meetings and calls as well as noted action steps taken. Counselor will provide quarterly updates to School Improvement Plan team. RtI chair will cross-reference documentation of case referrals with attendance data.
Counselor will then "check in" weekly with the student and review attendance records to ensure student is aware of the issue.		RtI overview for staff to ensure special needs are considered as a potential attendance and academic issue.					
Counselor will work with administrative staff to see if resources, such as transportation, are effectively being used.							
Counselor and classroom teacher(s) will review attendance improvement plan monthly to ascertain if special needs could potentially be an issue. RtI (or Child Study/ equivalent) chair will be present.							

Counselor will conduct a "check in" call with parents monthly to check on students who are on an attendance improvement plan.

K-12: Celebrating good attendance will be integrated into daily, quarterly, and annual events and notifications. This approach will enable a positive perspective on attendance to shape stakeholder perceptions of this improvement goal.

Homeroom classes with satisfactory (95 percent) attendance will be recognized via intercom on a biweekly basis.	Teachers, grade/department chairs, principal	Time allocated to biweekly announcements, Web page updates, and newsletter segments	✓	✓	✓	✓	Celebrations will be documented and reviewed quarterly by the School Improvement Plan team.
School leaders and School Improvement Plan team members will canvass local businesses to find sponsors for attendance recognition efforts. The School Improvement Plan team will sponsor an annual volunteer appreciation brunch to recognize volunteers, including local sponsors, who have impacted student learning in their work.	Local business partnerships School Improvement Plan team, principal	Volunteer coordination to affirm and engage external development efforts. Costs might include a recognition brunch, a "partnership wall of fame."					Donations from local partnerships will be documented and logged for future recognition efforts.

THE IMPORTANCE OF DIFFERENTIATED PLANNING

Schools vary in many ways. They encompass different configurations of grades. Most schools draw from the general population, but some are designed for particular kinds of students. Schools vary by size and purpose as well. In this section we consider how planning for school improvement is likely to be different depending on a school's track record. The section opens by looking at the planning required to turn around a chronically low-performing school. The next chapter investigates planning to sustain a successful school turnaround. The closing chapter looks at what educators can do to make a good school even better.

Differentiated planning does not mean that planners deviate from the seven basic planning steps identified in section I. The key to differentiated planning concerns the particular focus of the planning process. Different school track records present different challenges for planners. As challenges vary, so too will School Improvement Plan goals, objectives, and strategies.

CHAPTER 11

Planning School Turnarounds

PREVIEW

Since the passage of the No Child Left Behind Act in 2002, attention has focused squarely on how to turn around the lowest-performing schools. This chapter reviews some of the steps that have been taken by planners to achieve rapid and dramatic increases in student achievement. These steps involve a combination of "quick wins" and tough trade-offs.

COPING WITH A CONFIDENCE CRISIS

As Shirley Sizemore waited to see the superintendent, she debated whether to tender her resignation. She knew why Dr. McDade wanted to see her. Student achievement at Randolph Middle School had been declining for the past five years, and the community was putting pressure on McDade and the School Board to do something. No one wanted to reverse Randolph's downward spiral more than Sizemore, but she questioned the ability of her faculty to make significant improvements in student achievement.

Sizemore anticipated that Dr. McDade would ask for her opinion about why student achievement was declining at Randolph. What could she say? He realized as well as she did that Randolph's demographics had been changing since a second middle school had opened. Over the past five years Randolph's student body had become increasingly diverse. This year, for the first time in school history, more than half of Randolph's students qualified for free and reduced-price lunch. The number of English language learners also was steadily climbing.

Dr. McDade, of course, would offer one of his favorite quotes, "Demography is not destiny." She would have to explain why her faculty had been unable to rise to the challenge of demographic change. Sizemore knew that Dr. McDade hated excuses. If she was prepared to resign, she could take full responsibility for Randolph's decline, but she knew that replacing her would not automatically lead to improvement, not as long as the faculty continued to lack the confidence that they could make a difference for Randolph's newcomers.

As long as they were teaching students from well-to-do families, Randolph's veteran teachers had produced impressive results on state tests. As the student population began to change and test scores dropped, teachers expressed increasing uncertainty about how to reach students and motivate them to learn.

Sizemore wondered if she had failed to provide enough direction to her faculty as the numbers of nontraditional students rose. But how does a principal direct teachers who doubt they can teach certain students? Nothing in her preparation to be a principal had equipped Sizemore to address issues of agency and self-confidence. Perhaps she not only should tender her resignation but also suggest to Dr. McDade that he replace a significant number of Randolph's teachers.

———————

There is no doubt that Randolph Middle School needed to be turned around, and given its five-year slide, the turnaround had to be done quickly. The community was growing increasingly impatient. If Shirley Sizemore's assessment was correct that the Randolph faculty lacked confidence in their ability to address the needs of nontraditional students, a School Improvement Plan would require goals, objectives, and strategies quite different from those chosen by principals of more successful schools.

Although no one reason can explain why some schools are characterized by sustained low performance, lack of confidence on the part of teachers is frequently a contributing factor. Over time declining student achievement leads to demoralization and making excuses. Teachers begin to blame poor student performance on factors beyond their control—student apathy, lack of parental support, insufficient resources, inadequate leadership. The more teachers believe that the causes of low performance reside elsewhere, the more threatened they are by any teacher who manages to produce good results.

This chapter examines two schools—one rural elementary school and one urban high school—and the conditions that contributed to their prolonged decline. The steps taken by their principals to boost confidence and raise student achievement then are discussed in light of the process for planning school improvement.

A BOOST FOR BERKELEY[1]

Catherine Thomas only had a few weeks to size up the situation at Berkeley Elementary before the new school year began, and what the newly appointed "turnaround specialist" found was truly disturbing. Only one-third of the students in third grade had passed the previous year's state test in reading. Fewer than half of the fifth graders passed the state math test. These figures certainly were cause for concern, but what really upset Thomas was the depressed condition in which her predecessor had left the school.

At first glance Berkeley Elementary hardly fit the profile of a troubled school. Of the school's 352 students, only one-third were classified as economically disadvantaged. A little less than 90 percent of the students were white; the remaining students were African American. Located in central Virginia's farm country, Berkeley seemed far removed from the problems associated with urban schools. A closer look, however, belied Berkeley's bucolic surroundings.

As Thomas began to meet members of her faculty and discuss their perceptions of the school, she realized the teachers were unaware of how poorly their students were performing on the Virginia Standards of Learning (SOL) tests. The reason soon became clear—the previous principal had not shared test data with the teachers, and the teachers had not sought out the data on their own. The teachers were surprised when Thomas informed them that, because of Berkeley's low passing rates over the past three years, parents had gained the option to transfer their children to other elementary schools.

Further inspection provided clues regarding the likely causes of Berkeley's academic problems. No improvement targets had been set by Thomas's predecessor. If there was a School Improvement Plan for Berkeley, teachers were unaware of it. No systematic process for monitoring student progress was in place. Teachers had not taken advantage of available benchmark tests in order to track student achievement on the Standards of Learning.

Berkeley lacked any semblance of organizational infrastructure. No leadership team was in place nor were there grade-level teams or arrangements for teachers to meet periodically to identify struggling students. No coordinated plan existed to provide supplementary assistance to students other than those who were eligible for special education services. Thomas's predecessor had made no effort to develop a school schedule with designated time for instructional interventions and teacher planning.

When Thomas looked at the Berkeley faculty, she was dismayed to find a large proportion of first- and second-year teachers as well as some teachers without the proper credentials. To make matters worse, no effort had been made in the previous three years to provide teachers with professional development based on the needs of Berkeley students. Instructional materials were sadly out-of-date, and teachers had little access to technology.

As if these findings were not alarming enough, Thomas also discovered that the faculty was polarized. The previous principal had picked her "favorites" and given them the best assignments. The rest of the faculty grew resentful and distrustful. Thomas wondered how she would ever get all the teachers pulling in the same direction.

With little time to reflect, Thomas quickly reviewed the data she had gathered and concluded that she could not turn Berkeley around by herself. A plan was needed, but it would require buy-in by key faculty members. Thomas thought about her interactions with each faculty member and, based on her impressions, chose individuals she regarded as potential leaders with a commitment to school improvement. These teachers were assigned to be grade-level coordinators. They also formed the nucleus of her Leadership Team. Soon after forming the team, Thomas convened the group to review student achievement data and develop a ninety-day improvement plan.

Discovering that the teachers on the Leadership Team had no prior experience analyzing data, Thomas backtracked and arranged for training in data-driven decision-making. Once teachers felt more comfortable working with data, she had the team identify priorities and convert the priorities into achievement targets for the year. Then team members took a close look at all the programs offered at Berkeley. Programs that were judged to be ineffective were eliminated.

Knowing that the faculty was in desperate need of a morale boost, Thomas and her Leadership Team next considered what steps could be taken quickly to generate hope that improvements could be made. They decided to create a master schedule for the instructional day in order to guide the realignment of staff and resources. An important objective of the new schedule was to match Title I, special education, and reading resource teachers with targeted students. Instead of pulling students out of class to receive assistance, the new schedule enabled needy students to receive help in class. The new master schedule served as a symbol of sound organizational practice for the Berkeley faculty.

Members of the Leadership Team trained teachers on how to interpret student achievement data and identify areas in need of work. Whenever discussions drifted, team members refocused by asking, "Where do we need to be to achieve full state accreditation?" Stress was placed on the fact that every staff member had a vital role to play in removing Berkeley from improvement status.

Having gained some momentum from the creation of the Leadership Team, the new master schedule, and the initiation of school improvement planning, Thomas and the faculty were almost ready to focus on the strategies that would produce increases in student achievement by the end of the school year. First, however, Thomas needed to take care of some personnel issues.

A teacher who threatened another teacher was removed in September. An unreliable cafeteria worker was fired. A special education teacher without appropriate training was transferred, and the Title I math teacher left. An incompetent teacher was documented and dismissed. These kinds of actions are never easy, but Thomas knew that

Berkeley needed "the right people in the right roles" if speedy progress was to be made.

The primary goals for Berkeley's turnaround involved fostering a learning community, implementing benchmark testing in reading and math, and raising the percentage of students who passed the state tests in reading and math. The last two goals depended on achieving the first. Thomas expected her newly appointed grade-level coordinators to assume responsibility for promoting a learning community. Each coordinator convened a weekly meeting of the teachers in her grade level to discuss how well students were meeting learning targets, if any adjustments to the curriculum needed to be made, how students were grouped for reading and math, and whether certain students should be referred to the newly formed Student Intervention Team. This group of specialists was charged with providing targeted assistance for struggling students.

The implementation of benchmark tests provided teachers with data on how students were progressing. Thomas saw to it that each grade-level team had a pacing guide to show them where they needed to be in order to ensure that critical content was covered by the time state tests were administered in the spring.

When the first round of benchmark tests was given, teachers were disappointed with the results. Thomas rallied the faculty, telling them this information was exactly what they needed in order to help struggling students in a timely fashion. Student groups in reading and math were adjusted based on how the students performed on the benchmark tests, and appropriate assistance was provided to those who required re-teaching. Students actually began to set their own improvement targets for the second round of benchmark tests, and parents started to take an active interest in how their children were progressing.

By the time the third round of benchmark tests was given in March, teachers, students, and parents fully understood the assessment routine and why it was important. At each grade level, teachers knew exactly how many students required additional assistance in order to meet targets in reading and math. Thomas assigned the reading resource teacher to teach reading to a group of low-achieving fifth graders. Math instruction was reorganized so that a team of teachers that included a math specialist, a special education teacher, and the Title I math teacher could visit classrooms during math time to provide individualized help for students who were having difficulty. Careful analysis of test data indicated that Berkeley students had trouble with numbers and number sense; computation and estimation; and patterns and functions. This information enabled the Math Team to provide focused assistance when they visited each class.

To lay the groundwork for sustained success in reading, Thomas initiated a professional development program that focused on Berkeley's reading program and comprehension skills, the area of literacy development where Berkeley students did not score well. To avoid the mixed messages and confusion that can occur when too many "experts" are involved, Thomas contracted with one reading consultant to provide ongoing in-service training to all teachers.

When the school year ended, Thomas and the teachers at Berkeley acknowledged the strides that had been made and the energy and effort they had committed to the turnaround effort. Their reward came late in the summer when they were notified that Berkeley Elementary School had achieved state accreditation and met federal benchmarks under the No Child Left Behind Act.

TACKLING A TOUGH TURNAROUND[2]

Turning around a low-performing rural elementary school such as Berkeley is clearly a challenge, but accomplishing such a feat in a large urban high school can be even more daunting. High schools are more complex organizations involving larger numbers of students and teachers and a host of complicated academic and social issues. Nancy Weisskopf's successful efforts to turn around South Hills High School in Fort Worth, Texas, provide a good example of what can be accomplished with careful and creative planning.

When Weisskopf arrived at South Hills, she found the high school in decline. South Hills had opened in 1999 and initially developed a solid reputation, but shifting demographics and the failure of South Hills educators to respond effectively resulted in a sustained downward spiral. By 2008, more than 70 percent of South Hills students qualified for free or reduced-price meals, and discipline problems occupied an increasing amount of staff time. Of the school's 1,316 students, 83 percent were Hispanic, 11 percent were African American, and 6 percent were white. Many of the Hispanic students were English language learners. A shooting on school grounds convinced many parents of middle schoolers that South Hills was a dangerous place, and they opted to enroll their children at other Fort Worth high schools.

South Hills' sinking reputation was not helped by low academic achievement. The high school's state report card indicated that student achievement was below standard on twelve of twenty-one performance indicators, including math and science for most student subgroups.

Weisskopf's early impressions of South Hills' circumstances pinned part of the blame for the school's problems on a highly negative school culture. Teachers had filed grievances against each other as well as administrators. Weisskopf's predecessor was blamed for polarizing the faculty by favoring certain staff members. Adult "issues" had taken precedence over the needs of students.

Assigning Weisskopf to the principalship of South Hills was one component of a school district initiative aimed at turning around Fort Worth's most troubled schools. This initiative required new principals to replace 60 percent of the teachers at their schools. All teachers at South Hills had to reapply for their jobs and go through an interview process with Weisskopf. The interviews afforded Weisskopf an opportunity to look for individuals who believed they could make a difference for South Hills students and who were committed to collaboration and hard work.

Hiring capable and committed educators, Weisskopf knew, was just the first step toward turnaround. The teachers—some South Hills veterans and some newcomers—would have to be melded into an effectively functioning team. Toward this end, Weisskopf planned a three-day paid retreat at a local conference center. Instead of dwelling on the typical back-to-school details such as reviewing school policies and the Teachers Manual, she insisted that people focus on the big picture and South Hills' new mantra—"Student Success, No Excuses."

Forty-five minutes before the retreat began, Weisskopf asked the sixty teachers she had rehired from the South Hills faculty to join her and circle a fire pit at the conference center. She told them they were embarking on a new journey and needed to let go of the past. Each teacher was asked to take a piece of paper and write down what she was leaving behind. Together, they then dropped the pieces of paper into the fire pit. Following this highly symbolic act, the group walked together to the room where the retreat would be held. Weisskopf announced, "We're going through these doors together. If there's anything left to say, say it to me now because we're moving on."

The retreat was the first step to forging a new culture at South Hills. The second step involved a school-wide initiative to "brand" the high school. With input from students and staff, the decision was made to adopt the scorpion as the symbol of the reborn South Hills. "Scorpion Pride" placards appeared throughout the campus, and Nancy Weisskopf was dubbed the Scorpion Queen.

Weisskopf's plans for turning around South Hills depended a great deal on getting students to buy into the process. Six times during her first year as principal, she met with groups of students who were struggling to master various instructional objectives and asked them why they were having trouble. These sessions were videotaped and shared with staff members.

Student input became an important part of the planning process at South Hills. Weisskopf asked students, for example, if they were willing to try single-sex classes in certain subjects, but when they registered their opposition, she dropped the idea. She also learned from students that they resented having classmates who didn't want to learn. Because of this input, Weisskopf told teachers that the traditional practice of allowing unmotivated students to sit in class and do nothing had to stop. Teachers needed to insist that students keep up with their class work. Weisskopf also refused to permit repeaters to take classes with first timers. Instead, repeaters were required to attend a Plato Lab and complete their courses online. Negative role models were not part of South Hills' improvement plans.

Students told Weisskopf that they did not like being tutored right after school. She had wondered why so few students took advantage of teacher assistance. By listening to students, she realized they had a lot going on after school—from picking up their siblings at elementary school to playing sports to after-school jobs. Based on this feedback, Weisskopf and the faculty decided to provide tutoring once a week from 6 to 8 p.m. on Monday. Dubbed "Monday Madness," students took advantage of this new arrangement, especially when Weisskopf agreed to provide pizza and bus transportation.

To further demonstrate the important role of students in the South Hills' turnaround, Weisskopf launched the Scorpion Leadership Council. A dynamic Student Council adviser from California was hired and charged with locating student leaders capable of setting a positive tone for the high school. One of the Council's first initiatives involved developing "The Scorpion Way: Courtesy, Dignity, Respect."

"The Scorpion Way" became part of a concerted effort to reduce discipline problems at South Hills. A related move involved changing the system for student supervision. Instead of assigning assistant principals to different grade levels, Weisskopf planned a team approach to student supervision. She took one of the largest classrooms at South Hills and subdivided it into four offices for the assistant principals and a central waiting area, affectionately known as the "Shark Tank." This arrangement strengthened information sharing among the assistant principals and reduced the likelihood that students would play one administrator against another. The assistant principals worked out a rotation system: three days working on discipline, one day in classrooms, and one day in the main office. Teachers praised the new system because disciplinary referrals were handled efficiently and uniformly.

Much of school turnaround planning at South Hills centered on developing opportunities for teachers to collaborate on instructional improvement and interventions to assist struggling students. Teachers in every department were expected to conduct regular conversations about individual students and their progress. To facilitate these conversations, Weisskopf redesigned the school schedule in order to create common planning periods for teachers in each department.

To ensure that teachers were continuously aware of how students were doing in key content areas, common assessments were developed and administered every six weeks in academic subjects. A "Data Wall" on which the progress of every student could be tracked was created. At the end of the fall semester, Weisskopf met with each department to review the status of every single student. Teachers were asked to predict how each student was likely to finish the school year. For every student predicted to fail a course, an assistance plan had to be prepared. Sometimes assistance involved tutoring during the school day or at

"Monday Madness." Assistant principals were assigned responsibility for overseeing tutoring sessions. Students who missed a tutorial during the school day were "escorted" by an administrator to the next available session.

Because Weisskopf understood how crucial it was for ninth graders to get off to a good start in high school, she planned special measures for the incoming freshman. First of all, the ninth grade was organized as a separate "house" with its own group of teachers and campus building. Teachers of core subjects worked in middle school–style teams with the same set of students, thereby ensuring common planning and careful monitoring of progress.

Weisskopf did not believe ninth graders should be allowed to fail, so when a ninth grader received a failing grade at the end of a grading period, the student was required to attend school for an extra hour a day until a passing grade was earned. A late bus provided transportation home. If students ended the school year with a failing grade, they had to continue with their coursework into the summer until they achieved a passing mark. Instead of repeating the entire course, as they would have to do in a traditional summer school program, students concentrated only on the parts of the course they had failed.

Yet another step to ensure that freshman succeeded at South Hills was Freshman Camp. Staffed primarily by upperclassmen, the three-day summer program for rising ninth graders was designed to instill a sense of "Scorpion Pride" in newcomers and teach them the "basics" of high school survival. By the end of camp, every incoming ninth grader knew several older students to whom they could turn for support and advice.

When upperclassmen at South Hills experienced academic problems, they could expect to encounter Gerry Magin. A former coach Weisskopf had known for years, Magin was recruited specifically to work with students who were falling behind in their coursework. Gifted with the ability to relate to even the toughest students in a caring, avuncular way, Magin's full-time job involved keeping track of students who were failing courses, not turning in assignments, and missing too much school. He made home visits when necessary and insisted that his charges check in with him every week or two. Students understood that "Gerry," as he was universally known, refused to give up on them, no matter how far behind they fell.

All the careful planning and hard work Weisskopf and her colleagues had invested in turning around South Hills paid off. By the end of the year, disciplinary incidents had dropped from 4,720 the previous year to 1,752. The dropout rate shrank from 28.3 percent to 18.0 percent. Instead of missing twelve of twenty-one state standards, South Hills was deficient in only two—mathematics and science pass rates for African American students. Best of all, the community's pride in the high school had been restored.

KEYS TO EFFECTIVE TURNAROUND PLANNING

The planning required to turn around a chronically low-performing school differs in important ways from other kinds of school improvement planning. Chronically low-performing schools typically are places where confidence has eroded and commitment has waned. Schools such as Berkeley Elementary and South Hills High also face a withering array of challenges. To try to tackle all of these challenges simultaneously almost certainly will result in failure.

Building the confidence necessary to turn around a low-performing school therefore depends on targeting some short-term objectives that can be achieved quickly. Success, as they say, breeds success. Achieving some "quick wins" builds positive momentum, teacher efficacy, and faith in school leadership.

Catherine Thomas chose to develop a leadership team that could help her in grade-level planning and professional development. To facilitate grade-level planning and the analysis of data on student achievement, she created a new master schedule with time set aside for teachers to collaborate. Nancy Weisskopf undertook a similar course of action, redesigning the South Hills schedule to enable teachers in each department to plan together during the school day. She also reorganized her administrative team so they could deal more effectively with discipline problems.

Both Thomas and Weisskopf recognized the importance of team building. School turnaround cannot be accomplished by principals alone. Each principal invested time at the outset in identifying teacher leaders who were committed to school improvement and willing to take on additional responsibilities, including training their colleagues, data analysis, and troubleshooting. The effectiveness of a team, of course, depends on the abilities and dispositions of its members. Thomas and Weisskopf spent a lot of time making certain they had the right personnel on board. For Thomas, this meant documenting and removing staff members who were resistant to change or who lacked the requisite competence to handle school improvement. Weisskopf, on the other hand, was able to select her faculty before initiating the turnaround process.

All school improvement planning requires some degree of focus. There always seem to be more targets for improvement than time and resources to tackle them. This is especially true in chronically low-performing schools. Trying to address every problem at once is a sure recipe for failure. Planners must be prepared to make trade-offs in order to concentrate on a manageable number of goals and objectives.

Many schools are judged to be low performing because students are deficient in literacy and mathematics, so goals and objectives related to raising achievement in language arts and mathematics almost always are part of the school turnaround planning process. First steps often involve implementing some form of benchmark or formative testing so that teachers are able to monitor student progress. By collecting and analyzing student achievement data on an ongoing basis, teachers can pinpoint instructional objectives with which individual students are struggling. These students then can be targeted for immediate assistance.

Both Thomas and Weisskopf devoted considerable time and energy to promoting data-driven decision-making. They wanted teachers to become accustomed to checking student progress regularly and providing assistance on an "as needed" basis. Weisskopf, in particular, worked on implementing a range of interventions to accommodate the varied academic needs of South Hills students.

As a result of careful planning, Thomas and Weisskopf were able to reverse the downward spiral into which their schools were descending. Student achievement at Berkeley and South Hills improved during the first year of the turnaround process. Both principals understood, however, that the potential for slippage is always present. They would need to maintain their first-year gains while proceeding in the second year to tackle additional goals and objectives.

In the next chapter, we investigate some of the planning challenges that confront educators faced with the need to sustain initial success.

KEYS TO SCHOOL TURNAROUND PLANNING

- Achieve a few "quick wins" to build confidence.
- Address the need for committed personnel.
- Create opportunities for team building.
- Initiate regular assessments of student progress and arrangements for teachers to review assessment data.
- Focus on a limited number of goals and objectives (typically involving improvements in literacy, math, and discipline).

NOTES

1. This case is based on the following account: Catherine Thomas and Lesley Lanphear, "I see the light at the end of the tunnel," in Daniel L. Duke, Pamela D. Tucker et al., *Lift-off: Launching the School Turnaround Process in 10 Virginia Schools.* Charlottesville, VA: Partnership for Leaders in Education, University of Virginia, 2005, 43–55.

2. This case is based on the following account: Daniel L. Duke and Martha Jacobson, 2011, "Tackling the toughest turnaround—Low-performing high schools." *Phi Delta Kappan*, 92(5), 34–38.

CHAPTER 12

Planning to Sustain Success

PREVIEW

Turning around a low-performing school is just the first act of school improvement. Act 2 requires that initial gains are solidified and expanded. Planning for sustained success entails goals, objectives, and strategies that often differ from those characterizing school turnaround planning. This chapter looks at several examples of schools that grappled with the challenges of sustainability.

CAN WE NARROW THE GAP?

Reginald Brown thought about the previous evening's festivities. There he was with the entire faculty of Langston Elementary School, walking on the red carpet ordered by the School Board and entering the grand ballroom of the Westgate Hotel. The applause did not stop until Brown and the teachers were seated on the stage. Then the governor went to the podium and announced that Langston students had made sufficient gains on their state tests to become the first "Turnaround Triumph" in the state's new initiative to eliminate low-performing schools.

Reginald Brown was a veteran principal who had worked in a variety of challenging schools before becoming the principal of Langston. He knew that raising test scores was only the first hurdle in a very long race. He had looked at the data from the state, and he understood that Langston's glory would fade quickly if African American and Hispanic students continued to lag behind white students. The Langston faculty had demonstrated they could provide enough focused instruction and assistance to get almost every student to pass their math and reading tests. But could they cut into the double-digit disparities in test scores between whites and minorities at the school?

Langston's School Improvement Team was scheduled to convene the next day for its regular meeting, and Brown wanted to address the challenges of sustaining student gains and narrowing the achievement gap, but he was uncertain about how to broach these topics. He was well aware of the potential risks associated with focusing on achievement gaps. If such an effort resulted in a drop in achievement by Langston's white students, white parents would be quick to complain. They might even seek other schools. No one would benefit if Langston became a racially isolated school.

How could Langston narrow the achievement gap without holding back high achievers? Brown decided to open the meeting by posing the question, but he wondered if there was an answer.

It is one thing to reverse a downward trend in student achievement and quite another to set in motion practices that produce continuing improvement. The latter challenge is amplified when there also is an expectation that gaps in achievement between student subgroups will be narrowed or eliminated. Reginald Brown was more confident about the ability of his faculty to raise the achievement of all students than to raise achievement for all while simultaneously narrowing the gaps.

Brown's dilemma highlights an issue facing many school improvement planners. Should they focus on raising the achievement of all students and hope that gaps narrow, or should they concentrate on narrowing achievement gaps and pray that the learning of high achievers does not suffer as a result? There, of course, is no simple answer. In this chapter we look at the efforts of two principals and their faculties to do both—raise the achievement of all and narrow achievement gaps. Although neither eliminated gaps completely, they did make significant progress. Their experiences suggest how planners can refocus their efforts following an initial turnaround.

SUSTAINING GAINS AT GREER ELEMENTARY[1]

Some schools start out low performing. Others begin as successful schools and decline over time. Greer Elementary in Charlottesville, Virginia, fit the second pattern. There are many impetuses to school decline—high turnover of principals and personnel, cuts in funding, increasing expectations for student achievement. In Greer's case, decline resulted from the failure of faculty members to meet the needs of an increasingly diverse student population.

After several years of falling scores on state standardized tests, Greer found itself in "improvement" status. That is when Matt Landahl was asked by his superintendent to become the principal of Greer and turn the school around. It took him two years and a lot of careful planning, but Landahl eventually initiated the changes needed to arrest Greer's downward slide and begin raising student achievement.

After assessing the culture of Greer and the condition in which the school had been left, Landahl decided to adopt a highly directive leadership style. Teachers needed a clear sense of direction, specific improvement targets, and opportunities to collaborate. Landahl and his assistant principal developed a School Improvement Plan that focused on reading in the upper grades. Landahl understood that many educators might advocate for a focus on reading in the primary grades, but he did not want to send weak readers to middle school. If upper-grade teachers succeeded in improving reading instruction, there would be ample time to bring the rest of the faculty up to speed.

To support improvements in the reading program, Landahl cut back on the time devoted to math each day and increased the time for reading instruction to 150 minutes a day. To increase the likelihood that this large block of time would be used effectively, Landahl initiated grouping across classrooms. Ability groups were formed at each grade level, and teachers with the greatest expertise were assigned to the lowest reading groups.

To monitor progress, Landahl and his assistant principal engaged in regular "learning walks." They looked for evidence of focused instruction and student engagement. Following each classroom visit, observations were shared with the teacher and goals for improvement were discussed.

Students who struggled with reading were provided with carefully coordinated assistance. Instead of assigning students to a yearlong after-school tutoring program, Landahl decided to initiate twice-a-week help sessions in the second semester, prior to state testing. Otherwise, Landahl expected assistance to be provided on an as-needed basis in reading groups or on a one-to-one basis with specialists. Teachers at each grade level were required to meet on a weekly basis to discuss the progress of students and pinpoint individuals who were falling behind. Teachers were encouraged to examine samples of student work in these sessions in order to refine their diagnostic skills.

When the results of state testing at Greer were reported at the end of Landahl's first year, only 59 percent of African American students and 66 percent of economically disadvantaged students had passed in reading. Both figures represented a drop from the previous year. To make matters worse, the passing rates for both groups fell in math as well.

After reflecting on what had and had not worked in his first year, Landahl embarked on planning for Year 2. Still committed to focusing on reading, he increased the daily allotment for reading instruction and remediation from 150 to 245 minutes. During his learning walks the previous year, Landahl had noted that teachers of lower-reading groups were spending a lot of time dealing with discipline issues. He realized that the struggling readers in these groups often had been receiving help together since they entered elementary school. Landahl reasoned that "familiarity bred contempt," and he planned to have teachers in Year 2 focus on providing more one-on-one help to the lowest readers.

Having learned over the summer that many high-performing, high-poverty schools stressed writing as part of a well-balanced literacy program, Landahl decided that part of the 245-minute daily reading block should involve writing instruction and activities. His School Improvement Plan called for implementing a highly structured literature-based writing program.

Because math scores had also dropped in Landahl's first year, his School Improvement Plan included a goal involving the hiring and deployment of a math coach. Landahl's school system allowed principals to do site-based staffing, so he increased class sizes from eighteen to twenty students in order to create the new coaching position. The coach was assigned to work with teachers on new strategies for math instruction.

One of the most important components of Landahl's plan to turn around Greer involved teaching planning. He initiated a new schedule that provided common planning time during the regular school day for teachers at each grade level. No longer would teachers have to stay after school in order to analyze student data and develop instructional interventions.

Landahl made one other critical decision in planning for his second year as principal of Greer, but this decision was not formalized in the School Improvement Plan. He realized that much of his first year had been devoted to dealing with "adult dramas." He was determined not to repeat this mistake in Year 2. If some staff were uncomfortable with the changes at Greer, they would need to be replaced. Landahl needed to have everyone pulling in the same direction.

Landahl's assertive leadership and the teamwork of Greer's faculty were rewarded at the close of Year 2 when the district announced the results of state testing. Greer students, including African American and economically disadvantaged students, had made impressive gains, earning the school public recognition and enabling it to make adequate yearly progress. More importantly, the gaps between student subgroups had shrunk significantly.

While Greer was being held up as a model of what school turnaround planning could accomplish, Landahl was hunkered down with his Leadership Team trying to determine what would be needed to sustain success. The School Improvement Plan for Year 3 combined the continuation of certain initiatives with several carefully chosen changes and adjustments. Landahl and his colleagues understood that the blueprint for sustaining success should not be identical to the plan for achieving initial school turnaround.

One of the most important adjustments in Year 3 involved Landahl's approach to school leadership. By the beginning of school in Year 3, more than half of the faculty at Greer had been hired by Landahl. Feeling confident that a critical mass of teachers who supported his vision were in place, Landahl decided the time was right to distribute leadership more broadly. As he expressed it, "Success at Greer cannot be all about me."

Considerable responsibility for continuing improvement efforts at Greer was shifted to a series of teacher-led committees. Committees were established to address reading, writing, math and technology, scheduling, communication, school culture, and community relations. Many decisions that previously had been made by Landahl and his assistant principal were turned over to the committees. Among the accomplishments of the committees was the creation of a new daily schedule that facilitated assistance for struggling students and the delivery of teacher-led professional development on topics tied to school goals.

Year 3 school improvement goals called for continued gains in reading, new targets for mathematics, introduction of "assessment for learning" strategies, and staff collaboration around issues of school discipline and safety. Related to all of these goals was Landahl's interest in forging a new culture at Greer. He understood that school culture cannot be changed overnight, but he believed that the timing was right to press for higher expectations and greater academic rigor in all subjects. Putting to rest the prevailing belief that "our kids can just do the basics" became Landahl's personal mission.

During Year 3, Greer teachers continued to spend two hours and forty-five minutes on literacy, but an adjustment was made to enable some of this time to include reading in the content areas. This move was prompted in part by a drop in science and social studies achievement the previous year. Sustaining success, Landahl acknowledged, involved addressing some of the trade-offs that initially had been made to achieve school turnaround. Those trade-offs had included reduced time for instruction in science and social studies.

Another adjustment in the literacy block involved how students were grouped for instruction. Based on the success of ability grouping within grade levels, Landahl initiated ability grouping across grade levels. In order to implement this new format, all third-, fourth-, and fifth-grade teachers were scheduled to teach reading at the same time. A similar arrangement was made for first and second grades.

For students who struggled with reading, Greer teachers previously had relied on pullout assistance provided by Title I teachers and reading specialists. Landahl believed this arrangement was not ideal because students who left class to receive help missed material being covered by their classmates. He pressed for more "push-in" interventions delivered in class by reading specialists and other resource teachers. Additional help was available in after-school tutorials offered twice a week by Greer teachers.

To ensure that teachers tracked student progress, Landahl modified the format for weekly grade-level planning meetings. In Year 3, two meetings a month focused exclusively on analyzing data on student achievement. The remaining weekly meetings addressed curriculum issues, professional development, and general grade-level planning.

The adjustments made in Year 3 to sustain forward momentum at Greer produced gains in student achievement in science and social studies. With the exception of third grade, students also continued to improve in reading and mathematics. Slippage in third-grade pass rates, however, was a reminder to Landahl and his faculty that the road to school improvement is rarely as direct as educators would hope. Planning for Year 4 would need to determine the reasons for the third graders' disappointing performance.

STUART HIGH SCHOOL MAINTAINS EARLY GAINS[2]

When Mel Riddile became principal of J.E.B. Stuart High School in Fairfax County, Virginia, the school was a veritable United Nations. The student body of 1,500 consisted of Hispanics (40 percent), Asians (21 percent), Middle Easterners (14 percent), Caucasians (12 percent), African Americans (10 percent), and "others" (3 percent). Half of the students qualified for free or reduced-price lunch.

Riddile was expected to turn around Stuart. The average score on the Scholastic Aptitude Test for Stuart students was 951, the lowest in Fairfax County. Students performed poorly on state tests in eleven different subjects. Student attendance had fallen below 90 percent, and acts of violence, routine discipline problems, and gang activity had escalated to a point where parents worried for the safety of their children.

After three years of Riddile's leadership, Stuart's decline was arrested and achievement and attendance began to improve. Classrooms and corridors were more orderly, and school pride reemerged.

The turnaround at Stuart can be attributed to a variety of factors, many of which mirror the stories described in the preceding chapter. Riddile developed a plan that focused squarely on improving literacy and reducing misconduct.

All teachers, not just English teachers, were expected to help students improve their reading and writing skills. To determine how much help students needed, diagnostic reading tests were given. The lowest readers were assigned to teachers for one-on-one instruction. A reading coach was hired to provide teachers in various content areas with professional development training on strategies for improving literacy.

In order to ensure that instructional time was not lost dealing with behavior problems, Riddile made certain that all students understood school rules and the consequences for breaking them. Teachers received training in classroom management. A major campaign was launched to improve attendance. Parents were contacted when students were absent and asked to help ensure that their children attended school regularly.

These early initiatives produced promising results, but Riddile realized that additional improvements would be required if Stuart were to match the success of other Fairfax County high schools. Sustaining Stuart's turnaround depended on a new School Improvement Plan, one that addressed organizational structure, the school calendar, and academic rigor. Getting passing scores on state tests, Riddile understood, was not the ultimate goal, but simply the first step in a process to equip Stuart students with the knowledge, skills, and confidence to compete in the twenty-first century.

The principal responsible for achieving a quick and dramatic turnaround in student achievement is not necessarily the person best suited to sustain improvements. A "turnaround" principal may deplete his social capital by making tough decisions concerning school personnel and the allocation of resources. Under such circumstances, an "Act 2" leader often is needed to maintain momentum. As it turned out, Mel Riddile, like Matt Landahl, was up to the challenge of moving his school beyond the initial turnaround phase of improvement.

When Riddile assessed the organizational structure of Stuart High School, he determined it was not a good fit for the school's highly diverse population. Given the large number of English language learners in the Stuart neighborhood, the school needed a flexible structure rather than a one-size-fits-all arrangement.

Riddile developed a plan based on three semi-independent units. To meet the needs of roughly four hundred English language learners, he initiated a self-contained program that operated like an elementary school. Students spent most of each day with the same one or two teachers working on basic reading and language skills. Instructional materials included the kinds of basal readers and wall displays found in elementary classrooms.

As students began to read and converse in English, they transitioned to a second unit in which they worked on middle school content. The flexible schedule in this unit allowed students to work at their own pace, covering one subject at a time until they were ready to tackle regular high school courses. Students did not have to wait until fall semester to make the move to high school. When their teachers felt they were ready, students started working on the credits they needed to earn a diploma.

The third unit constituted the high school. Believing that all students, even students who recently learned English, should have access to a rigorous curriculum, Stuart offered both Advanced Placement courses and the International Baccalaureate program. Enrollment was open to any student, and a concerted effort was made to encourage every student to take at least one challenging course. Riddile's efforts to expand the number of challenging offerings at Stuart reflected both his idealism and his pragmatism. He believed that all students should be exposed to rigorous learning. But he also understood that focusing on remediation to the exclusion of advanced academic work risked the disaffection of Stuart's high achievers. The school would suffer if these students withdrew.

Creating a new structure for Stuart was a key component of Riddile's plan for sustaining achievement gains, but a new school calendar was needed to ensure that the structure functioned effectively. The existing 180-day school year did not provide enough time for students to make up English language deficiencies and still acquire the credits required to earn a diploma. Riddile believed the only answer was to expand the school year to 242 days, but in order to do so he had to secure the support of key stakeholders. After gaining the approval of his superintendent, Riddile was told he had to get the support of at least 70 percent of the Stuart faculty, student body, and parents. Two years were needed to gain this support. Riddile then went to the School Board, which voted in favor of the lengthened school year. The final step in the process entailed securing approval from the Virginia Board of Education.

Stuart's new school year included an eight-week summer trimester that provided enough extra time for students who were deficient in the number of credits needed for graduation to complete two additional courses. Other students used the trimester to continue working on courses they had failed to finish during the fall and spring semesters. The new calendar enabled students to complete five years of coursework in four years.

Riddile and his staff did not stop their improvement efforts with a new school structure and calendar. They understood that a continuation of early successes depended on constant refining and adjustment. Algebra and transitional English classes were lengthened to ninety-five minutes so that students had sufficient time to pass these essential courses. Students who continued to struggle with these subjects were required to attend two-hour help sessions until they began to earn passing grades. This policy resulted in a 50 percent drop in low grades after only a few months of implementation.

Another target for improvement efforts was the ninth grade. Riddile understood that getting off to a good start in ninth grade was a key predictor of success in high school. He initiated regular meetings with the staff of middle schools that sent students to Stuart. One of his goals involved developing a process for assessing the reading achievement of eighth graders. This data then was used by ninth-grade teachers at Stuart to determine how best to help incoming students. Riddile provided teachers with extensive in-service training in strategies for assisting low readers as well as a full-time literacy coach.

Rising ninth graders who were judged to be seriously deficient in reading were encouraged to attend a summer academy taught by Stuart faculty. This transitional program afforded students an opportunity to become familiar with a few Stuart teachers and with the layout of the large high school before their classmates arrived in September.

Five years were required to stabilize the early gains at Stuart. The results were indeed impressive. The average SAT score rose 104 points from 951 to 1,055. More than 80 percent of Stuart students passed each of Virginia's eleven required end-of-course tests. School attendance rose to 96 percent. Most striking of all, 97 percent of Stuart students graduated with a diploma, and nine out of ten graduates were scheduled to attend two- or four-year colleges.

KEYS TO PLANNING FOR SUSTAINED IMPROVEMENT

School improvement planning does not stop once a school has begun to turn around. Educators must come to regard planning as a continuous process, a basic component of school culture. Although there is no recipe for ensuring that schools maintain momentum, the examples of Greer Elementary and Stuart High School offer important clues concerning some of the issues that need to be addressed by planners.

Just because a program, practice, process, or policy helped to achieve school turnaround is no guarantee it will stand the test of time. Matt Landahl and Mel Riddile assessed their early initiatives in order to determine whether they needed to be fine-tuned or replaced. Landahl, for example, decided to modify how students were grouped for reading in the hopes that grouping across grade levels would promote greater vertical alignment and coordination of instruction. Part of the school improvement planning process should always include an examination of the effectiveness of measures introduced in previous plans.

Another key to sustaining improvement in low-performing schools involves identifying and implementing strategies for accelerating the achievement of low achievers. Given the fact that educators must not hold back high achievers in order that low achievers can catch up, the only option for closing achievement gaps is to find ways for low achievers to make up lost ground. Summer programs, for example, can supplement learning during the regular school year and reduce the learning loss that often occurs among disadvantaged students over the summer. Mel Riddile used the summer to afford students an opportunity for credit recovery. Matt Landahl initiated an extended school day twice a week so that struggling students could focus on specific problems. The only way most low achievers are going to catch up with their classmates is to spend additional time on learning.

The last chapter indicated that achieving school turnaround depended to a large extent on a laser-like focus on reading and mathematics. To sustain improvement, however, planners must move beyond these "basics" and consider ways to promote academic rigor across the curriculum. Teachers at Greer Elementary spent much of Year 3 addressing reading in the content areas. This expansion of their focus enabled scores on state social studies and science tests to rise. Stuart High School introduced an International Baccalaureate program along with more Advanced Placement options. All students were encouraged to enroll in at least one challenging course. Some School Improvement Plans also call for a phasing out of basic courses so that all students eventually must take only high-level courses.

Sustaining gains in middle schools and high schools requires careful coordination with feeder schools. Planners need to include feeder-school representatives in the planning process so that transitions for students can be as seamless as possible. Provisions should be made for vertical alignment of curriculum and information sharing about students in need of special assistance. Mel Riddile made a point of conferring with feeder middle schools before he established the summer academy for rising ninth graders. Middle school teachers and counselors helped identify students for whom the special transition program would be most beneficial.

Another important focus for post-turnaround planning entails cultivating greater teacher leadership. Initially, "turnaround" principals may be reluctant to distribute leadership because they do not know their faculty very well. Matt Landahl waited until his third year to delegate greater responsibility for planning to teachers. By that time, he had hired more than half of the Greer faculty and knew which teachers he could count on for support and leadership. This confidence led him to create an array of teacher-led committees to address improvement goals. No principal can maintain the improvement process on his own. Principals must be able to rely on teacher leaders to generate new ideas and see that the ideas are translated into action.

KEYS TO PLANNING FOR SUSTAINED IMPROVEMENT

- Assess turnaround initiatives and adjust as needed.
- Implement strategies for accelerating the achievement of low achievers.
- Address vertical alignment and transitions with feeder schools.
- Nurture teacher leadership.

NOTES

1. This case was based on the following account: Daniel L. Duke and Matt Landahl, 2011, "Raising test scores was the easy part: A case study of the third year of school turnaround." *International Studies in Educational Administration*, 39(3), 91–114.

2. This case was based on an account that appeared in Daniel L. Duke, 2010, *Differentiating School Leadership*. Thousand Oaks, CA: Corwin.

CHAPTER 13

Planning for Educational Excellence

PREVIEW

Many schools have managed to sustain solid academic achievement year after year. For these schools, the most appropriate goal may be to pursue educational excellence. This chapter considers the nature of educational excellence and how to plan for its pursuit. Various examples are provided to illustrate that excellence comes in many forms.

IS TEST PREP THE BEST WE CAN OFFER?

The headline in the Springdale newspaper did not come as a shock to Nan Stiggins. For years she had been reading articles critical of U.S. public schools and their performance in comparison to schools in other nations. She accepted most of the indictments, at least with regard to some schools, but she also knew that thousands of very good schools could hold their own against international competition. Wilson High School, where Stiggins had been principal for eight years, was one of these schools.

What worried Stiggins was how to move her school beyond the current focus on getting students to pass standardized end-of-course tests. She had seen the items on these tests and believed they covered mostly basic knowledge. If teachers were content to prepare students to pass these tests, students were unlikely to acquire the advanced knowledge and understandings necessary to think creatively and compete in a global economy.

Stiggins's concerns led her to confront Wilson's School Improvement Committee with a daunting challenge. "What can be done to provide our students with a truly exceptional education?" she asked. "Being a good school no longer is good enough."

The discussion that followed raised more questions than it answered. Several committee members felt that excellence was best pursued in college where students chose what they wanted to study. The best high schools could do, in their judgment, was to lay the foundation for advanced work.

A parent on the committee said, "You're right to press us to move beyond preparing teenagers to pass tests, but I'm not sure you have the resources to do much more." Stiggins agreed that resources were important, but she shared her belief that Wilson's faculty was capable of moving most students well beyond test prep.

The head of the English department pointed out that the faculty first needed to agree on what educational excellence looks like before they could start planning for it. Others nodded in agreement. "What if we can't agree?" Stiggins asked.

The group grew silent. After several awkward minutes, a guidance counselor asked, "Why is it necessary for all of us to agree? Maybe what constitutes excellence in math isn't the same as what's excellent in history."

Stiggins thought to herself, "This process is going to take some time, but I think it's worth it."

◆

Getting students to pass standards-based tests clearly is important. It is difficult to imagine anyone making a significant contribution without mastering the fundamentals. When mastering the fundamentals becomes the end, rather than the means to an end, however, the chances for advancement—on both an individual and a societal basis—diminish. Nan Stiggins grasped this concern, and it led her to press the School Improvement Committee to look beyond test preparation. Most Wilson students easily passed the state tests. They needed to be challenged, and so did the Wilson faculty.

The reasons were no further away than the daily headlines that linked the future of the economy to the capacity of the next generation to inquire and innovate. Policymakers decried the shortage of U.S. students majoring in mathematics, science, technology, and engineering. Parents wondered how students in other countries consistently outperformed U.S. students in various subjects. Even top performers from American schools were slipping in comparison to their international counterparts.

Planning to move a school toward excellence, as Stiggins began to realize during her meeting with the School Improvement Committee, presented many challenges. It is one thing to get students to pass standards-based tests. The standards are known. But, what about excellence? Opinions vary about its nature. How can improvement goals be set for something so hard to define and describe? Because the pursuit of educational excellence is qualitatively different from preparing students to pass tests, the planning process associated with it is likely to pose unique challenges.

THE NATURE OF EDUCATIONAL EXCELLENCE

Determining the meaning of educational excellence is challenging. The term has been invoked for a variety of rhetorical purposes ranging from efforts to narrow the achievement gap between white and minority students to initiatives aimed at making the United States more competitive in the global economy.

The movement to establish curriculum standards and tests to measure how well students are mastering them has been justified in the name of educational excellence. Many educators feel that the Common Core Standards represent an important step toward greater academic rigor. Standards, however, are more representative of fundamental knowledge than advanced content. Standards, after all, are associated with standardization—an assurance that all students have acquired "the basics." The standards used to drive state and local tests, in other words, have more to do with educational adequacy than educational excellence. Excellence pertains to what lies beyond adequacy.

It is much easier to define adequacy than excellence. Adequacy refers to what students need to make their way in the world—a certain level of literacy, the skills to calculate, an understanding of economic principles and the political system. Excellence, of course, requires a solid foundation in basic knowledge and understanding, but it is much more. Excellence represents performance at the highest levels. It is qualitatively different from adequacy, a level of performance to which many individuals can only aspire.

Often the real benefit of excellence lies in its pursuit, not its attainment. Pursuing excellence, in other words, leads to greater knowledge and competence, even if the highest levels of achievement are not scaled. One does not have to be an Albert Einstein, a Duke Ellington, or a Marie Curie in order to make a contribution to the world.

In order to pursue excellence, however, individuals must be able to recognize it when they encounter it. That is where schools can be of great service. Young people need to be exposed to various exemplars of excellence. Furthermore, excellence is always in relation to something—excellence in mathematics, excellence in musical composition, excellence in historical analysis, excellence in field hockey. The more young people understand about what excellence in various endeavors looks like, the better able they will be to pursue it. And some actually will reach the highest levels eventually.

Excellence, as the National Commission on Excellence in Education declared in 1983, is all about performing "on the boundary of individual ability in ways that test and push back personal limits" (p. 12). This is exactly what Jaime Escalante inspired his calculus students to do at Garfield High School in Los Angeles. These students did not have to go on to become world-class mathematicians in order to have benefited from their pursuit of excellence. What they gained in confidence alone would stand them in good stead for the rest of their lives.

This discussion of the nature of educational excellence has several implications for educators seeking to plan for excellence. First of all, the pursuit of excellence entails more than achieving high scores on standardized tests of fundamental knowledge.

Second, in order for excellence to be real and meaningful, it must be in reference to a specific enterprise or field of endeavor. Rather than striving to plan an "excellent" school, in other words, planners should focus on planning an excellent program in applied physics or American government.

Third, the pursuit of excellence requires that young people recognize excellence when they encounter it. An important part of planning for excellence therefore involves exposing young people to models of excellence and helping them to understand how these models differ from the typical or ordinary. It also helps for students to understand what individuals who achieve excellence had to go through in order to get there.

Fourth, although the pursuit of educational excellence is most often associated with high school studies, the groundwork for such pursuits is laid in elementary and middle school. Think of the successful varsity program that depends on youth league play and junior varsity participation to prepare players for the rigors of high school competition.

In the next section we take a look at several schools that were created with the express intention of promoting the pursuit of excellence.

MANY PATHWAYS TO EXCELLENCE

A variety of approaches characterize efforts to promote educational excellence. The traditional approach involves highly selective schools that require students to take an entrance examination. While such schools continue to exist, they have been joined by schools that provide students with broader access.

Schools associated with the pursuit of excellence frequently specialize in particular subjects. Some are relatively large magnet schools that draw students from across a school district. Others are so-called Governor's Schools that attract students from multiple school districts. Recently added are small academies and specialty programs created by subdividing large high schools. Yet another variation is the specialty school-within-a-school found in some comprehensive high schools. All of these options share a commitment to pursuing advanced work in a focused area of inquiry.

Manor New Tech High School.[1] Located near Austin, Texas, Manor New Tech High School (MNTHS) was launched in August 2007 as an opportunity for students to develop expertise in the STEM (science, technology, engineering, mathematics) subjects.[1] Planners subscribed to the precepts of the New Technology Foundation (NTF), an organization dedicated to addressing the knowledge and skills students need to thrive in the twenty-first century. The precepts include project-based learning, curriculum integration, and technology integration. These features are best implemented, according to the NTF, in small high schools of no more than four hundred students.

MNTHS opened with 156 ninth and tenth graders. The students reflected the demographic makeup of the rural Manor Independent School District—47 percent Latino, 28 percent white, 24 percent African American, and 1 percent Asian. More than half of the students qualified for free or reduced-price meals. The plan was to "grow" the school, adding eleventh and then twelfth grade, eventually reaching an enrollment of between three and four hundred students.

Planning for a school like MNTHS is somewhat different from planning for school turnaround. An express purpose of Manor is to continue to develop students' interest in particular subjects. The ultimate goal is to encourage students to consider careers in STEM-based fields. Because it cannot be assumed that students are interested in STEM subjects, student motivation must be continually addressed as lessons and activities are being planned. Concentrating on getting students to pass standardized tests and earn good grades, in other words, is not enough when the focus is advanced academic work in specific fields of knowledge.

Concern for student motivation led the planners at Manor to rely heavily on problem-based learning. Designing lessons around challenging, real-world problems engages students' curiosity and leads to the satisfaction that comes with successful problem solving. Teachers at Manor do not give students the solutions. Instead, they offer access to resources and guidance so that students can take responsibility for their own learning.

Every MNTHS student has a computer, which enables her to search for information, communicate with fellow students and teachers, and prepare projects and presentations. Typically students work on problems in teams. Planners felt it was important for students to get a taste of adult work experience and learn how to lead their peers in achieving project-based tasks.

Students sometimes get stuck on a difficult concept or operation. When this happens, instructors engage in a "stop and teach" moment or mini-workshop with a student team leader. The team leader then is expected to return to his team and instruct his teammates.

Another aspect of teamwork at Manor involves establishing group norms each time a new project is begun. Team members determine each person's role and responsibilities. An individual who fails to observe group norms can be "fired" by the team, an action that results in the individual having to complete the project on her own.

Projects frequently link concepts from STEM subjects with an authentic problem such as conducting an analysis of toxicity in a stream and proposing a cleanup strategy. Projects are presented to panels of community experts, thereby giving students opportunities to develop communication skills and receive feedback on their work in a public forum.

Each year teachers and administrators at MNTHS search for new ways to promote integrated learning. They believe students come to a greater understanding of subject matter when the disciplines are not taught as discrete subjects. Physics and algebra, for example, are taught together. Technology is integrated into every course. Projects almost always draw on knowledge from various fields. One project, for instance, may call for students to design a castle, thereby requiring them to combine history, literature, and engineering. Every student is required to take two years of engineering to enable them to see how mathematics and science are employed to solve a variety of practical problems.

In order to attend MNTHS, students must complete an application, but there are no specific criteria for gaining admission other than earning promotion to the ninth grade. A lottery system is used to select each class from the pool of applicants. This process was intended by planners to ensure that Manor would continue to reflect the diversity of the community.

Planning an innovative learning environment such as Manor New Tech High School's from scratch is considerably easier than trying to redesign an existing school. It should be noted, however, that planning at Manor did not cease when the school opened. If the pursuit of educational excellence in the STEM subjects is to continue at MNTHS, so must school improvement planning.

Maggie L. Walker Governor's School.[2] Founded in 1991, the Maggie
L. Walker Governor's School for Government and International Relations in Richmond, Virginia, serves as a magnet school for students
from twelve school divisions in the Richmond area. Unlike Manor
New Tech High School, Maggie L. Walker has a highly competitive
admissions process. Students must take three tests, complete an essay,
and undergo a thorough review of their academic record and recommendations. Typically, each class of 180 students represents about one
tenth of the applicants.

The mission of Maggie L. Walker is "to provide broad-based educational opportunities that develop gifted students' understanding of world
cultures and languages as well as the ability to lead, participate, and contribute in a rapidly changing global society." The school has consistently
been recognized as one of the top high schools in the United States.

Originally Maggie L. Walker was collocated with a Richmond
Public Schools comprehensive high school. Much of the planning in
the early years focused on coexisting with the comprehensive high
school, which had been designated for closure. When supporters of the
comprehensive high school succeeded in keeping it open, planners for
Maggie L. Walker started searching for their own facility. Eventually
they succeeded in securing the renovation of a high school that had
been closed.

Because Maggie L. Walker students perform very well on standardized tests, attend school regularly, and rarely engage in misconduct,
school improvement planning can focus primarily on making certain
that course offerings are up-to-date and challenging. Students are required to take four years of a primary foreign language, two years of
a second foreign language, and five years of social studies. Available
languages include Advanced Placement-level French, German, Spanish, Latin, Chinese, Japanese, Italian, Russian, and Arabic. A wide array of AP courses is also available in various subjects.

Arrangements with Virginia Commonwealth University and J.
Sargeant Reynolds Community College enable Maggie L. Walker
students to undertake college-level course work for credit. Maintaining
close working relations between Walker and these institutions requires
ongoing planning. The administration at Walker is intent on ensuring
that its students are well prepared to undertake college studies.

An important component of the Walker program, one that sets it apart from many high schools, includes the senior seminars and mentorships. This required course provides seniors with an opportunity to explore in depth a topic of personal interest that reflects the Walker mission. Every senior must participate in either a senior seminar or an off-campus mentorship. Each requires students to formulate a problem and the methods by which the problem will be investigated. Walker teachers expect students to collect and analyze data and arrive at their own conclusions. Student work must be presented in a professionally appropriate manner on Senior Showcase Day.

Because Walker serves school systems enrolling diverse populations, it is vitally important that the high school's enrollment reflects this diversity. School improvement planning at Walker frequently addresses ways to encourage broad-based participation without sacrificing the school's commitment to high-quality academic work. Although student applications to Walker are reviewed and graded by Walker staff members, the ultimate decision regarding which students are accepted rests with each participating school system.

No matter how successful Walker is—and the school has been extraordinarily successful in graduating highfliers who get into the best colleges—there will always be planning and program development as long as Walker pursues its vision of educational excellence:

> Students of the Governor's School for Government and International Studies will be analytical learners who construct meaning from ideas and concepts and who apply these principles to changing situations in their own lives. They will be citizens who seek to serve their communities, local, national, and international, with wisdom; they will be tolerant people of strong character who understand and celebrate diversity in the global community of the twenty-first century. (www.gsgis.k12.va.us)

Thomas Jefferson High School for Science and Technology. To provide a concrete idea of what is addressed in a School Improvement Plan for an elite school, we examined the 2011–2012 School Improvement Plan for Thomas Jefferson High School for Science and Technology.[3] Jefferson is another Virginia Governor's School and arguably the best public school in the United States. The school's website proudly proclaims that *U.S. News & World Report* ranked Jefferson the best public high school in the nation in 2007, 2008, 2009, 2010, and 2011. If the pursuit of educational excellence is to be found anywhere in the United States, it has to be at this school.

Jefferson is operated by Fairfax County Public Schools and attracts students from across Northern Virginia. Eighth graders interested in attending Jefferson must take an admissions test and be enrolled in Algebra 1 or a higher math course. Admission is highly competitive with only about 480 students admitted out of an application pool topping 3,000 students.

As its name indicates, Jefferson focuses on science and technology. Courses include organic chemistry, neurobiology, marine biology, DNA science, and quantum mechanics. Labs at the school are devoted to such fields as robotics, computer science, microelectronics, prototyping, optics, and oceanography. Labs often have corporate sponsors that provide Jefferson students with state-of-the-art equipment.

As part of its accreditation planning, Jefferson developed the following six goals:

1. Enhance TJHSST curriculum so that students develop research skills at all grade levels through vertical integration.
2. Continue to develop interdisciplinary lessons as needed.
3. Explore offering more flexibility in course selection, including high-level course work as an alternative to AP.
4. Initiate regulations for expected performance to remain a TJHSST student.
5. Review division course offerings in terms of vertical integration.
6. Explore and pilot alternatives to the current school calendar.

School improvement at Jefferson clearly focuses on the curriculum and maintaining high academic standards. One ongoing concern, for example, is that students who transfer into Jefferson may not have acquired the prerequisite knowledge expected of a Jefferson student. Just because a student takes a course with the same title as a Jefferson course is no guarantee that the student has met Jefferson's high expectations. One School Improvement Plan objective therefore involves comparing course expectations at Jefferson with expectations for similar courses elsewhere.

Teachers at Jefferson have found that even courses offered at the elite high school are not always aligned as well as they could be. Thus another focus for the School Improvement Plan is vertical integration. Teachers are called on to identify gaps in student background knowledge as students transition from one course to the next higher course.

Besides goals derived from the accreditation process, the Jefferson School Improvement Plan includes additional goals. One of these relates to academic ethics. A high-powered school such as Jefferson places students under a great deal of pressure to succeed. Such pressure can lead to cheating, plagiarism, and other unethical behavior. The School Improvement Plan calls on teachers to develop protocols for handling ethical violations and ways of communicating ethical expectations to students and parents.

Elite schools such as Jefferson often have difficulty enrolling a student body that reflects the diversity of the local population. Another School Improvement Plan goal for 2011–2012 therefore focuses on developing "ways to insure that the climate at TJHSST is welcoming and inclusive of the diverse populations found in Northern Virginia." Among the strategies tied to this goal is the use of parent volunteers from Jefferson as liaisons to elementary and middle schools. These volunteers are charged with raising awareness of the application process for Jefferson and answering questions regarding admissions requirements. Another strategy calls for raising money for scholarships so that students from less-advantaged families can attend summer enrichment programs in middle school. These programs are designed to serve as "stepping stones" into Jefferson.

Recruiting high-caliber faculty members for Jefferson is a high-priority goal in the School Improvement Plan. With many veteran teachers facing retirement in the near future, Jefferson needs a plan for replacing them. Strategies include inviting prospective teachers from other schools to visit Jefferson classes in order to learn about the school and advertising openings on broad networks, including private-sector websites.

One of Jefferson's goals is familiar to many school planners—securing resources to support professional development for teachers. Given the school's expectation that teachers will function "on the cutting edge" of their disciplines, ongoing training is essential. Because such training can be very expensive, the School Improvement Plan calls for seeking grant funding and external sponsorships to underwrite the costs of professional development.

The last School Improvement Plan goal addresses student academics. The target is to get 97 percent of freshman and seniors to present research at one of Jefferson's annual symposiums. Symposiums provide opportunities for Jefferson students to hear from noted scientists, share their own research, and gain experience presenting to their peers and teachers.

KEYS TO PLANNING FOR EDUCATIONAL EXCELLENCE

When educators think about school improvement, they tend to focus on making changes that will raise the achievement of low-performing students and narrow the achievement gap between student subgroups. These concerns, of course, merit attention, but so do efforts to challenge high-achieving students and promote excellence in various fields of study.

The first key to planning for educational excellence, as in the case of other planning efforts, is *focus*. Excellence is best considered in reference to a specific discipline or activity. Planning for generalized excellence may sound appealing, but it lacks the specificity to enable educators to concentrate resources and energy.

Once agreement has been reached regarding what to focus on, planners need to consider what constitutes excellence in the chosen field. Excellence can be a moving target, changing as new discoveries are made and new levels of performance are attained. Identifying individuals who exemplify excellence and can serve as models is helpful for students who aspire to exceed the ordinary. Understanding what these exceptional individuals did to achieve outstanding results can be invaluable for young people intent on pursuing excellence.

In most instances, planning for educational excellence involves programming at the high school level, but planners must remember that the foundations for pursuing excellence in high school are laid in elementary and middle school. If middle schools, for example, do not make it possible for students to complete Algebra 1, they will not be prepared to tackle the challenging mathematics at an elite high school such as Thomas Jefferson High School for Science and Technology. Once planners determine the fields in which they intend to pursue excellence, they need to work with elementary and middle school educators to create programs that pave the way.

Students must be highly motivated in order to make the commitment of time and energy necessary for pursuing excellence. Planners consequently should treat motivation as an important consideration. Goals and objectives that address ways to interest students in stretching themselves to the boundaries of their abilities and doing more than just "getting by" are critical components of School Improvement Plans focused on educational excellence.

The last key to planning for educational excellence deals with access. Given the nation's commitment to equity and educational opportunity for all, it is unacceptable for schools dedicated to the pursuit of excellence to exclude certain student subgroups. Although schools may require certain admissions requirements to be met, they must see to it that representatives of all student groups, regardless of their ethnicity and socioeconomic status, have the opportunity to compete for and gain admission. Providing such opportunities means that planners have to find ways to inform students and parents of admission requirements well in advance and provide special programs to prepare some students to compete for admission on a level playing field.

KEYS TO PLANNING FOR EDUCATIONAL EXCELLENCE

- Focus planning for excellence on a specific field.
- Determine what constitutes excellence in the field.
- Consider what foundations must be laid in elementary and middle school to prepare students for the pursuit of excellence in high school.
- Address ways to motivate students to pursue excellence.
- Take the steps needed to ensure a wide range of students have an opportunity to pursue excellence.

NOTES

1. Information on Manor New Tech High School was downloaded from the following sources: Hannah Gourgey, 2009, "Case study of Manor New Tech High School," http://www.utdanacenter.org/tcstem/manornths.php; and

"Learning tour: Manor New Technology High School," 2008, http://www .manorisd.net/portal/newtech/. Material was downloaded on November 14, 2011.

2. Information on Maggie L. Walker Governor's School for Government and International Studies was downloaded from the high school's website (www.gsgis.k12.va.us) on November 15, 2011.

3. The School Improvement Plan 2011–2012 for Thomas Jefferson High School for Science and Technology was downloaded from the Fairfax County Public Schools website (www.fcps.edu) on November 16, 2011.

REFERENCE

National Commission on Excellence in Education. 1983. *A Nation at Risk: The Imperative of Educational Reform.* Washington, DC: U.S. Government Printing Office.

grade-level planning, 248
grades, 53
graphic organizers, 189
grouping students, 97
group norms, 271

hands-on materials, incorporating, 121
Harlem Children's Zone (HCZ),
207, 226
high-achieving students, 276

implementation, 167; problems, 76,
78
impressionistic data, 46
improvement status, 253
individualized instruction, 189
innovation, 158
Institute of Educational Sciences,
99
instructional coaching model, 166
instructional improvement, 158–159,
246
instructional practices, 54
instructional rounds, 168
instructional time, 60
International Baccalaureate program,
259
interventions, 55, 95, 202; programs,
95, 202
interventions, instructional, 246

judgment calls, 6–7, 62

lack of confidence, 238
language, 187
leadership style, 61, 253
learning a new language, 186
learning targets, 165
learning walks, 253
lesson design, 161
lessons, organizing, 168

linguistically responsive practices,
187
literacy, 258
literacy block, 256
longitudinal data, 18
low graduation rates, 58
low-performing schools, 251, 261

managing and monitoring the plan,
36, 37
mapping, 47
master schedule, 246, 248, 256
math block, 121
math coach, 59, 254
math games, 126. *See also* games
math specialists, 120
mentoring students, 207
mobile learning devices, 148, 163
modeling, 142
monitor progress, 253

National Commission on Excellence
in Education, 268
National Dropout Prevention Center,
201, 206
National Institute for Literacy, 89
National Mathematics Advisory Panel
(NMAP), 115, 118–119, 122
National Reading Panel (NRP), 89,
91–92
National Research Council, 116
National Technology Foundation
(NTF), 270
ninety-day improvement plan, 241
No Child Left Behind Act of 2001,
2–3, 54, 237
norms of excellence, 146

observational data, 46–47, 156
observations, 141
online lessons, 123

About the Authors

Daniel L. Duke is professor of educational leadership at the University of Virginia. After teaching high school social studies and serving as a secondary school administrator, Dan Duke embarked on a career in higher education. For over three decades he has taught courses on educational leadership, organizational change, and school reform as well as conducting research on various aspects of public schools. After serving on the faculties of Lewis and Clark College and Stanford University, he came to the University of Virginia as chair of educational leadership and policy studies. Duke founded and directed the Thomas Jefferson Center for Educational Design and helped establish the Darden-Curry Partnership for Leaders in Education (PLE), a unique enterprise involving the Curry School of Education and the Darden Graduate School of Business Administration. He served as research director for the PLE until 2010. A prolific writer, Duke has authored or coauthored thirty-two books and several hundred scholarly articles, monographs, chapters, and reports. His most recent books include *The Challenges of Educational Change* (2004), *Education Empire: The Evolution of an Excellent Suburban School System* (2005), *Teachers' Guide to School Turnarounds* (2007), *The Little School System That Could: Transforming a City School District* (2008), *Differentiating School Leadership* (2010), and *The Challenges of School District Leadership* (2010). A highly regarded consultant, Duke has worked with over 150 school systems, state agencies, foundations, and governments across the United States and abroad. Recently he helped develop the Texas Turnaround Leadership Academy and the Florida Turnaround Leaders Program.

He has served as president of the University Council for Educational Administration and was chosen as Professor of the Year at the Curry School of Education.

Marsha Carr joined the faculty in educational leadership at the Watson College of Education Leadership at the University of North Carolina Wilmington after thirty-five years of service in private and public education. Carr, the youngest and first female school superintendent in her district, served for over a decade as a superintendent of schools in West Virginia. Prior to this appointment, she served as a pre-K–12 principal, director of curriculum/instructional technology, and a reading specialist. As a reading specialist, frustrated by the lack of available reading materials, Carr began to travel and study whole language in Australia and New Zealand educational systems. In 1993, she designed a twenty-book emergent level reading series named StoryMakers, which became an international success and was later published in two languages. Carr was named Teacher of the Year in Allegany County, Maryland, and was recognized by the Maryland House of Delegates as well as received the Maryland Governor's Citation for her work. In 1994, Carr was honored with the National Milken Family Educator Award, the most coveted educator award, and joined a prestigious family of outstanding educators around the nation. Carr has presented at over one hundred conferences and been published in numerous educational magazines and journals. She is the author of *Educational Leadership: From Hostile Takeover to a Sustainable-Successful System*. Presently Carr is leading research and is a consultant in the area of self-mentoring, a leadership development program Carr designed that is being piloted for new UNCW faculty, teachers and students in local school systems, and as an international study program in Belize. Self-mentoring promotes self-development as a leader through self-evaluative planning, self-guided techniques, and self-reflection strategies.

William Sterrett is assistant professor and program coordinator of curriculum, instruction, and supervision at the University of North Carolina Wilmington. Sterrett was recognized as a Milken National Educator, as a Title I elementary principal, in Charlottesville, Virginia, in 2008. Sterrett is the author of the book *Insights into Action: Success-*

ful School Leaders Share What Works (2011), and he enjoys working with schools and districts on issues related to instructional leadership, teacher leadership, and effective professional development. Sterrett earned his undergraduate degree from Asbury College (Wilmore, KY) and his PhD from the University of Virginia. Sterrett can be followed on Twitter via @billsterrett.

Made in the USA
Lexington, KY
08 May 2019